P9-CJM-342

WHY WE LIE ABOUT AID

Development and the Messy Politics of Change

PABLO YANGUAS

Why We Lie About Aid: Development and the Messy Politics of Change was first published in 2018 by Zed Books Ltd, The Foundry, 17 Oval Way, London SE11 5RR, UK.

www.zedbooks.net

Typeset in Bulmer by T&T Productions Ltd, London
Index by Rohan Bolton
Cover design by Michael Wallace
Cover photo © Mikkel Ostergaard/Panos

A catalogue record for this book is available from the British Library

ISBN 978-1-78360-934-5 HB
ISBN 978-1-78360-933-8 PB
ISBN 978-1-78360-935-2 PDF
ISBN 978-1-78360-936-9 EPUB
ISBN 978-1-78360-937-6 MOBI

MIX
Paper from
responsible sources
FSC
www.fsc.org   FSC® C013604

Printed and bound by CPI Group (UK) Ltd, Croydon, CR0 4YY

WHY WE LIE ABOUT AID

About the author

PABLO YANGUAS is a research fellow at the Effective States and Inclusive Development Research Centre and Global Development Institute, University of Manchester, as well as an international development consultant. He received his PhD in Government from Cornell University after studying History and Archaeology at the University of Seville. His research centres on the political economy of foreign aid, the politics of development policy, and public sector reform, and has appeared in academic journals such as *World Development*, *Development Policy Review*, *Third World Quarterly* and *Journal of International Development*. As an advisor, he specialises in politically smart and adaptive foreign aid with a focus on anticorruption programming.

Contents

Acknowledgements

This book draws upon a decade of study, research, and work, a time that I have been privileged to share with too many friends and colleagues to list here.

My first words of appreciation have to be for my mentors: Tom Callaghy at the University of Pennsylvania, Nic van de Walle at Cornell University, and David Hulme at the University of Manchester. They are all responsible for turning a hapless history major out of Seville into a bona fide international development researcher. I hope that this book can make up for all my stubborn questions, my obscure obsession with Weber, and my general inability to follow sound career advice. My best ideas are but echoes of their massive contributions to the political economy of development.

The research that substantiates this book was made possible by support from the Einaudi Center and the Peace Studies programme at Cornell University, and from the Effective States and Inclusive Development Research Centre and Global Development Institute at the University of Manchester. Of my many good friends and influences at Cornell, Phil Ayoub, Don Leonard, and Igor Logvinenko were my closest co-conspirators in this business of asking tricky questions about international and comparative politics, while Jaimie Bleck was, from that very first day at the Ithaca airport, a contagious source of enthusiasm and sheer joy about Africa and Africans. Over time, I have also benefitted from the wisdom of teachers and senior colleagues: Peter Katzenstein, Sam Hickey, Kunal Sen, Richard Batley, Heather Marquette, Merilee Grindle, Brian Levy, and David Booth will all find traces of their own work in this manuscript, which is all the better for it. My editor at Zed Books, Ken Barlow, offered encouragement and astute guidance in the long journey from inception to submission, and, together with two anonymous reviewers, provided useful feedback on the final text. Whatever flaws remain are probably the result of not listening to them closely enough.

I am continuously amazed at the willingness of practitioners to talk to junior researchers. Most of my insights into development grew out of conversations in Nairobi; Freetown; Monrovia; Tegucigalpa; Accra; Kampala; Dhaka; Washington, DC; Paris; Madrid; and London. I especially want to thank Alan Whaites, Nick Manning, Kathy Bain, Beatriz Novales, Nic Lee, and Isabel Castle, not just for their trust and inspiration, but also for demonstrating what aid can be like when smart, capable, and principled people take the reins. A whole book cannot do enough justice to their hard work and commitment, or that of their hundreds and thousands of peers across the development community.

Finally, as is often the case, no one feels the pressure and costs of writing a book quite as strongly as the author's family. My wife, Mar, has always been my biggest supporter, even when work has taken me far away from her. In the time between conceiving this book and submitting the final manuscript, our two children, Victor and Martina, were born. It is to them that I dedicate the book: may you grow up to see a more internationalist and humane world than the one captured in these pages.

Manchester, August 2017

Introduction

A scandal in Kampala

There are not many public scandals about foreign aid, but Ireland was rocked by a particularly big one in 2012, when Irish Aid suspended its entire assistance programme in Uganda. In October of that year, it was revealed that four million euros destined to help rebuild the country's war-torn northern region had been siphoned out to a personal account by the Office of the Prime Minister[1]. The revelation quickly escalated into a full-blown public debate about the future of development cooperation in Ireland. The *Tánaiste* – deputy prime minister and minister for foreign affairs in charge of Irish Aid – was 'absolutely disgusted' about the corrupt misappropriation and demanded that all the money be paid back in order to maintain future aid to Uganda[2]. Some politicians called for an investigation by the legislature to 'get to the bottom' of the scandal, while others used the opportunity to call for significant cuts to the aid budget. Newspapers printed opinion pieces questioning the logic of foreign aid in a time of financial bailout and fiscal austerity, and prime-time specials were aired on television detailing the context in which Irish money had been so blatantly stolen.

After a while, inevitably, the scandal subsided. The Ugandan government repaid the misappropriated funds in January 2013[3], and Irish Aid personnel quietly got on with the business of figuring out what went wrong and how to avoid similar scandals in future. The Irish government maintained the suspension for a while in protest at the lack of judicial action against the Ugandan officials responsible, but by 2014 foreign aid was again flowing into school rehabilitation, strengthening local responses to HIV/AIDS, and promoting access to justice for the very poor[4]. Perhaps one of the more significant consequences of the Irish Aid–Uganda scandal was exposing the public to very important, but also very complex, questions about the nature of development assistance. Should we give aid to countries with questionable democratic institutions? Should we work with potentially corrupt leaders in order to reach the poor and disenfranchised? Is it moral to send money abroad when there are still so many who need it at home? What should we expect to achieve in exchange for our aid?

Irish society is to be applauded for asking these questions, just as it surely needs to be excused for not finding any definitive answers. After all, foreign aid is a tiny slice of any country's national budget, hardly worth covering in prime-time news or newspaper editorials; even its scandals – with the exception of the above – are seldom publicised beyond official reports and specialist conferences. The fact is people know remarkably little about how foreign aid actually works. Instead, they are treated to shallow polemics supporting either end of the political spectrum: in Ireland, as in any other donor country, aid is a convenient black box with which progressives and conservatives can safely play to their bases. On the left, increasing the aid budget is a clear signal of charity and solidarity, just as, on the right, cutting it is an easy way to evoke fiscal responsibility and a business mentality. Politicians and pundits can so easily play with foreign aid because it has no constituency other than its professionals and – perhaps a distant second – its recipients in foreign countries. As a result, we are often treated to a pantomime of extremes in which development assistance is framed as either feeding starving children or fattening corrupt dictators. There is only room for nuance when treating aid as an instrumental resource: buttressing a country's international reputation or its ability to maintain and expand its influence abroad. But that is hardly a conversation about what development cooperation means on the ground.

The opaqueness of the aid world is at times calculated, which is partly the fault of its own professionals. It is also, I believe, self-defeating. The fact is that aid is neither salvation nor damnation, not just charity and definitely not just waste. Like many policies at home, foreign aid is messy: its principles and goals are subject to bias and short-sightedness as much as genius and foresight; its projects are managed by hacks and mercenaries as much as artists and visionaries; and its outcomes are incredibly difficult to evaluate with scientific accuracy, prone as they are to the vagaries of economics and politics. At the end of the day, the more internal documents you try to decipher, the more frustrated idealists you talk to, and the more local processes of change you try to unpack, the clearer it becomes that the defining characteristic of aid is its intrinsic humanity. Neither sinner nor saint: just human. Fallible, obviously, and gullible, quite a bit; but also entrepreneurial and subversive, an instrument for promoting change in the most difficult environments, which, after all, is what development is really about.

Aid: what you see is not what you get…

The minute one takes a critical look at our public conversations about aid, it becomes evident that they are hardly ever about

development: most of the time, they are about money, sometimes they are about partisan competition. According to surveys,
Americans wildly overestimate the amount of money their government spends on development assistance. When asked to guess
the percentage of the national budget devoted to aid, the most frequent answer falls between 20% and 25%, when the actual figure
is roughly ten times smaller. Part of the reason for this mismatch
between perception and reality has to do with the fact that foreign
aid is not so much a policy field as a political football for government and opposition to kick around in search of votes and cheap
rhetorical wins. Despite the fact that aid is a minute part of public
spending in industrialised democracies, with most of it going to
allied governments and strategic countries, many conservative
politicians keep calling for cuts to aid budgets. But the other side
is not blameless either. Just as right-of-centre governments tend
to use aid cuts as a bribe to reactionary backbenchers, so left-of-
centre governments use aid increases as a way to establish their
progressive credentials and appease critics from the radical left.

Money matters for aid debates, with conservatives and progressives playing a never-ending game of tug of war over spending. But there is a dirty little secret behind this political cha-
rade: the money, by itself, means nothing. Take, for instance,
the massive increase in aid budgets approved by Spain's left-
wing government in 2004. This did not automatically result in
increased development effectiveness. Far from it: the money
was spread out over too many programmes, often managed by
people lacking the skills and tools to make the best use of it.
The truth is that in development, money does not equal results.
A 50% increase in the budget of an ineffective programme does
not miraculously make it effective, it just makes it wasteful.

Since the 1950s, a succession of economists, intellectuals, and advocates have called for raising foreign aid contributions up to 0.7% of the donors' total national income, a threshold that only a handful of European countries have crossed. While the origins of the 0.7% mantra have clear humanitarian roots, the actual decision to meet the target is really more about our own domestic aid politics than about actual development: we are not debating the process of development but the size of our budgets. While the size of the budget draws much public attention, it is really what you do with it that matters.

International debates don't fare much better than domestic ones. Global conversations about development assistance have spent a couple of decades circling around the idea of 'aid effectiveness', as formulated by donors and recipients in successive high-level meetings in Paris, Accra and Busan. This agenda follows a very restrictive interpretation of effectiveness – donor agencies not making life hard for recipient governments – which distracts from any real understanding of the politics of reform. Just as domestic debates about aid are often really about money and the left–right political divide, global debates are usually informed or surrounded by broader diplomatic questions and the nature of interactions between developed and developing states in the international system.

One tragic repercussion of our short-sighted aid debates is an entirely wrong set of incentives for aid organisations and professionals. Domestic politics in donor countries has led to a strictly technical interpretation of development in the public eye, which forces aid practitioners to spend more time justifying their expenses than actually understanding and engaging with the difficult political contexts in which they operate. Our definition of development calls for engineers and accountants, not political operators, so we force aid professionals to turn every programme and intervention into a procurement document attached to a machine-like presentation of inputs and outputs. In the United Kingdom, business cases and the value-for-money (VfM) imperative have forced development professionals to consistently misrepresent the political risks attached to their publicly funded interventions. Across the Atlantic, the United States Agency for International Development (USAID) has been similarly hounded by the less enlightened elements of Congress.

Because we pretend development is a set of technical fixes, we force aid professionals to devote more time to management and reporting than actual development. Because aid budgets are a political football back home, we also force aid agencies to ensure that budgets are in fact spent so as to avoid the constant threat of cutbacks. That is why some development organisations have become veritable money-pumping machines. Nowhere is this more evident than at the World Bank, where professionals are evaluated on the size of their projects and their ability to get money out of the door. This disbursement incentive can be stifling, and over time it privileges those areas of assistance more amenable to bean counting and technical prediction, such as massive building projects – dams, roads, power stations – or giving tangible commodities such as medicines and books to poor people. The reality is that roads get built but not maintained, drugs are stored until they expire due to faulty prescription systems, and books are delivered but teachers don't show up because they don't get paid. Aid has been forced to chase quick wins, instead of supporting the establishment of the kinds of sustainable institutions that underlie effective governments, free societies, and fair markets.

... But you may be getting more than you expect

Development is a struggle. We know this intuitively, at least when we think about our own countries. Many landmarks of history are eminently political: the Glorious Revolution in England, the American Civil War, the transition to democracy after four decades of dictatorship in Spain. These are events and processes whose repercussions are felt even to this day: Britain's parliamentary monarchy with all its quirks, the legacy of racial tension in the United States, and strident left–right divides in modern Spanish politics.

Development is contentious. It takes time. It also needs reformers, people willing to challenge the status quo in order to build something different. Looking into the modern history of developing countries, one frequently encounters key individuals making difficult choices. In Sierra Leone, Valentine Collier was an old-school civil servant, who shook the country's post-war politics when he became anticorruption commissioner and decided to take the job seriously, in spite of personal and political repercussions. In Liberia, a young man called John Morlu turned the General Auditing Commission into a political threat to Africa's first female president, whose weak political position led her to remove this political thorn from her side. In these cases, and in many others, reformers waged dangerous political battles with little expectation of personal profit. Most importantly, they were able to do so because they had support from one or more donor partners.

Throughout the last few decades, aid has often been a catalyst for change, inspiring local actors to do things differently and sponsoring those who want to improve the lot of their compatriots. You will not read about these stories in the media, or even in the reports produced by the donors themselves; controversial programmes usually close all too quickly, their political repercussions silenced in favour of expenditure reports and spreadsheets full of arcane indicators. The real developmental implications of our assistance have been masked because our own perceptions did not allow us to see them and our political debates forced development practitioners to misdirect. As a result, we end up with approaches such as the Sustainable Development Goals (SDGs), lists of small fixes that are supposed to be the linchpin of development when in fact they are symptoms of underlying political problems. Giving all children malaria pills does not help reform the public health systems that leave them exposed to infection, just as getting girls to attend school offers no guarantee that they will receive a real education that enhances their social and political opportunities later in life. Targets such as the SDGs address some of the most pressing needs of the very poor around the world, but they do very little to promote reforms of the institutions that have kept them poor.

Foreign aid is not a good investment: risks are generally high, dividends far too uncertain. No wonder many people in donor countries such as Britain, the United States or Spain think that development assistance is a waste of money. At the same time, aid is exactly the right kind of investment, one that citizens of developed countries should be proud to make. There is a potential for aid to be enormously valuable, despite the myriad ways in which our politicians and our own misperceptions shackle it to ineffective models and practices. This value is evident in the countless development struggles that it supports around the world, the stories of personal sacrifice in search of a greater public good.

Why another book about aid?

Over the last ten years, I have met many aid practitioners in national donor agencies, such as the UK Department for International Development (DFID), and multilateral organisations, such as the World Bank. I have heard professionals complain about incentives that are just wrong, felt their seething frustration at politicians and public servants who just don't get what development is all about, and witnessed their efforts to try to do things differently. I have also met the people working for change in developing countries: politicians trapped between a vision of a better future and the reality of partisan politics, civil servants fed up with corruption and defiant in the face of political reprisal, and local activists tirelessly waging a war that they know they won't win. These are the real protagonists of development: the starving and sickly faces that we see on television will be their beneficiaries, as reformers (and the aid professionals who support them) work on a daily basis to level the playing field for the powerless to find their voice.

Over the years, it has struck me that these stories of contentious support for reform are often missing from major publications about aid and development. Academics have long recognised the political dimension of development assistance, but the nature of the data they use and the high-level theories they develop often constrain them to very broad generalisations. Daron Acemoglu and James Robinson, for instance, devote virtually no space in their massive book *Why Nations Fail* to what it would take for outsiders to support a transition from extractive institutions to more inclusive ones[5]. Researchers and practitioners who *do* write about aid usually focus on critiques of the aid system and its lacklustre performance when it comes to delivering results. I agree with all the arguments about fundamental misconception and even malpractice, from James Ferguson's *The Anti-Politics Machine* to Tania Li's *The Will to Improve*, all the way to Bill Easterly's many critiques of the planning mentality that condemns many aid interventions to failure[6]. But I want to go a step further than these authors by looking for the determinants of these failures: the aid debates that are not really about aid, the contradictory demands forced upon aid organisations, and the diplomatic imperatives shaping global discourse. I also take issue with those who condemn the aid system as a whole as 'dead', as Dambisa Moyo so provocatively claimed[7], for that very same line of reasoning could be turned on so many policy initiatives in donor countries that we still consider worthwhile and morally desirable. The fact that development is a long, hard struggle for change means that aid's impact will also play out over the long term and will be highly contested. Finally, I entirely disagree with suggestions that what we really need is an 'aid exit strategy', to use Derek Fee's appealing formulation, as that kind of frustration over modalities and quick fixes has little to do with the persisting reality of reformers fighting for change on the ground[8].

My argument is that aid has a role to play in development, supporting the many reformers who choose to pursue the greater good against sometimes insurmountable odds. This is a role that is consistent with our own interpretations of policy in donor countries and compatible with our most basic human values beyond partisan divides. However, it is also a role that requires a fundamental revision of how we think, speak, and debate about aid at home and internationally, moving beyond the idea of a transaction – 'one pound in exchange for one educated child' – in order to fully acknowledge the reality of contentious change. It will not be easy, as it has not been for so many reformers in our own countries. What we stand to lose in terms of comfort, we would more than make up for in intellectual honesty and moral responsibility. This is a pragmatic, sceptically hopeful book, mindful of the pressing challenges ahead but grounded in the conviction that there is a better way of addressing them than what we currently have. Aid is not dead unless we kill it.

Despite the overwhelming incentives against a contentious interpretation of development in our own domestic and global debates about aid, politics has in fact managed to enter mainstream development discourse under the guise of 'governance' and 'political economy'. For me, the crucial year in this process was 1997, when the World Bank released a world development report devoted to the politics of the state[9], and the Labour government in Britain established the UK DFID as a cabinet-level ministry. Over the following eighteen years, both organisations – one multilateral, the other bilateral – would become occasional leaders in the promotion of a more political understanding of development. But this was the result of small groups of bureaucratic insurgents fighting to persuade their managers and colleagues, and their successes have been limited and short lived. On the one hand, the academic profession of politics has failed to supply practitioners with a mental map matching the elegance and persuasiveness of economics[10]. On the other hand, expediency has called for compromises in the road to politically smart aid, with nuance turned into facile categories and process turned into product[11]. Above all, there is no public narrative supporting this kind of politically smart work.

Many sceptics and practitioners will be left wondering whether such a political approach to development assistance is a sure way to kill the aid industry entirely. But guess what? Foreign aid is dying anyway: the rise of South–South cooperation, the growing number of developing countries transitioning to middle-income status, and the new-found ability of many of these to access sovereign debt markets is a recipe for the gradual but inevitable demise of aid. Across the developing world, conventional donors such as the United States, Norway, and the World Bank are losing relevance in their ability to influence policy change, chiefly due to the slow but gradual erosion of their relative weight in governmental accounts. Money used to be the way to open the door for reform in many countries around the world, but that door is now closing as Brazil, China, India, and South Africa become key development players.

Money is not the challenge of development in the twenty-first century: policy effectiveness is. One has only to look at a place such as Ghana, a consolidated democracy with party alternation, a promise of untold wealth from natural resource extraction, and yet a persistently ineffective public-sector subject to entrenched patrimonial politics[12]. The reality of aid in the twenty-first century is that the most obvious problems to be fixed – maternal mortality, vaccination, literacy, and so on – are either fixed already or will be fixed by countries themselves in the coming decades. It is the intractable problems – almost all of them institutional – that will take decades or even longer to fully address. If aid donors really want to contribute to development in the twenty-first century, they need to focus on effectiveness instead of volume, strategy instead of tactics, and long-term pro-poor empowerment instead of short-term pro-poor results. From this perspective, the case for politically smart aid almost makes itself: the only way to avoid irrelevance might be for donors to finally take sides in the messy politics of change.

Cast of characters, methods, and biases

This is a book about donors, politicians, and reformers.

I use 'donor' as shorthand for the aid agencies that fund most development interventions in developing countries: the public organisations – national and international – that channel overseas development assistance, and that participate in such fora as the Organisation for Economic Co-operation and Development's (OECD's) Development Assistance Committee. Non-profit organisations (NGOs), philanthropists, foundations, corporations, etc., appear here and there in my cases, but they are not the main subject. The various cases in this book feature a number of bilateral aid agencies, such as the United States Agency for International Development (USAID), the Spanish aid agency Agencia Española de Cooperación Internacional para el Desarrollo (AECID), or the Swedish International Development Cooperation Agency (SIDA). However, most of my argument is derived from observing the UK DFID, which I consider to be the preeminent and most influential among national aid organisations. Likewise, while I pay some attention to multilateral aid institutions such as the United Nations Development Programme (UNDP), I devote most of my attention to the World Bank, which enjoys a central intellectual and financial presence in development debates. Of course, these donors are not monolithic organisations, so most of the time I refer to specific missions, units, and even individual practitioners within them, who are usually the agents of change within otherwise inertia-driven bureaucracies.

Political leaders are crucial for understanding aid, as they shape the kinds of approaches that they can fund as well as the implementation and eventual success of any intervention. Aid donors are severely constrained by the vagaries of partisan politics. I use 'conservative' and 'progressive' as basic labels for those politicians who pursue, respectively, a retrenchment or expansion of aid: the former often behave as 'aid hawks', who want to monitor every single penny spent, while the latter serve the role of 'aid champions', who want to expand aid budgets. In developing countries, political leaders are the gatekeepers and veto players of development interventions, determining whether reform happens or not. In my cases, they often pop up as antagonists of the reformers who seek to advance new ways of doing public policy. It is those reformers who are my true protagonists: the men and women who take up reform agendas and dare to challenge the status quo in pursuit of development.

I explore the contentious interactions between leaders, reformers, and donors in brief examples from countries such as Ghana, Nigeria, and Uganda, but mainly through in-depth studies of Sierra Leone, Liberia and Honduras. Sierra Leone and Liberia are two small West African states that endured state collapse, military coups, armed rebellions, and civil war throughout the 1990s. Their claim to celebrity was for a while defined by tragedy: warlord-turned-president-turned-war criminal Charles Taylor, conflict diamonds, child soldiers. However, what I study in this book is the donor-sponsored attempt to rebuild these states after the end of their civil wars in the early 2000s: the decade or so between 2000 and 2012 in which they became veritable laboratories for foreign aid. Across the Atlantic, Honduras was ravaged not by war but by natural disaster. In 1998, Hurricane Mitch devastated much of the country, prompting a massive inflow of international support. The challenges were not the same as in Sierra Leone and Liberia, although some of the underlying problems – elite factions, corruption, exclusion – do resonate. Honduras was also a laboratory for aid effectiveness, giving rise to one of the most coordinated and politically salient donor groups in the developing world.

For all of these cases, I draw on my experience as a researcher and practitioner. In that sense, the chapters of this book compile experiences and insights spanning a decade of work. I visited Sierra Leone in 2010 and Liberia in 2011 as part of my PhD research at Cornell University, which I began in 2007. I worked briefly in Honduras as a short-term consultant for the World Bank in 2013. Since that year, I have researched DFID, the World Bank, and other aid agencies as part of my job at the Effective States and Inclusive Development Research Centre (ESID), a DFID-funded programme. Through ESID, I also came to research public-sector reforms in Ghana and Uganda. In 2016, I became an advisor for a DFID-funded anticorruption project in Ghana. All of this makes for an odd collection of biases: I am both academic researcher and policy practitioner, advising some of the very organisations that I have studied. Donors have funded my research, though my publications are uniformly critical of their practices. I have a foot in academia and a foot in aid policy, and that is the standpoint from which I write this book.

The opportunity to reflect on a decade of research and work has led me to write something that looks very much like an ethnography of the politics of aid. Over the years, I have reviewed hundreds of programme documents, interviewed a couple hundred informants in donor and recipient countries, and conducted participant observation both as a member of various intellectual communities working on foreign aid and as a consultant on the ground. For this book specifically, I have tried to rely chiefly on data and documentation, triangulating from as many sources as possible. Interviews and testimonies – always anonymised – are often used solely as illustrations to support the main narrative. But many of the political challenges of development are seldom documented in written material, which makes oral histories a requisite component of this kind of research. While people in the know might be able to discern some of the individuals that I have talked to, I am confident that they would not be capable of attaching a name to any particular quote. Anonymity is essential for a study of the politics of aid, as so much day-to-day work relies on questioning or bending the rules imposed by public aid discourse.

Structure of the book

This book is structured along three broad themes: the politics of aid in donor countries, the politics of development in recipient countries, and the attempt to bring about a smarter kind of aid system.

Chapters 1 and 2 explore the constraints that donor-country politics have imposed on aid agencies. Using illustrations from USAID, DFID, and AECID, I argue that most of our debates on aid have less to do with development than with conventional partisan politics. The lack of a strong constituency for foreign aid makes it particularly vulnerable to instrumentalisation and manipulation by loud voices that are involved in much broader arguments between conservative and progressive philosophies of the state. Chapter 1 shows how aid budgets rise and fall, and how policies are adopted and abandoned, not as a result of the reasoned examination of development challenges, but in response to partisan advocates seizing windows of opportunity to wage a proxy war. Chapter 2 shifts to a recent consequence of this unbridled partisanship: the blind pursuit of managerial certainty as a standard for foreign aid. Since the financial crisis of the 2000s,

and especially since the rise to power of conservative governments in the United Kingdom, Canada, and Australia, VfM considerations have come to redefine how donor agencies work and
think, gradually displacing the more transformational but less
measurable interventions that are part and parcel of development.

Chapters 3 through 5 delve into the implications of transformational change, documenting a politics of development assistance
that simply does not fit within the narrow confines of aid debates
in donor countries. I use three specific cases to illustrate the key
ingredients of this political approach. In Chapter 3, the rise and
fall of DFID-funded Sierra Leone Anti-Corruption Commission
perfectly illustrates the challenges of development as a process of
institutional change that creates winners and losers. In countries
where clientelism and patronage are rife, such as Sierra Leone,
political leaders tend to oppose, obstruct, or undermine reforms
that threaten their discretionary abuse of public office. This reality places donors in the unenviable position of having to side with
either political leaders or institutional reformers. Sometimes aid
contracts have strict conditions attached, aimed at persuading or
coercing recalcitrant politicians into supporting change, as I document in Chapter 4. But even when donors appear to be strict,
as in Liberia's Governance and Economic Management Assistance Program, they are still vulnerable to their own coordination
problems and the skilful way in which recipient-country leaders
play them off against one another. The fact is that aid agencies
have particular identities and espouse particular values, which
can cause tension in times of political uncertainty. As I discuss
in Chapter 5, Honduras had arguably the strongest donor coordination group in the world, known as the G-16, yet this group
found itself in the politically uncomfortable position of having to

mediate between government and civil society, and then between the different sides of a palace coup that had a radical president ousted from the country. Aid interventions, by their very existence, legitimise some actors and delegitimise others, and donors are not always equipped to navigate the political implications of their actions.

Lastly, Chapters 6, 7, and the Conclusion turn the lens back on the aid system in order to explore whether a different approach to development assistance is possible. Chapter 6 documents the rise of the Thinking and Working Politically community, which advocates a more context-sensitive and politically smart approach to aid programmes. I present evidence of two politically smart interventions in Ghana and Nigeria to demonstrate that this kind of work is feasible and potentially transformational. However, the agenda is weakened by its disconnect with dominant aid incentives, its lack of a public narrative, and constant arguments over basic concepts. That is why in Chapter 7 I sketch out the contours of a different analytical approach, 'contentious development politics', and discuss whether there is room for a more eclectic and pragmatic theory of aid within the development studies community and donor societies in general. The Conclusion closes the book with a brief reflection on ethics and leadership. I ask whether the moral underpinnings that enabled and expanded the aid system for six decades – humane internationalism – are even possible in a twenty-first-century world of political nativism and isolationism. My own response is hopeful but pragmatic: a new moral vision is being developed by practitioners and reformers, but its ultimate success will require coordinated action from those of us who believe in aid as a messy tool for promoting development.

ONE | The theatrics of aid debates

On 16 April 2004, a young and idealistic politician read his inaugural speech as prime minister in the Spanish parliament. José Luis Rodríguez Zapatero had reached the premiership almost by accident, riding a wave of social anxiety over the previous government's political mishandling of a terrorist attack that struck Madrid days before the election, and which galvanised the year-long popular protest over Spain's involvement in the invasion of Iraq. Zapatero's Socialist Party reached the polls armed not with an agenda but a vision for progressive change, both domestically and internationally. He followed a simple creed he had inherited from his grandfather, who had fought seventy years earlier against the military faction of General Franco: 'a limitless thirst for peace, a love of goodness, and the social betterment of the meek'[1]. At home, they would use the power of government to build a more equitable and progressive society, enacting laws on dependents, marriage equality, or gender parity. Abroad, they would push an optimistic multilateralism that countered the post-September 11 narrative of clash of civilisations.

By the turn of the twenty-first century, Spain had become a rising actor in the international scene; two decades of democratic consolidation and economic growth had enabled growing trade relations and a more vocal role within the European Union (EU).

History had bequeathed it cultural and economic ties with both Latin America and North Africa, which made it a useful intermediary for the EU's new common foreign policy. Conservative prime minister José María Aznar had used his parliamentary majority since the year 2000 to actively seek a higher profile for the country. In the months following September 11, he became a staunch ally of President George Bush, lending Spanish troops to the North Atlantic Treaty Organization (NATO) invasion of Afghanistan, and then featuring in the infamous Azores Declaration on Iraq, together with Bush, Britain's Tony Blair, and Portugal's José Manuel Barroso. For the United States, these three leaders were their Western European allies in the Iraq dispute, and their support in the UN would be essential for the legitimation of any invasion. This granted Spain's conservative government a perhaps disproportionate amount of international clout as well as a growing level of domestic dissent. The anti-war protests that swept the world in early 2003 had a very partisan bent in Spain, amplifying the voice and presence of a new generation of Socialist Party leaders.

Against the backdrop of his predecessor's military adventurism and support for Bush's 'war on terror', Zapatero desired to fundamentally change course in Spanish foreign policy. While acknowledging the difficult security challenges facing Western countries, he believed that enhanced cooperation, not conflict, was the key to overcoming them. This included not only practical collaboration in matters of defence and prosperity, but also a grander aspiration to bring cultures – or, as he later put it, civilisations – closer together. His foreign policy was built around a strong pro-European commitment, a focus on Latin America and the Mediterranean, a loyal but critical relationship with the

United States, and an unequivocal alignment with international law and organisations. It would also, crucially, 'make development cooperation an essential element of our foreign policy'[2]. At the time, Spain's gross domestic product (GDP) placed it right outside the G-8 in international rankings, but the legacy of Franco's dictatorship and the focus on internal democratisation and growth had left the country punching below its weight on the international scene. In contrast to Aznar's choice of military and security tools for raising the country's profile, the new prime minister would focus on more charitable and humanitarian means[3].

Two months before his election as prime minister, Zapatero was invited to speak before the Spanish Coordinator of Development NGOs and the 0.7% Platform[4]. These civil society organisations represented the strongest voices of a small but vibrant development sector that was highly dependent on the national aid budget. Towards the end of the conservative government's second term, the amount of overseas development assistance disbursed by Spain had stagnated at 0.24% of GDP. This was a not insignificant contribution of around $2 billion to international development, but it fell short of the decade-long aspiration to achieve the symbolic 0.7% target (which in Europe had been reached only by Nordic countries). At that meeting in February 2004, Zapatero promised to substantially increase foreign aid to 0.5% of GDP by 2008, with a further goal of 0.7% by 2012 if he was re-elected. Not only that, he would change the official name of the ministry under which the Spanish aid agency was located to 'Ministry of Foreign Affairs and Cooperation' to signal his commitment to a foreign policy focused on peace and poverty reduction. In a hearing at the parliamentary commission on international cooperation in June 2004, the new minister for foreign affairs argued that 'a democratic society can only feel proud of itself when all human beings, men and women, around the world, enjoy the political, economic, social and environmental rights that we all want to enjoy'[5].

Once in office, the new prime minister demonstrated that his electoral promises were not empty ones. Albeit more slowly than anticipated, Spain's relative aid contribution doubled from 0.24% in 2004 to 0.46% of GDP in 2009. In absolute terms, this represented a jump from around $2 billion a year to $6.9 billion at the peak of 2008[6]. In order to manage this increase, Zapatero enlisted the support of the Socialist Party's former head of NGO relations, Leire Pajín, who at 28 years of age became Spain's youngest ever Secretary of State for International Cooperation (four years earlier, she had become the youngest elected MP in the country). With some experience in the NGO sector, Pajín became the face of a new era in Spanish aid, defined not only by the growing budget, but also by a closer working relationship with civil society and reforms of the central agency responsible for disbursing and overseeing all aid expenditures[7]. This last element was crucial, given how decentralised and chaotic Spain's aid system was, with virtually every public organisation from the ministries all the way down to universities disbursing foreign aid in one way or another[8].

In Spanish politics, Zapatero would be known in the following years for his love of symbols and subversion as a way of advancing a progressive agenda. Appointing a 28-year-old to oversee the country's foreign aid was just another powerful gesture in a list that included a cabinet with total gender parity and the appointment of a pregnant MP as defence minister. Some of these symbolic gestures were virtually costless, while others carried with them a hefty price tag. Changing a ministry's name doesn't seem major, until one realises the thousands of emails, web addresses, and mastheads that needed to be changed overnight. And this was nothing compared to the suddenly ballooning budget that Spain's aid agency would have to coordinate. However, that did not seem to be a major concern in those optimistic days of March 2004. A new progressive government was in place, and new progressive priorities would follow. Ultimately, the actual impact of the increased aid budget was a secondary consideration. The gesture – the signal – was what mattered most.

Zapatero's case illustrates a broader trend in the politics of donor countries, where public debates and political argumentation on foreign aid are rarely – if ever – about development. Instead of a substantial conversation, the voters and taxpayers are usually treated to a particular form of performance politics in which aid serves as a proxy for deeper, more ideological clashes between conservatism and progressivism. Political posturing takes over reality. The goal of this chapter is to illuminate these theatrics by unpacking the dominant discourse, revealing its most frequent tropes, and asking why it is that, of all public policy domains, foreign aid is so prone to be affected by completely unrelated calculations.

Is aid a partisan issue?
Before delving into the political theatrics of aid, let me offer an important clarification: basic development goals are not partisan. Whether we lean more to the left or right of the political spectrum has no effect on our desire for certain things, such as a paying job, good health, political freedom, low criminal activity, an impartial justice system, and certain means of helping those in need.

These are all things that both progressives and conservatives would find desirable: they could disagree about the particulars, the form of regulation, or who exactly deserves what, but it is hard to disagree with development as the pursuit of fair markets, efficient states, and personal freedom. It is important to get this clarification out of the way because our public debates about aid are already incredibly politicised. But therein lies the key: our debates are largely about the volume and means of aid, not about the goals of development.

Going back to the Spanish case, the impact of Zapatero's socialist government on Spanish aid policy was not actually that exceptional. Political scientists have spent decades looking into the determinants of aid budgets and allocation, exploring all sorts of variables running the gamut from colonial history to domestic social expenditure. One of those variables under examination is the impact of political ideology and partisanship, stemming from the folk expectation that leftist governments are more likely to give aid generously than right-wing ones. This is an interesting conjecture, because there has long been an assumption in Western democracies that foreign affairs (which encompass foreign aid) are above purely partisan squabbles. However, the historical record flies in the face of that assumption. Nordic countries, many of which have been governed by social democratic parties for decades, are among the most generous donors. Denmark, Norway, and Sweden have never dipped below the 0.7% threshold in the last twenty-five years, and at times have devoted more than 1% of GDP to overseas development assistance. Conversely, countries lacking strong social democratic parties, such as the United States and Japan, have consistently ranked below OECD averages in their relative aid contributions. This distinction was summarised by David Lumsdaine, who argued that governments project their domestic orientations onto the international scene. As with social spending at home, left-wing parties are more likely to increase aid spending abroad[9].

When taken outside specific cases, however, the evidence is much less conclusive, as different variables and statistical models are taken into account. A recent article does not find government ideology to be a significant determinant of aid disbursement when compared with other domestic and international variables[10]. Earlier research found that the mere existence of a left-leaning party in power should not have an unmediated, direct effect on aid budgets: it is instead the development of a socialist welfare state and government social spending that mediates whether social-democratic governments actually spend more money on aid[11]. That was the defining feature of Nordic countries compared with countries such as Austria, where left-wing parties had long governed without establishing strong welfare states. Yet another statistical analysis finds a significant correlation between changes in the economic ideology of ruling parties and the increase or decline of aid contributions, with a particularly marked effect on assistance to the least developed and lower income countries[12]. The influence of partisanship on aid is not limited to the size of the budget alone. In the United States, for instance, aid to African countries is more likely to follow economic need and democratic achievement under Democrats than under Republicans: ideology in this case is the world view through which policymakers interpret the problems and needs of developing countries[13]. It is, therefore, not uncommon to see self-identified progressive political parties such as Zapatero's increasing aid budgets while self-identified conservatives slash them. On purely ideological grounds, development cooperation can be seen as the foreign arm of the welfare state, as familiar to internationalists on the left as the military is to internationalists on the right. It makes absolute sense for fiscal conservatives and advocates of market liberalism to suspect the extension of state bureaucracy, which can only be financed through taxation or debt.

One might ask, however, whether the policy preferences of these parties are, in fact, representative of their voters and supporters. A project looking into the World Values Survey and the Gallup Voice of the People survey to assess contextual and individual determinants of public opinion on foreign aid in nineteen donor countries found that an individual's self-described position in the left–right spectrum had 'a significant effect on support for foreign aid'; agreement with closely related statements such as 'the poor are lazy' or 'the poor can escape poverty' also had statistically significant effects[14]. In the United States, the Pew Research Center asked in 2013 which federal government programmes the public would increase, decrease, or maintain at the same level. Of the nineteen categories surveyed, foreign aid had the biggest partisan gap, with 45% more Republicans than Democrats supporting a decrease; the gap was in fact wider than for high-profile controversial issues such as unemployment benefits or public healthcare[15]. This hyper-partisanship probably explains the widespread misperception among American voters about the size of their aid budget, which they estimated as 26% of the total federal budget in a 2015 Kaiser Family Foundation survey[16].

The United States may be an exception in the donor community. Across the EU, voting publics are generally supportive of aid. A 2010 special Eurobarometer survey found that 89% of Europeans considered development cooperation to be highly or very important, a result that is roughly consistent with previous surveys. There was some variation across countries, with Swedes twice as likely to consider aid 'very important' as the Portuguese, for instance. However, the 90% pattern of support was remarkably consistent across EU members, regardless of the political party in power[17].

So, donor publics tend to be broadly in favour of aid, despite being exposed to precious little information about international development and foreign aid. What, then, would motivate someone like renowned development economist Paul Collier to claim that '[t]he key obstacle to reforming aid is public opinion'[18]? It seems that there is a dichotomy between the long-term preferences of donor publics, which are likely supportive of helping the poor in developing countries, and the short-term debates of donor politics, in which political representatives run the gamut from the enthusiastic to the apocalyptic. Where does all the vitriol come from? And how does controversy come to displace actual voter preferences, let alone actual development outcomes?

The tropes of aid controversies

Our political debates about foreign aid could be seen as a very repetitive kind of performance, where roughly the same actors speak roughly the same lines with clockwork regularity. There are tropes on both the left and the right. The left-wing argument about aid, which was clear in the case of Spanish Prime Minister Zapatero, is about a vague form of internationalism, the kind supported by self-styled 'citizens of the world', who feel compelled to aid those starving children that feature in NGO ads. I will come back to the depth and veracity of this form of solidarity when I resume the story of Zapatero's aid budget in Spain. But the most pervasive, insidious, and – by far – entertaining claims definitely come from some corners of the conservative movement, where foreign aid has become a safe punching bag for those seeking to make a point or simply call for attention.

The most basic of all arguments against aid is also a more technical one: aid does not work. That is the basic premise of half a dozen books by economists William Easterly and Dambisa Moyo, who subscribe to the view that it is free markets, and not planned intervention, that gets people out of poverty. Easterly has called aid 'the cartel of good intentions' and supplied conservative commentators everywhere with a killer fact: since the 1960s, Western countries have spent $2 trillion in overseas assistance with little to show for it – many Africans, in particular, are still desperately poor. A killer fact indeed, but perhaps less so when we put it into perspective. Yes, $2 trillion sounds like a lot of money to any reasonable taxpayer, and absent any definitive evidence of impact it is likely to make us feel indignant and even betrayed[19]. But let us do the math here. Spread out over five decades (say, 1965–2015), the total amount of aid that OECD countries have given averages out to $40 billion dollars per year. One way to further divide the pot is by looking at how many countries have received this aid. Let us be really conservative and consider just the top fifty recipients: that $2 trillion suddenly becomes $800 million per recipient, per year. For some countries, such as Guinea-Bissau or Malawi, that looks like a lot of money. But consider the GDP of Nigeria, which in 2013 was sitting at around $520 billion. And then consider that $800 million is equivalent to the combined wage bill of football clubs Manchester City, Manchester United and Chelsea for the 2016–17 season. I will revisit the issue of whether aid does or doesn't work, but for now let us just agree that throwing numbers around is not necessarily the most useful way to talk about development.

A second trope, and a more worrying one, is that too much of foreign aid is stolen or wasted. Writing for *The Daily Mail* on the eve of her first parliamentary appearance as Secretary of State for International Development, MP Priti Patel declared that 'British aid is being wasted and stolen'[20]. The title for her piece was actually 'Too much of YOUR money is simply stolen or squandered', which seems a bit abrupt for someone about to take over the UK's foreign aid budget. Of course, she was forced to make some concession in the article, acknowledging the achievements of a global aid system that delivers successes 'of which we can all be proud'. But she committed to imposing even stronger checks and controls on the system (which I will discuss in the next chapter). It is no coincidence that Patel chose *The Daily Mail* as an outlet for her opening declaration of intentions. On the same page as her article, the paper boasted about leading the way 'in reporting how British taxpayers' money has fallen into the hands of the corrupt, been wasted on gimmicks and – in some cases – been lavished on projects that do not exist'. The paper has consistently published fantastical headlines linking aid to corruption, dictators, and waste. In March 2016, it launched a petition to the UK government and Parliament called 'Stop spending a fixed 0.7 per cent slice of our national wealth on Foreign Aid', which gathered 230,000 signatures. When the petition reached Parliament, it was dismissed by most MPs involved in the debate, much to *The Daily Mail*'s dismay[21].

The third trope that I want to highlight is about highly paid aid professionals. In the United States, conservative think tanks such as the American Enterprise Institute (AEI) and Heritage Foundation often write about the byzantine and incestuous relationships between aid agencies and the private experts and providers who implement their projects. In a piece for the AEI, former Pentagon official Michael Rubin wrote about the growth of a 'USAID mafia, in which USAID employees retire to contractors who use their expertise to win contracts', and then 'flip contracts to subcontractors, each of whom take their cut for overhead, staff, and consulting fees'[22]. Rubin's concern is somewhat undermined by the much bigger mafia of defence contractors, who consistently overcharge the Pentagon. However, the characterisation of aid types as scheming and money-grubbing is not unique to the United States. In the United Kingdom, *The Daily Mail* has again led the charge against what it calls 'foreign aid fat cats', who have apparently built a '£1.4 billion empire ... with YOUR tax money'.[23] The *Mail* decries the rise of contractors who bid for DFID projects and implement them on the ground, which leaves a lot of the money back in the United Kingdom instead of in the hands of poor people. The paper went so far as to name and shame a few 'poverty barons', who have formed a 'consultancy cartel' of mostly British firms implementing contracts for the government. The language is similar to that of the 'Beltway bandits' who contract for USAID: specialised for-profit organisations that actually implement most projects of American aid in developing countries. There is a profound irony to this complaint, in that it is conservatives who have reduced staffing numbers within DFID and USAID to the point that the agencies can barely implement their own projects, and, consequently, it was conservatives who pushed the government into relying on private providers. Such a market-based system for aid should make aid deniers smile, but, apparently, some people are incapable of finding even the barest silver lining.

These three tropes are so powerful, and so prevalent, that it is a wonder average citizens are not opposed to foreign aid entirely. Together, they paint a rather grim picture: aid ends up either lining the pockets of exploitative consultants or being wasted on non-existent projects – or it just doesn't really work. Taken in combination, these arguments form a powerful discourse through which outspoken corners of the conservative movement seek to create an aversion to foreign aid among voters. It is political communication at its most astute. The terminology is appealing, the statements are clear and direct, and the repetition is relentless.

In the United States, foreign aid is seen as a good thing by a relatively small percentage of the centre–left of the political spectrum, and, even then, it is always with a caveat. In 2010, the Brookings Institution welcomed an announcement by President Obama on global development policy, which included 'the elevation and strengthening of the US Agency for International Development' as the country's 'lead development agency'[24]; however, the authors made sure to acknowledge USAID's need to rebuild its internal processes. It was a rather meek celebration of the aid system, and hardly a proportional counter to conservative attacks: barely a few months later, for instance, 165 Republicans in the House of Representatives supported a plan to defund most of USAID[25]. In the United Kingdom, some Labour MPs did confront Priti Patel about her claim that much of British aid was wasted and found that she was unable to provide specific numbers. In March 2016, the Department for International Development actually responded publicly to five of the most outrageous claims made by *The Daily Mail*. However, most of the pro-aid conversation is confined to the pages – and mostly the website – of *The Guardian* newspaper, whose Global Development section is funded by the Bill & Melinda Gates Foundation.

The right-wing tabloids in the United Kingdom and the right-wing think tanks in the United States have basically won the debate, and there is little that aid proponents can do about it. Instead of speaking to the public, then, progressive experts and pundits are left talking to one another and responding in a purely reactive way to conservative misrepresentations of aid. They cannot defeat conservatives at the aid discourse game for three reasons. First, the right has spent more time coming up with catchy and flashy tirades on everything that it hates, from welfarism to political correctness to multinational organisations. Second, progressives are prone to responding to criticism with fact, when the truth is mostly peripheral to the three tropes about aid that I have discussed. Instead, it may be more helpful to develop a counter-narrative about aid, a point that I will develop below. Third, aid proponents are in the trenches fighting to preserve overseas development assistance and the small sector it nurtures, while aid detractors are waging a much broader war, one in which attacking aid is an almost insignificant proxy for bigger, more ambitious objectives.

A small battle in a much bigger war
The reality is that these claims, and the controversies that they feed, are not really about development. Aid fights are just a useful, instrumental version of bigger and more bitter partisan fights between small-government conservatives and welfare-state progressives. The proof of this is the fact that aid detractors seldom miss the opportunity to make a larger point about public policy in general.

When Priti Patel made her opening statement as Secretary of State for International Development in 2016, she was speaking about more than just British aid. Her article began with a simple claim: 'The aid budget isn't my money, or the Government's money. It's taxpayers' money – your money. We politicians have a duty to spend it well, in ways that not only help the world's poorest, but also help us here at home'. Together with this avowed commitment to serving the taxpayer, Patel justified her tough stance on the aid system by relying on 'some core Conservative principles': wealth creation instead of dependency, people instead of the state, investment and trade instead of intervention, and paid work instead of passive assistance. When in 2011 the Republican Study Group (a group of over 170 small-government conservative representatives) proposed a drastic defund of USAID, they did it as part of a larger plan to save $2.5 trillion in federal spending over a decade[26]. This plan resonated with another proposal the previous year, which came out of the Heritage Foundation. This sought to cut $343 billion from the federal budget[27]. The Heritage plan included cutting over $2.5 billion from USAID's Development Assistance Program, but this was small fry compared with the over $8 billion in suggested cuts to education grants, $15 billion in farm subsidies, and $45 billion in the federal highway system. It was not an anti-aid proposal, even if it was reported as such by sympathetic observers of USAID. It was an anti-government spending proposal. When fiscal conservatives take a look at foreign aid, what they see is an extension of the welfare state that they criticise so much at home: benefits and entitlement for the poor, and not even our own poor, for that matter.

Likewise, progressive investment in foreign aid is usually a small appendix to an expansion of public spending on domestic policy. The strengthening of USAID under President Obama is almost an afterthought when seen in the context of the biggest economic stimulus in modern American history and the introduction of massive health care reform under so-called Obamacare. In Spain, Prime Minister Zapatero's commitment to aid was part of his vision for a progressive foreign policy, but his real interest lay in welfare state reform and expansion, with a particular emphasis on vulnerable groups and people with special needs. It is not a coincidence that the UK Department for International Development was made an independent ministry under the Labour government of Tony Blair, or that the person overseeing its original mandate and vision was Clare Short, a famously progressive Labour MP who resigned on principle during Britain's involvement in the Iraq War. The 0.7% goal is likely to be supported by politicians and voters who like the idea of a bigger role for the state in managing markets, education or the environment. For most people who are broadly supportive of development assistance, the aid budget is not a core concern: it is the icing on the cake.

In that sense, the aid budget displays a significant level of what economists call elasticity: its own changes are sensitive to changes in other variables, such as welfare state expenditures or the overall size of a government's budget[28]. A study looking into the various motivations for tinkering with aid budgets by four European governments found clear evidence of how secondary aid considerations are. In Belgium, for instance, development assistance was 'political small change', used by cabinets to balance other considerations between political groups[29]. The degree of elasticity relative to non-aid-related factors makes this a unique sector in Western public policy. But why is that? Why can politicians play around with aid budgets and targets to such a large extent without actually paying much attention to aid itself? The answer is actually straightforward: foreign aid does not have a constituency.

Modern industrialised democracies operate on the basis of the aggregation of interests. At a high level, aggregation happens through elections and representative democracy: voters choose their preferred representatives, and these elected officials make policies. While there can be more or less of a disconnect between voter preferences and politicians' choices, it is difficult for an elected representative to go squarely and openly against a clear public priority. At a lower level, interest groups create a more persistent and perhaps impactful form of representation: industry associations, chambers of commerce, trade unions, advocacy groups, community associations, NGOs, and lobby and pressure groups of every ilk. In more liberal states such as the United States and the United Kingdom, these groups tend to operate through the logic of pluralism: money equals voice, and interest groups compete with one another for access and influence. In the more welfare-oriented states of continental Europe, in contrast, a system called corporativism redirects grievances to established commissions bringing together business and workers. However, the broader point stands: our public policies tend to be representative of societal interests.

Wild changes in regulation and government budgets often generate societal backlash. If you cut education budgets, teachers are likely to voice their opposition, protest, and maybe even go on strike. The same goes for nurses, doctors, or waste-collection workers if their respective sectors are under threat. Similarly, if you promise an increase in the regulation of a private market, companies may organise a lobbying effort (which may or may not have a public dimension) to persuade government to stay its hand. Financial markets are another way through which private investors and firms can influence public policy, by signalling their preferences to governments playing around with regulation. When the welfare state is up for debate, relevant interest groups promptly take sides: conservatives are usually backed by businesses, finance, libertarian movements, or religious organisations, while progressives find support in unions, students, NGOs, artists and celebrities. The battle lines are as clear cut as they are predictable for every sector of public expenditure. Every sector, that is, except aid.

The invisible constituency

Who are the constituents of foreign aid? Whose interests is the aid budget serving? This is a surprisingly difficult question, with at least three completely different answers.

The seemingly obvious answer is that foreign aid represents the preferences of taxpayers in donor countries. From this standpoint, aid is just another category of public expenditure covered by taxes, such as roads or public schools, and therefore it is subject to the usual demands of policymakers being accountable to voters. The logic of representative government leads us to expect a world in which foreign aid budgets respond to popular preferences. But, of course, we know that this is not necessarily true. Even if support for aid splits along partisan lines, as it does in the United States, that does not necessarily mean it is a core issue for voters, let alone a question the broader public ever ponders between elections. There are at least three reasons for this. First, aid budgets are generally small, especially when compared with health care, education, pensions, defence, or debt servicing.

Western governments cannot balance budgets with aid money alone. Second, the effects of aid are distant to donor publics. It is easy to overlook what is happening with aid projects in Malawi when everyone's attention is drawn to school performance or unemployment figures in their own country. Third, and perhaps as a result of the first two reasons, the general public knows very little about aid. It is a very specialised policy area, and under-standing its effects requires knowledge of developing country contexts. For donor taxpayers, aid can be as opaque as national security, but it lacks all the attention the latter receives.

A more enlightened and well-meaning answer to the question of who is served by foreign aid focuses on those receiving it. In abstract terms, we are talking about the very poor in developing countries, even if actual aid gets channelled through govern-ments, NGOs, or private companies. This is the response for people who care about whether aid actually promotes develop-ment. It is a curious form of accountability, because the ultimate beneficiaries have no say whatsoever on the levels of aid or how it is managed. However, there are experts and professionals in donor countries who take on the mantle of representatives of the foreign poor. This makes the answer a bit more complicated, because then we would have to add the caveat that aid serves the interests of developing-country populations as seen through the eyes of donor-country NGOs, experts and scholars. The fact is that there is no clear chain of accountability between aid providers and recipients, at least at the macro level. Those implementing projects on the ground will set up sensitisation and dissemination workshops to make sure that the voices of their local partners are being heard. But this rarely filters up to the corridors of power in donor governments, so we cannot say that the poor are the real constituents of aid in any but the most aspirational of senses.

If not donor taxpayers or aid recipients, then who? Which actors are most invested in foreign aid as a public policy in donor countries? It turns out that American and British conservatives are not far off the mark: it is the aid 'mafia' and the 'fat cats' that have the most to gain and lose from changes in aid budgets. Dropping the insulting language for a moment, donor countries have grown small but vibrant ecosystems around their respective aid agencies. NGOs are often recipients of donor money and implementers of development projects. For-profit businesses flourish in those aid ecosystems centred around tenders and competitive bidding, such as the United States and Britain. And these core implementing partners are surrounded by a cloud of think tanks, academics, and consultants, who are also likely to benefit from aid money channelled through academic research, campaign advocacy, or policy advice. All of these actors are invested in the continued reproduction of their aid ecosystems, so they are most likely to become vocal defenders of aid budgets whenever conservatives threaten to slash them. But most of them are also committed intellectually to the task of development assistance. Easterly may paint them as ideological or even self-serving 'planners', but the fact is that many of them could earn a much larger salary working in a more conventional for-profit sector. Those populating the aid ecosystem are the true constituency of foreign aid.

It bears mentioning that there is in fact a fourth category of people who may have an interest in foreign aid policy, but not for the reasons one imagines. For many politicians and policymakers, foreign aid is just another instrument in the toolkit of foreign policy, which can be wielded to improve trade relations, gain international recognition, or attain regional influence. This explains the remarkable consensus among political elites in the United Kingdom, for instance, where the 0.7% target was actually secured by a Conservative government. But let us dispel the notion that this role of aid has much to do with actual development. If aid can serve as a proxy for fiscal conservatives to fight their budget wars, it has an equally instrumental worth for those policymakers who see it as just another item in the menu of foreign affairs.

At the end of the day, even if we can associate partisanship with certain preferences about aid, these rarely go beyond the relative size of the budget. There are many loud voices out there who claim to speak for taxpayers, or for the poor who receive our help, but that does not mean that aid systems are accountable to anyone but a relative narrow political and policy elite. Detractors of foreign aid usually fall in the fiscal conservative camp that decries state interventionism and the economic and moral pitfalls of welfare dependency. They engage with development issues only tangentially, and always as pundits or provocateurs. Proponents of aid, in turn, are usually the very same people whose livelihoods and very sense of professional identity depends on its continuation: their involvement in the aid ecosystem makes them almost blindly supportive of larger budgets, and it is unclear whether their claim to speak for 'the people' actually holds up to scrutiny. Finally, we have the foreign policy types, who just see aid as a form of soft power on the world stage. With such protagonists and motivations, it is little wonder that public debates about aid have only a marginal relation to the problem of development. Even those inside the aid industry can fall prey to this rarefied atmosphere, in which a trench mentality usually precludes open and pragmatic debate.

It's not the size of the budget, but what you do with it

The case of Spain between 2004 and 2010 perfectly illustrates how disconnected aid policy debates in donor countries can be from the actual challenges of development. I began this chapter with the promising rise of a new progressive prime minister, José Luis Rodríguez Zapatero, who delivered on his promise to make foreign aid more central to Spanish foreign policy. As I mentioned above, the numbers did indeed get bigger: up to 0.46% of GDP by 2009, more than tripling the absolute volume of Spanish aid to about $7 billion a year. But the figures hide a more complex story, one that exposes the limits of partisan pandering to a very insular constituency utterly disconnected from the broader public.

When Spanish aid officials found themselves with a rapidly growing budget in the early years of Zapatero's government, they quickly realised that the central development cooperation agency (AECID) did not have the capacity to absorb all of this money. AECID is a public organisation, chiefly staffed by a mix of senior-level political appointees and lower-level civil servants. The appointees are usually drawn from the diplomatic corps, and they tend to be more interested in international affairs than development proper. As to the civil servants, they are as likely to work in aid as they are in education or agriculture. Some of them do stay with AECID for a long time and become seasoned veterans. But, at the end of the day, the Spanish aid system is populated by project managers, not aid experts. Faced with an overnight deluge of money driven by political fiat, one civil servant recalled, they resorted to the only conceivable solution at the time: pumping the money out by increasing contributions to multilateral organisations such as the UN and the EU, and giving out grants to Spanish development NGOs to actually carry out development work.

The development NGO sector in Spain is thriving but fragmented[30]. There are myriad small charities and organisations that apply for public funding to carry out development projects, some as small as funding a single school in an African village. There are bigger players, too, such as the Spanish chapter of Oxfam, or umbrella organisations such as the Development NGO Coordinator. The latter was one of the co-hosts of Zapatero's speech in which he pledged to reach the 0.7% target in the days before the 2004 election. The sector as a whole is deeply dependent on the public aid budget to operate, but their relationship with AECID is symbiotic: this agency supplies the funding, and they supply the advocacy and implementation. It is a mutually beneficial relationship, so when the budget tripled in the space of four years, it was logical for the government to turn to the NGOs[31]. There was a problem with this choice, however. The sector did not actually have the managerial or technical skills to absorb all of this money and redirect it towards effective development interventions. Without large, capable organisations able to benefit from economies of scale, the influx of funds multiplied overheads and basically overwhelmed NGOs' capacity. At that point, the sector could have had an honest debate about this conundrum and advised the government to diversify its funding strategy, or at least adopt a more gradual approach that would enable them to grow technically as they grew financially. However, they were so dependent on the state, and so enamoured of the largesse of a progressive government that catered to them, that they kept quiet. By doing so, they set themselves up for failure.

The perils of flooding the NGO sector with aid money should have been apparent to Spain's aid policymakers, starting with Secretary of State for International Cooperation Leire Pajín. But she demonstrated neither the willingness nor the capacity to address the challenges of effectiveness. Pajín herself had been president of the small development NGO International Solidarity, which was politically close to Zapatero's Socialist Party. Her expertise and political acumen made her a shoo-in for Secretary of State, but Pajín always saw the Spanish aid agency as a stepping stone to bigger things. She never became quite the energetic leader that the sector needed. In 2008, she left the post to become the secretary of organisation of the Socialist Party, making her the third most powerful politician in the country. She left behind an inchoate reform agenda that had not quite fixed the sector's absorptive problems or turned AECID into an effective manager and watchdog for them. Her successor in the agency was another socialist politico, Soraya Rodríguez, who had no background in international development.

When the financial crisis hit Spain in 2010, the aid budget stagnated, and when a year later the conservative People's Party came back to power, it was the first item to be slashed. In a matter of two years, the volume of Spanish cooperation dropped by two thirds; no one outside of the aid industry itself batted an eyelid. Development had never really been a priority of the socialists, and by that time there were bigger fish to fry. Just as it had been swollen out of proportion by the years of progressive largesse, Spain's aid ecosystem now became anaemic, another victim of the hammer of fiscal austerity as wielded by an uninterested conservative government. NGOs were the ones who felt the cut the hardest: drunk with the wild inflows of funding under Zapatero, they had never really diversified their portfolios. When the axe fell, it took with it many projects and jobs.

What is striking about the Spanish aid rollercoaster of 2004–10 is the extent to which the effectiveness of development coopera-tion was an afterthought for both progressives and conservatives. At no point were actual experts put in charge of the aid budget by the different governments. The central development agency, AECID, was never overhauled to grant it the managerial and technical capacity to oversee a much larger sector[32]. Even aid's constituents, the NGOs, lacked the willingness to rock the boat by openly addressing the challenges intrinsic to a development bubble that would prove fatal for them. This is what partisan-ship theatre did to Spain as a donor. This is the distance between actual development and the kinds of public conversations that we have in donor countries.

TWO | The banality of certainty

When George Bush became president of the United States in February 2001, USAID was in shambles after a decade of political neglect and hostility. During the 1990s it had lost roughly half of its budget and personnel to congressional Republicans eager to score political points against President Clinton. The end of the Cold War and the ensuing internationalist euphoria had also undermined USAID's old role as an arm of American diplomacy throughout the developing world. During Bush's campaign, there had been no indication that he would reverse this trend in any significant way. In January 2000, the prestigious journal *Foreign Affairs* published an article by his then foreign policy advisor, Condoleezza Rice, with the title 'Promoting the National Interest'[1]. Outlining the principles of a new Republican foreign policy in the post-Soviet world, Rice openly attacked Bill Clinton and the democrats for mistaking 'humanitarian interests' or those of an 'illusory international community' for the national interest. Peace, markets and prosperity were the core pillars of a vision that did not mention the word 'aid' even once. This is perhaps unsurprising coming from a woman who at the time was Senior Fellow at the Hoover Institution, one of America's preeminent conservative think tanks. No one expected things to take a positive turn for the DC-based aid community.

Shortly after taking office, President Bush appointed Andrew Natsios as administrator of USAID. Natsios was a former Republican congressman who had worked in the Agency during the administration of Bush's father, George H. W. Bush. Between 1989 and 1993, he was first tasked with directing USAID's disaster assistance, and then all food and humanitarian assistance. During the Clinton years, he worked as vice president of World Vision, a large NGO. Because of this, it would be easy to see him as a member of the kinds of industry cliques that I described in the previous chapter. But before joining USAID, Natsios had been a Republican congressman for over a decade, so he was hardly a progressive member of the aid intelligentsia. During his confirmation hearing before the US Senate, he did reject calls for replacing USAID with a grants scheme targeting NGOs and church groups; however, the vision he offered instead was one of limited aims tailored to the agency's limited means: focusing on conflict prevention and resolution, working more closely with the private sector, and reducing poverty through agricultural development. The appointment of Andrew Natsios heralded the arrival of a modest, almost managerial, approach to American foreign aid that was consistent with Rice's emphasis on promoting the national interest. Few people could have anticipated how quickly the time of modesty would give way to unprecedented largesse.

As it turned out, and against all odds, George Bush ambushed the entire foreign policy establishment with proposal after proposal to increase – not cut – America's engagement with the world's poor and disenfranchised[2]. Even before running for office, Bush and his wife, Laura, had become interested in making relief to Africa's poor a key element of his foreign policy – a perfect example of what would be known as Bush's 'compassionate conservatism'. Once in office, and particularly in the wake of the September 11 terrorist attacks, Bush wasted no time in pushing this moral agenda. First came the announcement, at the 2002 International Conference on Financing for Development in Monterrey, Mexico, that the budget would be raised from US$10 to US$15 billion a year, with the goal of supporting governments who pursued good governance and the rule of law. Around that time, the White House also commissioned a report on HIV/AIDS from the National Intelligence Council, which it used to justify the creation in 2003 of a massive programme, the President's Emergency Plan for AIDS Relief (known by its acronym, PEPFAR), the first of the large funds in the world of aid targeting a specific problem. Then came the creation the following year of an entirely new aid agency, the Millennium Challenge Corporation, to manage the new chunk of the budget devoted to recipients with good institutions and policies as well as monitor their progress against a set of political and legal benchmarks. And then there was the entry of the Pentagon into the aid business during the wars in Afghanistan and Iraq. All told, the American aid budget grew more between 2001 and 2006 than at any other time since the Marshall Plan that helped lift Europe from the ashes of World War II.

The unexpected availability of funds and the high level of political commitment at the very top should have made Andrew Natsios's work relatively easy[3]. His mixed background as a politician-turned-aid administrator, together with his experience working with relief assistance, should have made him a shoo-in for Bush's new era of compassionate conservatism. Instead, a few years after leaving his post as administrator, Natsios published a scathing essay on the legal and bureaucratic hurdles imposed by Congress on USAID: 'The Clash of the Counter-bureaucracy

and Development'[4]. In it, Natsios borrowed a concept from public administration scholar James Q. Wilson to describe 'the compliance side of aid programmes', the array of hearings, watchdogs
and auditors which ensure that every cent and penny spent on
development assistance achieves its stated purpose. The problem, as Natsios wrote, is that not all areas of public policy are
equally quantifiable, and this poses a particular problem for aid:

> The counter-bureaucracy ignores a central principle of develop-
> ment theory – that those development programmes that are most
> precisely and easily measured are the least transformational, and
> those programmes that are the most transformational are the least
> measured[5].

In other words, we can count how many vaccines we give to children in the Central African Republic, but we cannot easily assess
how effective our conflict-resolution and development interventions are in ensuring those children do not die a violent death.

As Natsios noted, the counter-bureaucracy has forced many
aid programmes to turn towards public health in search of measurability. Those that cannot are forced to come up with inventive
– and sometimes outright preposterous – ways to either demonstrate impact or distract from what is actually happening. Because
the counter-bureaucracy demands certainty, almost everyone in
the aid community feels compelled to underplay complexity and
uncertainty. This chapter explores that fundamental challenge to
how we talk about development assistance, documenting the rise
of the counter-bureaucracy, and supplying an almost century-old
concept that can explain why the current demand for evidence
and transparency is leading to a mix of banality and opacity.

Aid on the defensive

There is a clear appeal to arguments that aid does not work and should be scrapped, and one does not need to be a Republican congressman from the 1990s to appreciate them. Perhaps the clearest, and certainly the loudest, denunciation of the limitations and side effects of development assistance is the 2009 book *Dead Aid*, by Dambisa Moyo[6]. After a two-year stint at the World Bank (1993–5), Moyo spent a decade working in the financial industry. There is a certain irony to the fact that she chose the time of greatest debacle in private finance to criticise foreign aid, of all things. Nevertheless, her catchy title and incendiary message catapulted her to the *New York Times* Best Sellers List, and even to Oprah's list of 'twenty remarkable visionaries'. Moyo used two very persuasive kinds of evidence to make her case. First, in a statistical analysis she found no correlation between receiving foreign aid and experiencing economic growth; in fact, she found a link between receiving aid and getting poorer and having more corrupt rulers. She supported some of her statistical claims with vignettes of dictators, aid waste, and economic downturn. Overall, her case may not hold up to methodological scrutiny by social scientists, but it did have a clear bottom line. More importantly, it resonated with that of other well-known voices.

One could see Moyo as an interloper in a cottage industry dominated by William Easterly, an economist from New York University, who between 2001 and 2014 built an increasingly hostile polemic against aid. One need only look at the evolution of his book titles to get a sense of his own intellectual journey. *The Elusive Quest for Growth: Economists' Adventures and Misadventures in the Tropics* has a literary, almost fanciful title, and documents for a specialist audience some of the key challenges in securing economic growth in developing countries[7]. *The White Man's Burden: Why the West's Efforts to Aid the Rest Have Done So Much Ill and So Little Good*, in contrast, has colonial resonances, and the subtitle's meaning could not be clearer to the uninitiated[8]. Finally, *The Tyranny of Experts: Economists, Dictators, and the Forgotten Rights of the Poor* is just a clear attack on the aid industry and its complicity with the political and economic oppression of poor people in developing countries[9]. Easterly's books share a lot of DNA with Moyo's hit: distrust of economic planning coupled with faith in individual ingenuity and market solutions. In other words, your run-of-the-mill conservative economic philosophy. While development assistance has well-documented shortcomings, Moyo and, increasingly, Easterly are perhaps a bit too enthusiastic in their critique of what could be considered overseas welfare programmes. They have too much faith in people and the invisible hand of the market, when most development challenges are institutional and therefore political, as I will discuss in the next chapter.

Easterly and Moyo are but two of the protagonists of what Nilima Gulrajani called 'the great aid debate' of the 2000s[10], but they were probably the loudest ones. The only comparable author offering a dissenting view was Jeffrey Sachs, an advisor to the UN and head of the Earth Institute at Columbia University. Sachs was the aid optimist to Easterly's pessimist in what looked at times like a petty dispute between two white middle-aged New York economists: a showdown between uptown and downtown Manhattan. Sachs, too, made the *New York Times* Best Seller List with *The End of Poverty: How We Can Make It Happen In Our Lifetime*, a somewhat self-aggrandising book in which he claimed to have saved Latin America and Eastern Europe from hyperinflation in the 1980s, and called Bono (yes, the singer from U2) the real expert on poverty after traipsing with him around the world speaking out for the voiceless[11]. Unfortunately, Sachs also became somewhat infamous for the failure of his Millennium Villages Project, which was documented by journalist Nina Munk in her 2013 book *The Idealist: Jeffrey Sachs and the Quest to End Poverty*[12]. Despite all of these limitations, Sachs has been virtually the only positive voice about aid in global public debates. British economist Paul Collier has had his moments in the spotlight as a supporter of intervention[13], but by and large academics and practitioners tend to write books about aid not working, rather than about its successes. The growing public narrative on aid's many failures came to a climax with Dambisa Moyo just as the financial crisis of 2007 turned into a full-blown austerity crisis across many donor countries.

In the previous chapter, I detailed what this crisis did to the aid budget of Spain, a heretofore generous donor. Interestingly, the financial crisis did not create similar dips in aid budgets across the board: the general OECD trend since 2007 is one of slow growth, not decline. But the effects of the fiscal crunch have been felt in a more indirect manner, through the austerity-related policies sponsored largely by conservative governments in donor countries. This indirect punch found its most dramatic expression in the folding back of key bilateral aid agencies into ministries of foreign affairs. The Canadian International Development Agency (CIDA) was, at least in my experience interacting with donors as a researcher, a well-respected donor organisation, and a key contributor to the goals of aid effectiveness in developing countries. In March 2013, the Conservative government decided to absorb CIDA into the Department of Foreign Affairs, Trade and Development, which from that moment on would add the 'Development' appendix to its title. Although the notion of the merger had been around for a while, the 2013 decision stemmed from a political and budgetary calculation outside the aid agency proper: the ostensible goals of the government at the time were enhancing policy coherence and aid effectiveness by bringing the different arms of Canadian foreign policy closer together. Months later, the move was mirrored across the Pacific Ocean, when Australia's conservative government decided to fold AusAID into its own Department of Foreign Affairs and Trade (DFAT). Newly elected Prime Minister Tony Abbott justified this decision on grounds very similar to those invoked by his Canadian peers: 'we want Australia's aid program to be fully integrated into our overall diplomatic effort'[14]. Abbot's centre-left predecessor had actually strengthened AusAID's independence as recently as 2010 by making it an executive agency. However, AusAID's growth and increasing international reputation had alarmed those who echoed Condoleezza Rice's concern for promoting the national interest. The climate of austerity created a perfect opportunity for the new conservative government to rein in the Australian aid bureaucracy as well as make budget cuts that would not create political opposition. Just like Mariano Rajoy in Spain, Abbot's goal was to use the AusAID merger as a way to make hundreds of staff redundant and save more than AU$4 billion over four years[15]. Of course, there was no love lost between AusAID and DFAT, but that did not mean the aid community could do much to stop the tidal wave of austerity.

The absorption of AusAID by DFAT was legitimated by an overarching change in aid paradigm for the country, which Minister for Foreign Affairs Julie Bishop kindly shared with the world in a June 2014 YouTube video[16]. The cornerstone of this new approach was 'performance management': the government would impose tougher benchmarks on aid recipients and private implementers to ensure that taxpayers got the maximum VfM out of their hard-earned Australian dollars. These 'exciting and important reforms to the Australian aid programme', Bishop said, were a response to a changing world in which aid played a relatively smaller role in developing countries compared with access to financial markets and trade relationships. Crucially, a central role of foreign aid would be to foster private sector growth in order to plant the seeds for future trade partnerships. Under the new paradigm, humanitarian and human development interventions would not be an end in themselves, but a stepping stone towards economic growth. The language of this approach sounded appealing and very much in sync with the philosophy of Silicon Valley: the Australian government would finance an 'innovation fund', participate in an international 'innovation ventures programme', and establish a 'development innovation hub' that would put it at the 'cutting edge' of development assistance. The bottom line was crystal clear: 'Funding will be directed to projects that make a real and measurable difference'. This emphasis on measurability and impact is a recurrent theme of aid policy under conservative governments in the twenty-first century, and I will return to it below.

If Julie Bishop's concept of aid as a catalyst for trade resonates with Priti Patel's own goals, it is because the roots of her conservative discourse on aid can be traced back to the United Kingdom's political transition from Labour to a coalition government of Conservatives and Liberal Democrats in 2010. When Prime Minister David Cameron came into office, he did not challenge the core elite agreement on the key role that aid plays in Britain's foreign affairs. Nor did he question the autonomy and bureaucratic independence of the Department for International Development, even though its creation had been one of the signature decisions of Tony Blair's government in 1997. Indeed, the Coalition government of Britain between 2010 and 2015 was the first to reach the 0.7% target, which it then made into law. The arrival of fiscal conservatives was not felt in the overall budget, nor did it lead to the subordination of aid to more conventional foreign policy goals. What it did, much like in Australia, was introduce an array of new principles that shook the foreign aid system to its core, forcing it to play by rules that were far too managerial to truly capture the reality of development.

The absorption of CIDA and AusAID and the UK's new managerial philosophy are different expressions of the same underlying philosophy. In contrast to the perceived profligacy of centre-left governments, which was conveniently accused of worsening the financial and fiscal crisis of the late 2000s, new conservative governments arrived in office with a clear plan to make every penny count. There is remarkable consistency in the language used across donor countries, usually a combination of the following: performance management, results orientation, efficient delivery, transparency, and accountability. There are also hubs, funds, innovation, and pilots, but chances are this is as much a reflection of this new philosophy as it is an expression of Silicon Valley envy.

The brave new world of value for money

In 2010, the British government launched a Bilateral Aid Review 'designed to improve the allocation of UK aid to ensure that [its] objectives are achieved in the most cost-effective manner possible, maximising VfM, and based on a solid understanding of what works and what does not'[17]. In the words of a 2011 technical report,

The Review was the first stage of a process to embed this new approach to results and value for money. Subsequent stages will include the development of Operational Plans for countries and regions and consideration of the business case for individual interventions. All new projects will be subject to a rigorous investment appraisal process prior to approval which will test the evidence underlying the intervention and its value for money more thoroughly[18].

It is worth unpacking the different elements of this agenda one by one in order to fully realise the seismic change that the Coalition government brought into British aid. But first let us examine the guiding principle behind all of this: VfM. The concept can be traced back to a 2004 Treasury handbook on 'Regularity, Propriety and Value for Money', which was primarily intended reading for accounting officers, the senior-most officials in public organisations of Her Majesty's Government[19]. The handbook included a one-page chapter on VfM, defining it as 'the optimum combination of whole life costs and quality'. This principle is core to the work of the National Audit Office, which inspects public expenses. Its 'Successful Commissioning Toolkit' defines VfM somewhat more clearly as 'the optimal use of resources to achieve the intended outcomes'[20]. The principle thus applied to all public organisations in British government, and in 2011 DFID released its own 'Approach to Value for Money' based around a '3E Framework': economy, efficiency, effectiveness, and cost-effectiveness. (I suppose someone must have found 3Es and 1C-E too convoluted for an abbreviated title.) The document went to great lengths to dispel any notion that cost-cutting was the only consideration: instead, the aim was to achieve better results on the basis of stronger evidence and a more open and competitive process of public procurement[21].

VfM sounds eminently reasonable. It is the kind of due diligence we expect from modern liberal states: accountability to taxpayers' demands that governments keep an eye on how public funds are spent, assurance that these funds are, in fact, employed for their stated purposes, and transparent management of public funds are all necessary for avoiding corruption and waste. In that light, VfM is not only reasonable but perhaps even morally desirable. However, not all areas of public policy are equally amenable to the same calculations and standards of proof. When procuring bricks to build a school, for instance, we can easily compare the costs and estimates of different providers in order to choose the most economic, efficient, effective, and cost-effective option. As we move to less tangible goals, however, the simple logic of VfM begins to unravel, and at a certain point the demand for hard evidence does not necessarily lead to accountability.

Some of the ideals and aspirations that we hold dearest are the most difficult to measure in practice. Take, for example, women's empowerment: scholars and activists consider it a *sine qua non* for achieving inclusive development and correcting some of the worst instincts of patriarchal cultures by incorporating women into the economy, social life, and politics. But how do we know when we have achieved women's empowerment? What do we measure? There is plenty of evidence that gender-blind or gender-neutral policies can create structural discrimination against women. Combatting these types of structures takes decades, maybe even generations. So, how can an aid programme on women's empowerment fit a VfM mentality? Where is the evidence? Where are the indicators of success? What counts as a 'result'? The same dilemma applies to any other area of assistance that deals with culture, informal norms, and institutions. What does an 'effective' anticorruption programme look like? Do we count the number of investigations, or how many of these investigations are effectively prosecuted, or how many cases lead to civil or criminal punishment? Or do we measure the willingness of whistle-blowers to report illicit or inappropriate behaviour from their peers? I will come back to this issue throughout this book, but let me make the following point clear right now: a VfM logic of assistance privileges results that can be easily measured, and interventions that can be easily managed.

The 2010 Bilateral Aid Review process is an exemplar of this pernicious set of incentives. It introduced a series of layers of compliance that turned DFID's work upside down: instead of starting with political analysis and strategic considerations about the needs of recipient countries, many of which suffered from structural problems, the Review forced country offices to start with results, making the best pitch that they could on whatever achievements they could actually measure. A new operational plan template was introduced to guide DFID's portfolio in each country from that point on. This was not so much a strategic document as a VfM framework listing individual interventions, their projected cost, and their intended results. For over a decade, key thinkers within DFID had been pushing for a more politically astute approach to foreign aid, incorporating rigorous systematic analysis into the planning process. In 2007, these advocates had secured the adoption of a Country Governance Assessment framework that all field offices would have to carry out as part of their programming work[22]. The operational plan had no room for this kind of analysis, though, and in 2011 the assessments

stopped being mandatory. Country offices were now encouraged
to 'draw on evidence in their existing analysis documents' instead
of commissioning new work as long as 'key changes in context
[were] reflected in the results proposed'[23]. Country teams faced
with these demands did an admirable job trying to reconcile them
with the reality in which they operated. Consider the 2011–15
operational plan for Sierra Leone, a fragile country with weak
institutions and profound structural problems[24]. Buried at the
beginning of the section on 'Delivering Value For Money', one
can find this pearl of a reality check:

> The operating environment in Sierra Leone presents challenges
> to achieving value for money in a number of ways:
> - Poor quality and limited data
> - Rapidly changing environment, requiring speedy policy devel-
>   opment to address or take advantage of opportunities
> - Weak delivery capacity in Government of Sierra Leone partners
>   and variable quality service providers available
> - Changing costs of doing business; many products and services
>   are imported requiring foreign exchange subject to currency
>   exchange rate fluctuations
> - Uncertainty over availability of goods and services resulting in
>   delays in procurement, and impacting on price
> - Weak fiduciary environment

What better proof of the fundamental contradiction between
working in difficult places (where aid is needed the most) and
wanting to control the impact of every penny?

While the operational plan model replaced actual strategic considerations with a collection of numbers, VfM made its greatest

mark in British aid through the business case model. I was lucky to start my doctoral research a couple of years before the Coalition government dragged DFID kicking and screaming into this brave new world, and thus I was exposed to the old model for designing aid interventions: the project memorandum. There was never total consistency amongst the project memoranda that I got my hands on, but they were always interesting documents, full of analysis, history, and just general bits of useful knowledge. They reflected, to my uninformed eyes, an exploratory philosophy that took context seriously, animated not by the question 'what will we achieve' but rather by 'what needs to be achieved'. In today's world of heightened counter-bureaucracy, it is easy for outsiders to forget how daring and transformational DFID was as an aid agency in the early 2000s, taking on difficult sectors and explicitly political topics, and even engaging in the wholesale reconstruction of weak states. It was probably a manager's nightmare, but at least it was interesting, and the project memoranda reflected that. Then along came the Bilateral Aid Review and the VfM agenda, and DFID stopped looking so interesting, at least to the untrained eye. I blame the business case model for that.

A direct outgrowth of the VfM approach, DFID's business cases follow the five-case model developed by Her Majesty's Treasury, a structured set of questions that justify the expenditure of taxpayers' hard-earned money[25]. There's a strategic case, which sets out the context for intervention; an appraisal case, which lays out alternative options; a commercial case, which describes how the project will be tendered and a bid selected; a financial case, which deals with how the money will be disbursed and accounted for; and a management case, which details the particular arrangement between DFID, the actual implementer of the project, and whatever other partners are involved. Like the operational plan, this template makes intuitive sense, and the clear structure and requirements ensure that all projects will be evaluated on the same standards.

However, there are two basic problems with the business case model. First, the standards may not be good enough. Consider how much space is given in an average case to justifying the procurement, accountability, financial risk, and managerial concerns, in contrast with the actual definition of the problem that the project is supposed to address. The structure of the business case signals to practitioners that they ought to devote more time to justifying themselves than actually thinking about what needs to be done and how best to do it. Second, the standards may create a pernicious incentive to 'game the system' by drafting cookie-cutter business cases that satisfy the compliance overlords. For instance, one of the things I find most amusing in appraisal cases is the (probably fabricated) opposition between three options, only one of which is desired. It usually runs like this: under option A, we will do a little bit, but not very much; under option B, we will commit to a medium-size project with clear partners and objectives; and under option C, we will do absolutely everything. It does not take a genius to see the smoke and mirrors, but one has to applaud the cunning of practitioners who have to persuade the counter-bureaucracy that there may be only one reasonable course of action available.

The jadedness regarding the business case model is most deeply felt by DFID's own field personnel, especially by those who are more inclined to think about the bigger picture. Across country offices in Ghana, Uganda and Bangladesh, as well as in Whitehall, DFID advisors that I spoke to between 2013 and 2015 betrayed

a mix of disillusionment and perplexity at the government's decision to apply stringent VfM standards to the thorny, non-linear,
and often unpredictable problems of development. One governance advisor lamented how the business case model had extracted
the politics from projects, reflecting a new direction for DFID that
focused on the 'easy bits' of development. Every single advisor that
I talked to pointed to UK politics and the Conservative demand for
'evidence' as key driver of this new model. They were well aware
that the Bilateral Aid Review in the United Kingdom, as well as
similar processes elsewhere, did not stem from a desire to actually
improve development outcomes so much as to demonstrate that
aid was being spent in a perfectly accountable way. By using that
word, I don't mean accountable to taxpayers, let alone recipients,
but rather that every single pound and dollar spent overseas was
accounted for. The truth about business cases? 'Essentially, they
are procurement documents', a senior advisor told me. 'It's all
about numbers, often very spurious numbers'. And this spurious-
ness goes further than the numbers.

An important component of the VfM agenda is transparency,
understood in a profoundly naïve and expedient kind of way.
Consider the World Bank, which in any given year undertakes
thousands of projects around the world. Due to a commitment to
total transparency, the Bank publishes on its website all of its programme documents. Delving into the virtual stack of paperwork
can be tiresome, and involves sifting through hundreds of files,
all following similar templates; but this is obviously designed to
satisfy the zealousness of those aid hawks most concerned with
accounting and results. DFID has a similar imperative to publish,
which leads to all business cases and evaluations becoming, in
principle, public documents. A closer look at what these reams of

pdfs contain, however, reveals an interesting paradox: the more that aid agencies publish, the less they actually share about how development interventions really unfold. As extensive as a World Bank Program Appraisal Document can be (and some of them are over a hundred pages long), it generally does not say much about why a project was designed in a particular way, other than via some bland generalities. The months and months of preparatory work cannot possibly be included in any official document, especially when the format is so strongly defined by an animosity to complexity. For the most part, this leads to programme appraisal documents and business cases that are plainly safe: defensive in their presentation, arcane in their reliance on management jargon, and almost predictable in their formulaic approach to justification. It is hard to find holes in documents that are engineered to withstand assault by aid deniers, if one is not already familiar with the context in which these programmes are supposed to unfold.

Perhaps the gravest unintended consequence of the aid counter-bureaucracy is the displacement or obfuscation of the politics of development. As a senior DFID advisor told me, official documents usually deflate the probability of any political risk, which also leads to an underestimation of their impact in final evaluations. 'The incentives – rightly or wrongly – do not lead to honest explanations for why things are done', he said. 'Few people would like to hear anything that rocked the boat'. A DFID economist acknowledged that political analysis had less of a role to play in the business case than in the old project memorandum; moreover, when political-economy studies are commissioned as part of the design process, they are never included in the business case. I heard similar complaints from World Bank specialists in country offices and in Washington, DC. As one of them told me, 'you can try to incorporate as many political considerations as you want in the original design of a project. The important thing is to make sure that there are measurable indicators in the results framework'. When the World Bank does commission political analyses, 'it hides behind consultants to avoid accusations from the host government', another staffer said. She also pointed to a common strategy to keep politics out of the Bank's 'transparency' requirement: a report by Bank personnel with their names on it will be archived and released, whereas consultant reports will remain internal documents or 'deliberative drafts' that never qualify for publication. I have personally been on the wrong side of this particular paradox, writing a lengthy and detailed report for a World Bank country office that to all intents and purposes does not exist. It is impossible to know how many other political studies about development interventions have also vanished, like tears in rain.

The mirage of certainty

Most people have never heard of early twentieth-century economist Frank Knight, but he made one of the most significant conceptual distinctions in economics: one that is particularly relevant for understanding the fundamental flaws at the core of the VfM agenda. It all begins with the notion of risk. All of us have a common-sense understanding of risk, which we witness or experience when we make financial investments, walk into a tricky neighbourhood, or give extreme sports a try. Gamblers and people addicted to games of chance are particularly aware of the role of probability in determining outcomes and calculating odds based on the available information; some of the best poker players can easily guess their opponents' chances of winning given the cards in their hand and on the table. Probability is the bedrock of statistical analysis, allowing us to understand patterns in big data and formulate predictions about the likelihood of certain events or outcomes occurring. It also plays an important role in the economic analysis of choices by firms and individuals, where models have actors make choices based on the probabilities that they attach to different outcomes. Almost a century ago, Frank Knight called this objective probability: when we know how many options there are, and how likely they are to become real, we can calculate the probability – or risk – of different choices. Flip a coin a thousand times and you will end up having close to a 50/50 split between heads and tails. A common die has six sides, which means a 1/6 probability of getting any number between one and six. Add another die and you have to do some basic math: there is only a 1/36 chance of getting two of the same number now, making it a riskier bet, but still a calculable one. And so on. By betting on any given probability, you are taking a certain risk: a bet of double sixes is simply much riskier than a bet of seven in whatever combination.

But what happens when outcomes are not so easy to calculate? Imagine you are asked to play poker with a special deck of cards that contains an unknown number of duplicates, or to bet on a die roll with an unknown number of dice. Without accurate information on the probability of different outcomes, it is impossible to make a risk estimate about different choices. In a sense, you don't actually know what your choices are. This is what Frank Knight called subjective probability, or uncertainty[26].

Economic models work under assumptions of risk, but they begin to fall apart under conditions of uncertainty. This became painfully clear in the 2008 financial crisis, as it had in previous financial panics and market crises. Indeed, the concept of 'Knightian uncertainty' has been used to explain why the 1930s financial crisis led to the disintegration of the post-World War I economic and political order, leading in parallel to the rise of fascism and of the welfare state[27]. Knight's insight is a powerful one, because it undermines one of the bedrock assumptions of modern economic theory, calculability. The moment risk turns into uncertainty, economics gives way to a different profession: philosophy if we are lucky, astrology if we are not. A crisis of Knightian uncertainty does not have an obvious way out, and, absent the scientific analysis of risk, what we are left with is some kind of ideology. That is why northern European countries and the United States responded to the 1930s by creating welfare states, whereas Germany responded by electing a fascist regime. The most powerful of the ideologically committed actors provided a vision for a way out, and people followed.

Fast-forward seventy years, and the rise of the counter-bureaucracy and VfM can be explained according to a similar logic. The 2008 financial crisis introduced Knightian uncertainty into public policy in donor countries, undermining economic forecasts and the basic formulae that justified public spending and interest rates. The conservative answer to the crisis had all the trappings of a risk calculation: austerity would lead to fiscal stability, which in turn would reassure financial markets. It looked like a reasonable bet, and the successive electoral victories of conservative parties across Europe made it seem as if voters were rewarding the best poker players in partisan politics. However, austerity was never a scientific choice: it was an ideological one. The same applies to VfM. Is it too much of a coincidence that VfM considerations in Australia, Canada, and the United Kingdom were pushed by conservative governments? Was it really that unexpected to have aid deniers seize the financial crisis as an opportunity to bash agencies even harder? The rise of the aid counter-bureaucracy is perhaps the clearest proof that what began in the late 2000s was an ideological project charting a very particular way out of Knightian uncertainty. And that is how we have arrived at today's paradoxes. The current landscape of foreign aid is subject to the tension between what a DFID advisor called 'two fundamentally competing models': aid as a public good, which may solve some basic, superficial problems, and aid as a contested and political resource, which can be used to help tackle some of the complex, underlying problems of development. Whereas the former model is designed to manage risk, the latter operates under the assumption of uncertainty.

The notion of VfM as calculated risk is patently ridiculous when subject to any kind of scrutiny. Consider the very first conceptual step: we want to get some value out of aid. That seems fair. But how do you attach value to development outcomes? How much is a vaccinated infant worth? Is it more or less than a woman empowered to start her own small business? What is the value of a new procurement law? What about a more effective ombudsman? And a community policing programme? I am not being facetious here: these are some very common development interventions. By any reasonable measure, they are all very desirable. All of us would like to have healthier children, greater gender parity, cleaner governments, or more responsive police officers. But the VfM agenda forces aid practitioners to attach value and risk calculations to each of these desirable goals, which is not an easy task. Imagine all of the potential factors that may influence the success of a new public procurement law: the willingness of political parties to agree on a law; the government's capacity to properly enforce it, which entails funding an oversight body; the professional skills of public auditors, who will keep track of procurement processes; the ability of businesses to adequately comprehend the new requirements and participate in open tenders; the personal relationships between public officials and business owners; the willingness of ministers to take cuts or allow their subordinates to take cuts; and so on. Now try to attach a probability to every possible combination of factors. I'm afraid you will soon exit the land of risk and enter the realm of uncertainty. And this is a problem because of Andrew Natsios's warning at the beginning of this chapter: 'those development programmes that are most precisely and easily measured are the least transformational, and those programmes that are the most transformational are the least measured'.

VfM instruments are clearly designed to calculate and mitigate risk rather than deal with uncertainty. A business case outlines assumptions, expected benefits, and different cost scenarios. A risk matrix identifies potential stumbling blocks, outlining their severity and probable impact on the project. A results framework details every single output to be produced by the project at different milestones as well as what weight they will have in achieving the desired outcome. All of these tools serve to justify development interventions by artificially constructing a manageable set of risks. They are essential to getting a project approved, funded, and evaluated in a positive light. Calculability is more than just due diligence; it is a religious dogma. However, the incentive to minimise risk leads to two kinds of projects: either the 'easy bits' of service delivery that DFID advisors complain about, or somewhat falsified interventions that have to conceal any uncertainty under an elaborate disguise of spurious numbers and misleading portrayals of the reality on the ground. The end result is the perverse kind of accountability that I mentioned earlier, that is, business cases that do not capture reality, risk matrices that deflate actual risks, and evaluations that just measure due diligence.

My personal favourite is the anticorruption strategy template that DFID began using in 2010. Despite the crucial challenges of corruption in most countries where UK aid operates, these so-called strategies had nothing to do with tackling those challenges, and instead focused exclusively on ensuring that not a single aid pound was misappropriated along the way. I like to ask my students how much corruption they'd be willing to tolerate in aid projects: 10% is often the limit of their comfort zone. Their certainty starts to dissipate, however, when I ask them what to do when it is hard to measure accurately how much money is being lost. It vanishes entirely when I mention interventions so worthwhile – such as child immunisation – that even a 10% success rate can be considered a net public good.

The risk-versus-uncertainty conundrum is not just an analytical one: it has clear ethical implications for what donors choose to do, and how they justify their choices. The calculability of the VfM agenda carries with it a very specific ethical theory that does not stray far from classic utilitarianism[28]. We learned from John Stuart Mill to think about the greatest happiness for the greatest number of individuals as the pinnacle of ethical decision-making: by calculating the overall value (or 'utility') of alternative courses of action, we can identify the most satisfactory one. It is easy to see traces of this moral philosophy in VfM, where the goal is to measure the expected utility to aid recipients as well as aid taxpayers. Hence the different scenarios posed by business cases, or the results frameworks that all projects must have. However, utilitarianism leads to some odd and not at all intuitive conclusions, such as the so-called trolley problem: the ethical dilemma of what to do when a trolley is being led by its engineer without knowing that further down the tracks there is a group of five unconscious people, who will die if the trolley is not stopped. To this, admittedly far-fetched, scenario, utilitarianism offers only one rational answer: kill the engineer to stop the trolley[29]. After all, one dead person is surely better than five dead people, right? But who among us would be ready to pull the trigger, taking responsibility for a murder in order to stop an accident? There is a certain allure to simplistic utilitarianism, as demonstrated by audiences' fascination with the terrorism-themed TV show *24*, in which protagonist Jack Bauer constantly pushes moral boundaries to stop unstoppable threats. But, in reality, there are very few – if any – ticking-bomb or unstoppable-trolley scenarios with predictable consequences and clear choices. At the end of the day, utilitarianism rests on the same assumption of calculability as Knightian risk: in order to make the best choice, we must be able to calculate all of the probabilities involved. Outside of the kind of thought experiments devised by moral philosophers and Hollywood writers, it is very hard to make calculable moral choices, especially when faced with development challenges.

Is it right to finance a failing health system so that more patients can be saved from preventable diseases, even if 50% of the total aid funds get lost to waste or corruption? Are the lives of those patients saved worth more or less than what we would get out of the money if it stayed in donor countries? Can we ensure that our own use of public funds at home will be 100% VfM? What if politicians here choose a patently useless project to fund just because it is expedient or good public relations? How can we be sure that the risks of foreign aid are less desirable than the risks of domestic policy? The answer, of course, is that public policy everywhere tends to unfold in a context of Knightian uncertainty, and that public choices tend to be guided by ideology (protestations from Dambisa Moyo and Bill Easterly notwithstanding). And just like public policy at home, foreign aid is guided by – usually covert – moral principles, even when they are disguised as calculability and due diligence.

The VfM agenda and its proponents, however well meaning, are forcing foreign aid agencies to choose between irrelevance and subterfuge. Either practitioners will look after their career prospects first and design the kind of low-risk projects that politicians like to talk about but rarely lead to sustainable development, or they will obfuscate the very real politics of development in order to comply with the twin demands of accounting and transparency. This condemns donor publics to a superficial understanding of development, which can only give wings to fiscal conservatives and aid deniers who, as we saw in Chapter 1, are more likely to use foreign aid as political ammunition than worry about the plight of developing countries. We will have certainty, yes, but a kind of certainty that is ultimately banal in its lack of practical and moral value. Above all, this mirage of certainty will blind us to the core political challenges of reform and development, which is the subject of the next chapter.

THREE | The ugly politics of change

Towards the end of the civil war that had ravaged their country for an entire decade, Sierra Leoneans had little reason to trust their government. Corruption among public officials was widely seen as one of the main causes of the conflict, and the political elite seemed unlikely to renounce the old ways when hostilities finally ceased. According to a survey conducted in mid-2000, 95% of Sierra Leoneans believed that corruption was 'rampant' in government departments, and about two thirds thought that their government was not doing much to control this epidemic[1]. For a problem that was deemed to be so destructive for the country, there was remarkably little faith in the ability of political leaders to do something about it.

In 1999, even before the civil war was officially over, President Ahmad Tejan Kabbah decided to launch a 'war against corruption'. He did so after receiving warnings from his main financial backers – bilateral and multilateral aid donors – who needed some sort of assurance that funds would not go to waste in an unreliable system of public finance[2]. In order to provide such assurances, the president established an Anti-Corruption Commission (ACC) with the assistance of the UK Department for International Development (DFID). Signed into law on 26 January 2000, the Anti-Corruption Act established a new Commission for Sierra Leone, which was designed by an international consultant and borrowed heavily from foreign models as well as best practices espoused by Transparency International. Its objectives were to enlist public support in the fight against corruption, to promote and strengthen administrative systems and processes within ministries and agencies, and to investigate and prosecute a list of nine corrupt offences[3].

Some limits to this expansive brief were built into the new organisation. Even if the Commission was formally independent of 'any person or authority', it was the president's prerogative to appoint the commissioner and his deputy. The decision to prosecute, moreover, was controlled by the Office of the Attorney General and Minister of Justice, who was a member of the cabinet. Finally, the ACC did not have the ability to threaten or impose compliance sanctions on public agencies that failed to implement its recommendations. These were not unreasonable limits, and they ensured that the Commission did not become a state within the state. But its effectiveness would rely on the political will of the president to enforce new anticorruption standards on public officials. Luckily, President Kabbah definitely talked the talk. Beyond him, the ACC could also rely on the sponsorship and support of the United Kingdom through its High Commission and DFID country office in Freetown.

At the time, there was much hope that the ACC would rise from the debris of civil war and state failure to begin the long and arduous process of cleaning up the Sierra Leonean government, making it more accountable to its people. However, the decade that followed is a perfect illustration of the challenges that reformers face. This chapter explores the fundamental political barriers to development, which the aid community has grappled with for the better part of six decades. Before we delve into the politics of assistance proper – which is the subject of Chapters 4 and 5 – we need a basic vocabulary for defining what development is and what it entails.

Development as institutional change

The relationship between political analysis and the aid industry is much like teenage love, swinging between passionate infatuation and painful rejection at an alarming pace. The academic study of the politics of developing countries has been nothing if not consistent, with a good five decades of cumulative research into the political economy of development by economists, economic historians, anthropologists, sociologists, geographers, and political scientists. One can go even further back if we look into the foundations of social science: Max Weber, Karl Marx, and even Adam Smith can all be counted among the founding fathers of political economy. Much more recently, a public interest book by Daron Acemoglu and James Robinson, *Why Nations Fail*[4], caught the attention of politicians such as British Prime Minister David Cameron; the book even made it into airport bookshops, which is no small feat for two academic economists. Acemoglu and Robinson's key contribution was shedding light on the distinction between extractive and inclusive institutions: whereas the former concentrate wealth and power in the hands of a few actors, the latter create a rules environment in which anyone can prosper. Collusion versus free market; corruption versus rule of law; dictatorship versus democracy.

Why Nations Fail is perhaps more interesting to the general public than to academics, because the relative weight of its contribution diminishes when compared with the intellectual foundations on which it rests. Acemoglu and Robinson are heirs to an intellectual tradition called 'new institutional economics', whose most celebrated figure is the late Douglass North. An economist with a background in the humanities, North was fascinated with history and, in particular, with figuring out the mystery of why societies become more complex and institutionalised over time: tribes organising into empires, barter leading to the stock exchange, and so on. He wrote mostly about economic history and the rise of the modern Western world[5]. However, North's most enduring contribution is perhaps his articulation of the concept of institutions, which he defined as 'humanly devised constraints that structure political, economic and social interaction'[6]. Or, to use the widespread shorthand, the 'rules of the game'[7]. This definition has led to some really interesting realisations.

The first realisation is that institutions affect actors, whether they are firms, politicians or schoolchildren. They limit what we can do, and tell us what we can expect from different courses of action. Steal and you will go to jail. Cheat on a test and you will fail. The second realisation is that actors tend to adapt to their institutional environment. While there are rule breakers everywhere, most of us have actually internalised the myriad institutions governing our lives, to the point that we are likely to stop at a red light in the middle of the night even if there are no pedestrians, no other cars, and no police to see us. The third realisation is that once actors have adapted to a certain institution, they become invested in its reproduction. Once I have devoted enough time and effort to playing by certain rules, I want all of my peers and competitors to play by the same rulebook: no one gets a free pass, and violators will be prosecuted. As the number of actors invested in reproduction grows, institutions become 'sticky' and quite hard to change.

To clarify, what I have just presented is a basic summary of new institutional economics. Sociologists, anthropologists, and political scientists all have alternative and more or less competing definitions of institutions, depending on whether they focus on historical trends, culture and ideas, or increasing returns[8]. But most of these alternative approaches tend to emphasise the 'stickiness' of institutions, whether because of the weight of history, or simply because dominant social norms prevent us from imagining an alternative future. Change is hard in institutional theory, and it is usually split into two kinds: small, incremental change that reflects institutional evolution over time; and large, disruptive change that occurs in times of crisis. Institutional change is either humble and boring, or ambitious and scary, and it is almost always contested. Change brings about a new order of things, which may please some people but scare or harm others. Whether one talks about new ideas, new regulations, or new technologies, there tend to be winners and losers when it comes to institutional change.

Now let us go back to the idea of development. What are we really talking about? It is a term of art more than one of everyday conversation, and in the twenty-first century it is probably associated with software more than politics or public policy, except within the large but insular international development community. Even members of this select group tend to disagree about what development means. Is it economic growth? Industrialisation? Urbanisation? Human rights? Democratisation? All of the above? My own response is less expansive, but hopefully more interesting: development is institutional change on a societal scale. It is the transition from old rules to new rules, and the often-difficult path that lies between them. Like any form of institutional change, development also creates winners and losers. To quote sixteenth-century development consultant Niccolò Machiavelli:

> And one should bear in mind that there is nothing more difficult to execute, nor more dubious of success, nor more dangerous to administer than to introduce a new order to things; for he who introduces it has all those who profit from the old order as his enemies; and he has only lukewarm allies in all those who might profit from the new[9].

Despite its auspicious beginnings, Machiavelli would have told donors such as the United Kingdom to prepare for the worst as Sierra Leone's anticorruption reformers set out to fulfil their mandate.

The ACC's rise and fall

The character of the Sierra Leone ACC as an organisation during its first five years of existence was shaped by the personality of its first commissioner. A British-sponsored candidate, Valentine Collier had been chief of the public service as secretary of the establishment in Kabbah's administration. In a way, he was a rational choice, considering that the administration envisioned the ACC's main task as prevention through oversight of the civil service. However, it was also an unpredictable appointment; when Collier was brought in, nobody expected that he would actually try to make the Commission work. In his first annual report to Parliament, the commissioner invoked William Reno's popular notion of the 'shadow state' as an explanation for corruption in Sierra Leone. In his determination to fight the 'inadequate incentives' prevalent in the public service, he expected to rely on the assistance of Sierra Leone's 'most reliable partner', the UK DFID[10].

The ACC was officially launched on 7 July 2001. A British consultant put together the conditions of service, code of conduct, standing orders, and competence-based training that would make the Commission into an effective organisation. As ACC officials described it, a new culture of integrity was instilled through in-house training of young staff recruited outside the public service system. Despite a paucity of experience and resources, by the end of 2001 the ACC managed to secure its first conviction, successfully prosecuting a sitting magistrate (although he would successfully appeal later).

Despite this initial zeal – or perhaps because of it – it soon became evident that 'many politicians, public officers, civil servants and their accomplices [were] still bent on betraying public trust and civic responsibility for personal gain'[11]. During a visit to Sierra Leone in February 2002, UK Secretary of State for International Development Clare Short received complaints from ACC officials regarding the failure of ministers and their subordinates to act upon the findings and recommendations relayed by the Commission[12]. The Commission's second annual report conveyed a mixed picture of acquiescence and hostility: support within the public bureaucracy 'was in the mean characterized by open apathy and in a fair number of cases outright non-compliance'. Likewise, the report complained of 'the rather lukewarm attitude of the judiciary' as well as 'the level of disinterestedness ... displayed by Parliament'[13]. In other words, none of the three branches of the Sierra Leonean government seemed willing to work with the Commission.

Prosecutions were by and large blocked at the Office of the Attorney General, except on those occasions where they served a political purpose for the administration[14]. In the words of a donor official, it was unclear whether President Kabbah was unwilling or unable to prosecute corrupt officials, especially when some of the suspects had helped him achieve power. By the end of 2002, over forty cases had been submitted to the Office of the Attorney General for prosecution, half of which had been discarded. Since there was no obligation to justify such dismissals, it was difficult to ascertain to what degree they were based on legal grounds as opposed to political ones. The fact that the position of Attorney General was entrusted to individuals who were politically close to Kabbah did little to encourage optimism[15]. In the ensuing years, a political clique within State House, dubbed 'The Untouchables', accused the ACC in cabinet meetings of embarrassing the government, and advocated for the appointment of a sympathetic lawyer to handle corruption prosecutions[16]. Leaked documents betrayed the president's desire to appoint a new commissioner[17]. By the spring of 2005, official cooperation had all but ceased between President Kabbah and Commissioner Collier, who was refusing to shield cabinet ministers and had no less than six of them under investigation[18].

Collier's misgivings with the president had gradually escalated to an open confrontation with the governing Sierra Leone People's Party. This came to a turning point in April 2005, when he said in a public forum that 'Parliamentarians were sick men in crutches ... acting hopelessly with disillusionment in addressing state matters'. A few days after these words were reported in the Freetown press[19], two MPs motioned to summon Valentine Collier so that he could answer for his remarks before Parliament.

On the 31 May meeting of the Parliamentary Committee on Privileges, the members' reactions to the remarks were full of indignation and dismay: the commissioner's comments had been 'derogatory', an 'affront [to] the dignity and prestige of Parliament'. 'Such negative statements, the committee observed, are far-reaching and misleading, especially in the eyes of the International Community.' MPs were unanimous in their belief that there were grounds for charges of contempt of Parliament, and so Collier was summoned to answer before Parliament on 13 and 22 June 2005. The following are some excerpts from the sessions:

Collier: 'Parliament has not criticized what we are doing and has not provided guidance or direction to us in the conduct of our work.'
Chairman: 'Mr. Collier, you have failed to take into due regard the constraints of Parliament. We legislate but don't have the personnel to make these documents. All our legislations [sic] come from Government. In other countries, Parliaments have their legal teams which carry out their legislative drafting work but this facility is not available in Sierra Leone.'
Chairman: 'If we don't respect our Parliament no outsider will.... The ACC documents are going to donor countries and when Parliamentarians in other countries read about our Parliament including what was said by you at that forum, it could be devastating to this country.'[20]

With these words, the chairman of the Committee on Privileges, which was supposed to act as an administrative check on public officials, betrayed the growing sense of unease that the Sierra Leone People's Party and the administration felt at the ACC's meteoric rise to prominence. Even without the political autonomy necessary to secure convictions of corrupt officials, the dedicated work of the Commission's staff in collecting reports and publicising them in the press was making a dent in the respectability of the Freetown elite. The aggrieved public officials did not sit idly by while the Commission exposed their abuses. By the time of the parliamentary inquiry, the list of grievances that the administration had against Collier was already long and somewhat fantastic. In a memo sent to the British High Commissioner in late 2005,

> The government accused Collier and his deputy, Andy Felton (a British national and DFID consultant), of causing the death of Gloria Newman-Smart, the former head of customs and immigration, whom the Commission had accused of corruption; of discourtesy to the President and parliament (which Collier allegedly described as full of rogues); of 'travelling in and out of the country without the permission of the government'; of paying journalists to 'write negative articles against the government'; and of giving a French public relations firm $50,000 'to write against the Sierra Leone Government'[21].

The position of the ACC's first commissioner became politically untenable. So, on 8 November 2005, the government of Ahmad Tejan Kabbah decided not to renew Valentine Collier as anticorruption commissioner, invoking as a justification the slim chance that MPs would confirm his appointment after his public confrontation with them[22].

Collier's replacement as commissioner was Henry Joko-Smart, an elderly law professor and brother-in-law of President Kabbah. The Sierra Leonean and donor officials who witnessed the transition agree that Joko-Smart's appointment was the outcome of a political decision to stall the anticorruption agenda, or at least the ACC's targeting of cabinet ministers. Joko-Smart himself had been penalised for corruption – unjustly, in his mind – during an

inquiry by a military regime in the early 1990s. Much like Kabbah, he had an instinctive disgust of investigations and prosecutions of high-level officials[23].

The first order of business for Joko-Smart was to clean up the
ACC itself, having decided that the attacks on the government
were a sign of the ACC's own corruption. The switch from external action to internal policing basically stopped all prosecutions
for a two-year period, a time remembered by one ACC official as
'the dark ages': 'We were just idle ... could not hold our head up
high ... people called us all sorts of things'. Joko-Smart ignored
his subordinates, accused them and DFID of being 'thieves', and
complained of British interference. Investigations ceased, and
civil servants working for the Commission began to come to the
office to do no work, with some even devoting themselves to distance learning instead. The ACC was put in a 'deep slumber', said
an official working there at the time. 'Nothing was happening.'

The fight against informal institutions

In order to understand the tremendous setback suffered by the
Sierra Leone ACC in 2005, it is helpful to go back to the work
of Douglass North. Earlier in this chapter, I summarised three
key realisations from his idea of institutions as 'rules of the game':
institutions constrain actors, who, in turn, adapt to them and, as a
result, the former become sticky and hard to change. But there is
a corollary to this conceptual framework, which is a most interesting twist. There is not just one kind of institution, but two: formal
and informal. Constitutions, laws, regulations and codes are all
examples of formal institutions: they are public, usually written
down, and enforced by official actors in a predictable manner.
However, underneath them is a thick substrate of social norms,

cultural values, policy ideas, and popular expectations. These
are the informal institutions, which are not always public and are
usually tacit, being communicated and enforced by private individuals and groups. Sometimes formal and informal institutions
overlap and reinforce one another; at other times there is a mismatch, with one side falling short of the other[24].

Inspired by father-of-sociology Max Weber, in the 1980s a
number of observers of African politics came up with the term
'neopatrimonialism' to describe political systems that had adopted
all the trappings of a modern state but retained a foundation of
informal institutions, such as clientelism, patronage, and ethnic
favouritism[25]. The pathologies of this hybrid state are well known
among development experts: copying the form without the function in an attempt to generally 'look like a state' results in rather
limited success at achieving the sorts of things that modern states
do[26]. Western forms are adopted because they are demanded by
financial markets, international financial institutions, and wealthy
donors. But the informal institutions behind this Western façade
are difficult to uproot. Sierra Leone's post-colonial history was
a clear example of neopatrimonial development: the transition
from a fragile multi-party democracy to a one-party state in the
late 1960s led to a system of political patronage and institutionalised corruption – what William Reno called the 'shadow state' –
that lasted until the wars of the 1990s[27]. The two military regimes
that dominated the civil war years were little more than organ-
ised bandits, who deepened the informal capture of public office
and resources, further eroding whatever foundations remained
beneath the Sierra Leonean state[28].

In the fight between formal and informal institutions, it is the
latter that often emerge victorious. Max Weber himself made

this point abundantly clear when discussing legal reform, stating that 'where it transforms a custom into a legal obligation (by invocation of the "usual") [it] often adds practically nothing to its effectiveness, and, where it opposes custom, [it] frequently fails in the attempt to influence actual conduct'[29]. The continued preeminence of informal institutions over formal ones does not preclude the initiation of reform, but it does severely hinder the prospect of actual implementation. Such is the staying power of informal institutions. As Douglass North put it: 'Although a wholesale change in the formal rules may take place, at the same time there will be many informal constraints that have great survival tenacity'[30].

When informal institutions have become sticky, there are few individual incentives for any one actor to support the enforcement of anticorruption reform[31]. The political conflict inherent in anticorruption reform is most evident in terms of its redistributive consequences. When political leaders rise on the backs of ethnic networks, there is very little incentive for them to treat all citizens equally. When senior policymakers can provide for their family and community through kickbacks on public contracts, laws about public tenders and bidding become an obstacle. And when teachers or health workers need to ask for bribes in order to supplement meagre salaries, it is hard to tell them to think of the public good instead of their immediate welfare. This is particularly relevant in weak states such as Sierra Leone, where public-spirited actors can do little against competing informal incentives. At the time, the country suffered from the 'institutional resilience in and of failed states' that plagues most post-conflict reconstruction efforts[32].

If change is so hard at an institutional level, what does it actually look like? How does development happen? Here, as anywhere else, beauty is in the eye of the beholder. Lawyers will say that a solid and consistent institutional framework is essential to development. Economists are likely to argue that what you need is to alter the incentive structure, so that individuals and groups will start behaving according to new rules. Anthropologists may point to cultural transformation as the ultimate form of change. Public management consultants will tell you to build more efficient organisations that can enable the right kind of leadership.

My own bias forces me to see development as a series of fights. It is just a larger form of 'contentious politics', to borrow a term from social movement scholars Charles Tilly, Doug McAdam, and Sidney Tarrow[33]. At any given point in history, in any given country, there will be incumbents, who benefit from dominant institutions (whether formal or informal), as well as challengers, who want to replace them with new ones[34]. By definition, challengers are at a disadvantage, enjoying fewer resources and access to the levers of power, so they need to change how people see themselves and how the battle lines are set. They try to build coalitions, seeking allies anywhere they can find them. They try to redefine issues so that lukewarm supporters can more easily get behind them. And they exploit crises and windows of opportunity to push their agenda across[35]. One can go much deeper into details, and I will in Chapter 7, but that is really the gist of it. Development is hard, it is costly, and it takes time. It is two or three steps backward for every step forward, and it does not follow a linear path. In sum, it is exactly the kind of reality that a foreign aid system based on value-for-money calculations cannot deal with. This does not, however, preclude donors from achieving some success on the backs of courageous local reformers.

The second rise of the ACC

Despite the mounting evidence of political interference with the Commission between 2005 and 2007, the United Kingdom had actually been reluctant to use the few sticks built into its assistance programme to Sierra Leone. During a visit to Sierra Leone in February 2002, UK Secretary for International Development Clare Short clearly stated the terms of British assistance, including 'a strong mutual commitment to the building of a competent, transparent and uncorrupt modern state'[36]. Then, in November 2002, she signed a ten-year 'Memorandum of Understanding' with President Kabbah, which highlighted corruption as one of the key commitments of governance reform. The conditionality attached to the Memorandum stated that the United Kingdom would continue to fund its multiple projects in the Sierra Leonean state as long as there was clear action on the part of the government in the enforcement of anticorruption legislation[37].

In late 2006, a team of DFID consultants was sent to Freetown in order to carry out the annual review of British support for the ACC[38]. The evaluators registered with dismay the impact that new leadership was having on the organisation. Joko-Smart had stopped carrying out the fortnightly meetings between department heads that had allowed the Commission to foster coherent strategies and policy. These had been replaced by monthly management meetings, as well as daily mini-management meetings dealing with minor administrative issues, for which no agendas or minutes were prepared. There was a significant underspend of about £750,000, suggesting that costly tasks in investigation, prevention, and community relations were not being carried out. In his meeting with the consultants, Joko-Smart claimed to ignore the contents of the project memorandum governing DFID assistance. He initially refused to let the evaluators meet department heads individually, and failed to provide them with documentation until the end of their visit.

The team found that the Commission had fallen behind in every component of the support framework: there was limited collaboration with ministries and civil society on prevention, no impact assessment of community mobilisation efforts, low numbers of – generally low-profile – prosecutions, and no new surveys on corruption. The Commission had voluntarily limited its organisational footprint in the country, and in so doing it had become unable to measure the results of its own work. It had become 'inwardly focused', with no attempts being made to establish stronger ties with the Office of the Auditor General or to pressure the Attorney General into processing cases at a faster pace. Meetings between the Commissioner and the Attorney General had, in fact, ceased after DFID decided to stop attending them. Informants from other state sectors reported the gradual disappearance of the ACC from the strategic policy level. Press conferences had begun to focus more on why prosecutions were not initiated than on the merits of the cases, and the Advisory Committee mandated by law to oversee the Commission had lost all relevance. The commissioner was accountable to no one but the president himself.

The conclusions of the review were simple enough:

> The recent leadership and management of the organisation has undermined any progress that had been made with previous donor support. It is our view that during the period under review, the necessary leadership in building and leading an effective ACC within an already difficult environment has largely been absent[39].

Considering the future trajectory facing the ACC under the stewardship of Henry Joko-Smart, there was only one logical conclusion: 'We recommend that DFID ends support to the ACC Sierra Leone'.

The report's drastic conclusions did not do much to improve DFID's frayed relations with the Kabbah administration. Initially, Britain had been willing to overlook the shortcomings of the anticorruption system (to some local officials, DFID had been 'possibly too willing to help'); but ever since Hilary Benn had replaced Clare Short as secretary for international development in 2003, Britain's relationship with Kabbah had taken a turn for the worse[40]. Nevertheless, despite the scathing ACC report, DFID was persuaded by the UK Foreign and Commonwealth Office not to withdraw its ACC assistance, for fear of the strong political signal it might send. Eventually, London managed to secure a middle road between suspension and acquiescence: official funding for phase two of support was scheduled to end in March 2007, and it was determined that on that date the commissioner would be notified of an offer of five additional months of limited assistance in order to implement some of the pending recommendations[41]. After that, continued noncompliance would result in a freeze of British support for the ACC.

In April 2007, DFID annual review found its way into the public eye, and the press presented it as an indictment of Joko-Smart's work as commissioner and, indirectly, of President Kabbah's commitment to the fight against corruption[42]. For some within the ACC, the report was lopsided, placing no blame on the British consultants who had worked within the Commission; for others, however, it was the natural outcome of Joko-Smart's refusal to work with donors. Later that year, the United Kingdom finally did what it had not dared to for seven years: it applied its conditionality, although not due to transgressions of the ACC assistance framework. Together with the EU, Britain withheld disbursement of budget support to the government in response to its failure to release public account audits going as far back as 2002[43]. Even though – as a donor official worried – not enough thought may have been given to the political implications of such a symbolic gesture in an election year, the freeze sent a powerful message to President Kabbah about donors' new-found serious-ness. Coupled with the ACC report, Britain's willingness to sus-pend budget support signalled to the people and political opposi-tion alike that the government of the Sierra Leone People's Party – and, by extension, the presidential candidacy of Vice-President Solomon Berewa – did not have the political will to address cor-ruption at a fundamental level[44].

The opportunity was not lost on Kabbah's rivals, chief among them being Ernest Bai Koroma. He was an insurance business-man, who had risen to become a candidate for the presidency under the opposition party, the All People's Congress. Koroma capitalised on public discontent and made the fight against cor-ruption the central theme of his campaign, promising 'zero tol-erance on corruption' and thereby sending a message not just to voters but, in particular, to donors. The ACC had acquired a sig-nificant public profile since its creation, and its success – or lack thereof – had become an important component for the assessment of politicians. It was precisely this high profile that made Koroma focus on the ACC during his campaign, throughout which he made all sorts of pledges, such as strengthening the ACC, draft-ing new legislation, and ensuring there would be no sacred cows in his cabinet. The only way for the opposition candidate to separate his party from the previous administration, and thereby to win the vote of Sierra Leoneans, was by committing himself to make the Commission effective.

Ernest Bai Koroma beat Kabbah's Vice-President Solomon Berewa in the second round of presidential elections in the fall of 2007. While the losing incumbent party blamed donors for its defeat, accusing them of emboldening the opposition and withholding budget support as political punishment, Koroma in fact won due to a split within the ranks of the Sierra Leone People's Party. This had led Charles Margai, son and nephew of the post-independence prime ministers, to form his own splinter party and then strike an alliance with the opposition[45]. As president-elect, however, Koroma did not renege on his electoral commitments. He once again pledged that he would prosecute corrupt officials, investigate crimes of the past, and reinvigorate the ACC. Specifically, he aimed at giving the Commission its long-sought ability to prosecute independently, without veto from the Attorney General[46]. The most powerful message that he could send was the removal of Henry Joko-Smart from the commissioner's office, which he did shortly after his election. Appointed in Joko-Smart's stead was a young human rights lawyer, Abdul Tejan-Cole, who would preside over an anticorruption renaissance in post-conflict Sierra Leone.

In his first annual report as commissioner, Tejan-Cole welcomed with relief the end of an 'annus horribilis' for the ACC. He also expressed his aspiration to persuade DFID to restore its support, and reported the establishment of a committee tasked with revising the Anti-Corruption Act of 2000[47]. The latter task he carried out without external funding, calling in favours from friends in the legal community. By late July 2008, a draft was ready for ministerial review and parliamentary approval[48]. The government did not make any major changes to the proposal; ACC officials argued that, because of its public commitment, it could not have. Free from interference from the executive, Tejan-Cole was able to place political pressure on MPs to pass the act by building an alliance with civil society groups. Caving in under popular demand, MPs adopted the Anti-Corruption Act 2008 without much attention to its contents, only later realising the true strength of this new law.

The revised act increased the number of punishable corrupt offenses from nine to twenty-seven. More importantly, it granted prosecutorial autonomy to the Commission, as well as the power to enforce compliance sanctions on public officials who refused to implement its recommendations. The ACC thus became, in many ways, a veritable 'state within the state': an administrative organisation independent from the civil service, with its own internal and external revenue streams, and the power to investigate and prosecute any public official within Sierra Leone; all this, ostensibly, with President Koroma's backing[49]. In the words of an ACC official: 'The government ha[d] given us a free hand'. Tejan-Cole also reorganised the Commission internally, giving the staff a new impetus with the addition of intelligence and legal personnel as well as an increase in salaries. The ACC moved ahead of other agencies, not only in terms of remuneration but also with regard to equipment, work plans, strategy, reporting, and recruitment. A strategic plan that contained guidelines and expectations was provided to donors, and DFID provided additional benchmarks that would have to be met in order to secure continued funding. As a result of all these changes since the arrival of Tejan-Cole, ACC staff developed an awareness of greater responsibility to the public: 'You don't want to be seen as a non-performer', one official said. 'Because of clear benchmarks you cannot afford not to work.'

The new commissioner wasted no time in terms of investigations, arresting the former ombudsman, Francis Gabbidon, in April 2008[50]. By February 2009, the ACC was investigating the sitting minister of energy and power, Haja Afsatu Olayinka Kabba, for an energy contract that may have wasted up to $100 million[51]. The Commission had also indicted the former director general of the Sierra Leone broadcasting system, Kashope Wellington, and the acting head of the Sierra Leone Road Transport Authority, Sarah Finda Bendu[52]. In September 2010, President Koroma suspended the head of the National Revenue Authority after the ACC launched an investigation into several offences. Shortly afterwards, the sitting minister of health, Sheku Tejan Koroma, was relieved of his office and charged with abuse of office and failure to comply with procurement regulations[53]. Gabbidon, Wellington, Bendu, Kabba, and Koroma would all be convicted by late 2010.

Convictions on charges of corruption can hardly be the sole indicator of success for the Sierra Leone ACC, but this successful prosecution of high-level government officials conveys the inability or unwillingness of political leadership to interfere with the ACC and its new-found prosecutorial autonomy. Beyond investigations and prosecutions, the Commission had intensified its outreach and communication activities. In addition, it enhanced its role as watchdog of the public sector, contributing a set of best practices on the use of government property, a code of conduct for local councils, and a number of service charters for government departments and service providers[54]. The ACC may have been unable to change prevalent cultural norms, and despite its new-found vigour it still faced significant resistance within the state apparatus. However, it was succeeding in transforming the basic incentive structure for public officials, changing their risk calculations. As one official put it, '[c]ulture can also be ambushed'.

Ten years after the Commission was launched, Sierra Leoneans expressed greater confidence in their government's willingness and ability to fight corruption. While 88.2% of respondents continued to view corruption as a serious problem, 57.3% believed the government was committed to curbing it; 63.6% saw the Commission as effective; 66.9% had confidence in its ability to fight corruption; and 69% believed that the new Act passed in 2008 had increased government accountability[55]. This is a far cry from the scepticism and disillusionment that prevailed when the ACC was launched.

Sponsoring institutional change

The ACC managed to recover from the 'dark ages' and reach even greater effectiveness, partly due to the role of the United Kingdom as the its chief sponsor and financier. The impact of UK aid can be seen as a three-step process: it established a parallel system of accountability; disseminated reliable, nonpolitical information about political interference; and indirectly forced political leaders to adapt to Sierra Leoneans' unmet expectations.

The fact that the Commission was created as a new organisation outside the public service generated both risks and opportunities. The greatest risk was that the ACC would brew resentment among public servants as a body of 'dollar boys', who were topping up their salaries with aid money, working in better conditions and facilities than most other public sector departments, and meddling in the affairs of lower-paid civil servants just for the purpose of shaming their day-to-day survival tactics. To some extent, this risk did manifest in the ever-growing antipathy that ACC officials sensed in their public service peers. But by establishing the Commission outside the conventional personnel and oversight structures of the bureaucracy, its officials also had the opportunity to rise above the demands of everyday corruption and pursue their anticorruption brief with an administrative culture of their own. Moreover, the explicit support of the country's main external backer meant that the ACC leadership could be bolder than other departments. Free from the need to please political leaders, both Valentine Collier and Abdul Tejan-Cole pursued anticorruption goals with dogged independence, even to the point of open political confrontation.

Parallel accountability enabled ACC officials to develop a highly public profile for the Commission, thereby altering public expectations about what public servants could and should do. For the first time since Sierra Leone's independence, corruption was broadly reported and publicly shamed as improper behaviour instead of invoked and manipulated for purely partisan purposes. Having a large donor publicly committed to institutional change provided sufficient new information for citizens to begin questioning their government. The online leak – unintended or not – of the 2006 ACC annual review offered Sierra Leoneans a non-partisan assessment of their president's commitment to fighting corruption. This clear signal was only strengthened when Britain and the EU jointly decided to withdraw budget support due to the government's lack of compliance with audit conditions. Whether they liked it or not, donors first raised public expectations and then supplied a scathing indictment of government performance.

In a way, therefore, Britain's overt support for the ACC nudged the institutional balance of power in favour of reformers such as Collier and Tejan-Cole.

Despite misgivings in London about enforcing aid conditionality and interfering with Sierra Leone's electoral process, the ACC report and budget support debacle managed to alter the structure of political incentives for party leaders in the lead up to the 2007 election. Ernest Bai Koroma, in particular, seized the ACC case as an opportunity to pledge a 'zero corruption' platform, staking his political success on the credibility of this commitment. The reason Abdul Tejan Cole was able to push so hard for a new Anti-Corruption Act was because he was able to spend not his own political capital but the president's[56]. It was Koroma's public commitment; Cole was just implementing it. Koroma had committed himself to such an extent because of his campaign platform, which was deeply rooted in public discontent with Kabbah's alleged unwillingness to sacrifice his party's 'big men' to reform. There is no reason to believe that Koroma was any less beholden to entrenched interests within his party than Kabbah was, and he was no stranger to restaffing key public positions along ethnic or clientelistic lines[57]. Yet corruption continued to feature prominently in the new president's agenda, even after inauguration[58]. Without the public expectations raised by the ACC's early years, and without the devastatingly clear message of nonperformance sent by Britain and the EU, there is no reason to believe that the Commission would have been strengthened under a Koroma administration.

Given all that we know about institutional change, Sierra Leone's ACC should not have worked. Between 2005 and 2007, when the government effectively managed to defang the

Commission by removing its energetic commissioner and promoting an inward-looking turn in its day-to-day operations, failure was indeed the ACC's likely fate. Enduring informal institutions had reared their ugly heads and beat new formal rules to the ground in an all-too-familiar pattern of failed reform. Yet, by 2010, the Commission had been reinvigorated; in fact, it had become one of the best-run state agencies in Sierra Leone. This drastic reversal of fortunes eventually secured the Commission a diversified stream of donor funding: besides DFID and the German Organisation for Technical Cooperation (GTZ), it started receiving support from Irish Aid, the World Bank, the EU, the UN Peacebuilding Fund, and the Open Society Initiative for West Africa[59]. Foreign aid flocked to the apparent success of the ACC, at least for a time.

This chapter has shown that aid can provide the right financial backing and political nudges here and there, but that, ultimately, local reformers must be relied upon to advocate and fight for institutional change. The politics are just too ugly and the landscape is simply too treacherous for aid donors to bear the burden of pushing development down the throat of a reluctant government. And yet, this is exactly what they tried to do right across the border in Liberia, as I will discuss in the next chapter.

FOUR | The limits of donor influence

Corruption had also become endemic throughout Liberia towards the end of its second civil war (1999–2003). The transitional government that emerged out of the 2003 comprehensive peace agreement was a compromise coalition of political actors, running the gamut from enlightened to exploitative, which made policymaking slow and ineffective. Nepotism dominated staffing decisions in the civil service, and the judicial system was either unable or unwilling to act as a check of any kind. Crucial positions within government were considered first and foremost a stupendous source of personal enrichment[1], and there was a widely held belief among the people that 'if you don't steal from the government you're seen as stupid'[2]. The US Department of State's annual human rights report on Liberia left no room for interpretation:

> Corruption was widespread during the year. The absence of salaries for government employees exacerbated the situation. Corruption was present in all sectors of society including the judiciary. Those who publicly admitted to corruption were often not charged or tried[3].

Liberia emerged from its fourteen-year-long conflict to find a plethora of aid donors willing to assist with reconstruction efforts. Well-meaning foreigners were not oblivious to the strong legacies of capture and corruption that threatened the entire reconstruction enterprise. In late 2003, a Joint Needs Assessment prepared by the UN, World Bank, and International Monetary Fund (IMF) concluded that the most challenging reform ahead would be 'the alignment of state practices according to the norms of transparent and law-abiding governance'[4]. In order to secure the foreign resources necessary to overhaul the Liberian state, the transitional government had to 'reassure donors that if they contribute[d] to the transition, their resources [would] be properly managed and make a difference'. A fundamental requirement for the general process would be a mechanism that had 'the authority to manage the transition process, enabling stakeholders to monitor progress, assess achievements, track the use of resources and obtain the information necessary to decide whether or not to release additional tranches of finance for specific purposes'[5].

It was exactly the same concern that had animated the British to establish an ACC in Sierra Leone. But while the aims were similar in Liberia, the means were not: absent a commitment by the government to keeping itself honest, aid donors had to resort to more intrusive forms of influence to fuel the engine of reform. This time around, the international community was ready to get dirty and play politics, doing whatever was required to help get Liberia out of the conflict and state failure trap. To that end, the donors that helped establish the transitional government also agreed to a broad reconstruction framework with it. When local partners began to betray a lack of commitment, major aid agencies stepped up the political pressure and eventually established an unprecedented mechanism for external support of institutional change: the Governance and Economic Management Assistance Program (GEMAP).

Contracts without conditions

When Liberia's aid partners demanded stronger institutional checks in exchange for their financial support, they were engaging in a practice known as conditionality. It is easy to imagine that most foreign aid functions as a donation. When the average Westerner gives money to a charity or NGO, for instance, she expects that the resources will be transferred to the poor in kind or through various forms of assistance. A lot of humanitarian assistance works along these lines, turning nonrefundable grants into medical treatment or food relief. However, the most frequent type of aid transaction by far is not a donation but a contract: DFID and USAID hire private providers and local partners for specific projects, while the World Bank's world-spanning portfolio of interventions is basically a set of financial agreements with recipient governments. These contracts serve to establish the terms of partnership, the anticipated objectives and means to achieve them, and the specific funding modalities and disbursement mechanisms that will fuel the intervention. Seen from this rather technical perspective, the aid system as a whole is one of the largest procurement processes in the world. However, contracts also include obligations, for the donor as well as (and especially for) the recipient. This usually takes the form of a carrot-and-stick approach, in which successive tranches of funding are dangled in front of recipients but will only be disbursed if certain conditions are met. That is what we call conditionality.

Aid conditionality is a tricky business. We could reasonably expect donors to exert a disproportionate level of influence over developing counties, owing to their position of relative power in terms of finance: in a contract between rich and poor, it seems obvious that the rich would have the upper hand. The data is clear on this matter. In some particularly aid-dependent countries, development assistance actually contributes a sizeable percentage of the national GDP. However, the reality of donor assistance betrays a more complicated picture, in which conditionality is seldom invoked, if at all. As I highlighted in the previous chapter, Britain did develop a comprehensive conditionality framework as part of its partnership with the government of Sierra Leone. However, it took seven years of mismanagement and corruption in the latter for the United Kingdom to pull the plug on only part of its support. Why is that?

Aid agencies are basically trapped between two competing demands. On the one hand, they need to be able to withhold or withdraw aid funds in order to enforce their conditions on less-than-committed local partners; failure to comply must be met with retribution of one kind or another in order to retain credibility. On the other hand, donor agencies are forced to constantly look over their shoulders at the home political environment, which can be disinclined to tolerate waste. In Chapter 2, I explored some of the lengths to which aid critics will go to make sure that every single penny is accounted for; failure cannot be tolerated. These competing demands place donors in the rather difficult position of needing to disburse money in order to keep the lights on back home, which means that enforcing conditionality can amount to shooting oneself in the foot. But here's the punch line: recipient governments know this, and they are not above using it to their own advantage. The years of structural adjustment in the 1980s and early 1990s brought this dilemma to the fore in development circles, calling into question the effectiveness of conditionality[6]. Instead, many assistance processes devolved into what Thomas Callaghy called the 'ritual dances of reform', an iterated dynamic of negotiation and disappointment in which recipient governments promised to reform, while international donors promised to believe them[7]. A pattern of 'permanent crisis' emerged throughout Africa, in which political leaders failed to pursue any policy or institutional reform that threatened the rents from public office captured by their clients[8].

Adding to the already difficult demands coming from domestic politics and recipient governments, in the 2000s the international community set in motion a new global agenda that threw yet another spanner into the contractual gears of aid. Responding to concerns regarding some common pitfalls of donor programmes, the Paris Declaration on Aid Effectiveness (2005) was a laudable effort to define guidelines for the improved design, implementation, monitoring, and evaluation of official development assistance[9]. The Paris Declaration did not really condemn aid conditionality, but it did subsume it under the principle of alignment of donor strategies and programmes with recipient ones. The text of the declaration calls on donors to '[d]raw conditions, whenever possible, from a partner's national development strategy or its annual review of progress in implementing this strategy'. Likewise, it suggests that aid actors '[l]ink funding to a single framework of conditions and/ or a manageable set of indicators derived from the national development strategy'. The following sentence in the declaration was surely aimed at appeasing some of the more idiosyncratic donors, telling them: '[T]his does not mean that all donors have identical conditions, but that each donor's conditions should be derived from a common streamlined framework aimed at achieving lasting

results'. Finally, the declaration allowed for exceptional circumstances in which conditions not included in the recipient's strategies and programmes could be legitimate, but only 'when a sound
justification exists and would be undertaken transparently and in
close consultation with other donors and stake holders'[10]. In other
words, conditionality under the Paris terms became a mechanism
for foreign aid donors to hold a recipient accountable to whatever
reforms and policies it 'owned.'

Ownership is as popular a buzzword as it is a difficult idea to
observe and measure, much less implement, in practice[11]. But
that did not prevent the emergence of a post-Paris zeitgeist in the
aid community that turned ownership into the keystone of 'good'
international assistance. The 2000 World Bank strategy on public sector reform, for instance, began with the basic premise that
'[r]eform will proceed only when a country's leaders are committed and in the driver's seat'[12]. But there is a clear flipside to the
principle of ownership: 'The effectiveness of governance assistance will always be limited', writes Stephen Krasner, because
'[s]ome leaders will find the exploitation of their own population
more advantageous than the introduction of reforms'[13]. Thus,
aid donors are faced with the demand to work with local actors
in pursuit of locally defined objectives and strategies, even when
those local actors may not actually act on behalf of the public
good, and might only be interested in development or reform to
the extent that it can lead to the short-term enrichment of a few
well-connected crooks.

The experiment of GEMAP

In early 2004, the international community and the National
Transitional Government of Liberia (NTGL) agreed to the

Results-Focused Transitional Framework, a detailed reform and aid coordination strategy[14]. The framework lacked a dedicated section on accountability and transparency, separating these reforms under different clusters and sectors: public official probity would be dealt with through civil service reform, whereas auditing and procurement transparency were included under public financial management. As a result, there was no overarching mechanism whereby donors could monitor or check the anticorruption efforts of the transitional government. This was only too convenient for a fractured coalition of big men animated by a sense of entitlement and retribution, whose time horizons had been shortened by a peace agreement-mandated end to their tenure by January 2006.

An European aid strategy drafted at the time lamented the fact that the transitional assembly was 'not a proactive political body', but a group 'more preoccupied with salaries and cars'. This 'culture of bad governance' posed a threat to revenue collection, dampening the prospects that the government could ever meet its stated objectives[15]. In fact, by 2005 the speaker of the National Transitional Legislative Assembly, his deputy the chairman of the Ways and Means Committee, and the chairman of the Rules and Order Committee were all suspended for fiscal and administrative misconduct[16]. The speaker had allegedly taken home about $90,000, but he was not alone: the director of national welfare and the managing director of the National Port Authority had both embezzled $600,000, while the head of the Bureau of Maritime Affairs had pocketed $3.5 million. Despite the widespread suspicions of malfeasance – or rather because of them – in June 2005, the transitional government established an Executive Task Force of Corruption, comprising nine governmental and nongovernmental commissioners. Its mandate included civic education, investigation and recommendation for prosecution, the elaboration of an anticorruption law and strategy, and the drafting legislation for the establishment of an anticorruption agency[17]. However, no reports were published by the Task Force, and no public officials were ever prosecuted under the NTGL regime. Instead of effectively hampering state capture, transitional legislators themselves engaged in a free-for-all capture of public resources: in November 2005, they passed a law allowing them to take government vehicles for personal use at the end of their terms, and the following month 'legislators leaving office stripped the capitol building of desks, computers, chairs, and carpeting'[18]. At that point, however, donors were no longer idly witnessing the pilfering of their aid money.

In order to address the shortcomings of the initial phase of assistance, in 2005 international actors designed the Governance and Economic Management Assistance Program (GEMAP) as a coordinated intervention along six lines of action: financial management and accountability; budgeting and expenditure management; procurement and granting of concessions; processes for the control of corruption; key governance institutions; and capacity building. In terms of administrative organisations, the GEMAP agreement mandated the transitional government to issue 'within two weeks' an executive order establishing an 'effective and independent nonpolitical ACC with full prosecutorial powers', headed by both Liberian and expatriate commissioners[19]. It also committed the government to the adoption of a new law guaranteeing the independence of the General Auditing Office. Such was the kind of 'immediate remedial action' that, according to the GEMAP agreement, all partners had decided the situation required. What the document failed to mention was that the emergence of such an 'agreement' had been far from uncontroversial.

In a twist of fate not deprived of a certain irony, the roots of what would become the intrusive GEMAP scheme lay in a series of audits, conducted in early 2004 by the European Commission after a direct request from transitional government Chairman Charles Gyude Bryant. At the time, public financial management was a key prerequisite for European assistance, but it was also becoming a growing source of concern for international financial institutions and the United States. Reports of widespread corruption and pilfering of state coffers were rattling the nerves of those external actors most involved in resurrecting the Liberian state and economy. Once finished, the audits provided an empirical justification for such fears. Before going public, the Europeans shared the reports with the IMF, the World Bank, and the United States, and together they began to discuss the possibility of an international intervention of some sort to counter such levels of corruption. At a meeting in Washington, the four donors decided to take the issue to the West African regional body and the UN. According to a joint World Bank–UN report on the origins of GEMAP, that particular meeting turned out to be a veritable 'grim occasion':

> Speaker after speaker focused on corruption as the main reason for Liberia's lack of recovery, so much so that the leader of the NTGL delegation, Minister of Planning and Economic Affairs Christian Herbert, felt obliged to intervene a second time to assure donors that the NTGL accepted the need for a more robust international role in public finance management. He characterised the problem as lack of capacity and asserted that there was no resistance to international experts coming in to work alongside counterparts in line ministries. Herbert called on the World Bank, the IMF and the US to provide this assistance[20].

With this admission of constraints, the minister provided a political justification for the intrusive aspirations of donors, who set out
to design an economic governance assistance programme that went
far beyond the usual kind of technical assistance (an initial draft,
in fact, granted the envisioned programme's steering committee
veto power over any government policy). Naturally, this initiative
aroused major resistance from the transitional government. 'They
wanted a take-over', recalled a Liberian official who participated
in the negotiations. The transitional government at first 'capital-
ized on tensions between partners', hurling around accusations of
international trusteeship. Bryant secured an uncomfortable ally in
the United Nations Mission in Liberia, which found itself trapped
between its reluctance to be overly political and its fear that the
government would only accede to a watered-down programme.
Donors responded to the government's continued obstructionism
with increasingly drastic measures: at first they raised the possibility
of withdrawing their aid, and when that did not work they resorted
to direct pressure on Chairman Bryant himself. Shortly thereafter,
the United States conveyed a more specific and powerful threat,
the withdrawal of its support to security sector reform, which
prompted the government to accede to the signature of GEMAP[21].
Six years later, a former negotiator on behalf of the Liberian government rationalised the decision by arguing that foreign controllers were just meant to confirm what they were supposed to be
doing anyway. 'We knew our weaknesses', he admitted. 'We were
prepared to play ball.'

GEMAP was an interesting mix of very different instruments,
which were themselves expressions of different aid relationships with the government. The shared authority over financial
processes, for instance, was almost exclusively an American

intervention. USAID's main concern with regard to Liberia's economic management was the leakage of public revenue, and what this foretold for the country's eventual graduation from foreign – and especially American – aid. To that end, under the first GEMAP component, in early 2006 USAID deployed expatriate financial controllers to four state-owned enterprises – the Liberia Petroleum Refining Company, the National Port Authority, the Roberts International Airport, and the Forestry Development Authority – as well as to the Bureau of the Budget, where they were supposed to contribute technical expertise as well as 'exercise cosignature authority over all financial commitments and payments or allotments of their company or agency, including the use/replenishment of petty cash'[22]. The only other donor employing executive authority in this fashion was the IMF, which in February 2006 seconded its own expert as chief administrator of the Central Bank of Liberia. Institutional assistance, in contrast, was dominated by multilateral donors. The European Commission, for instance, provided support for the Governance Reform Commission, the Public Procurement and Concessions Commission, and the General Auditing Commission[23]. Finally, all donors engaged in various forms of technical assistance to public financial management, deploying short- and long-term experts to state-owned enterprises; the Ministry of Finance; the Ministry of Lands, Mines, and Energy; the aforementioned commissions; and other public agencies throughout the Liberian executive. The result was a sprawling set of interventions aimed at improving financial management and curbing public corruption.

The GEMAP agreement was designed to maintain strong coordination into the implementation phase, while adopting a much less confrontational relationship with the government.

An infrastructure of donor coordination, monitoring, and joint oversight with the government was set up around an Economic Governance Steering Committee. Chaired by the head of state of Liberia, with 'a representative of a development partner' (the American ambassador) as his deputy, the Committee was meant to bring together all relevant ministries and agencies from the transitional government, along with its international backers: the African Union, European Commission, Economic Community of West African States (ECOWAS), Ghana, IMF, Nigeria, UN, United States, and World Bank. It would review GEMAP periodically 'against benchmarks, results, and resource needs' during its intended three-year implementation period, while also ensuring alignment and coordination by all international actors[24].

GEMAP was born out of explicit political pressure from donors. Regardless of the diplomatic tone that permeated the agreement, the reform context was one of mutual suspicion, if not outright hostility. Fortunately for them, donors were relieved of an uncomfortable local partner when Liberia's first post-conflict democratic elections were held in late 2005, ushering Ellen Johnson Sirleaf into the Executive Mansion shortly after GEMAP was signed and before the beginning of its implementation. Johnson Sirleaf publicly assumed the inherited GEMAP commitments as her own, and in so doing she gave donors the benefit of a retroactive ownership of sorts. Indeed, it seemed that the energetic new president – a former multilateral donor official herself – was willing to own GEMAP's aims to the bitter end. Pressure from the Executive Mansion on public servants, for instance, would be later identified in a mid-term review as one of the main sources of improvement in performance and revenue generation[25]. Moreover, the president dismissed a number of high-level officials suspected of corruption, such as the comptroller of the Ministry of Public Works, the deputy minister for health and social welfare, and the director of the Civil Aviation Authority[26]. She instilled new life into the development of central administrative organisations for corruption reporting and sanctioning, even if it was this process of institutional reform that eventually exposed the government's reluctance to embrace and enforce actual change.

Although it was touted by its designers as an innovative and even exemplary approach to development assistance, the GEMAP that oversaw Liberian public finances between 2005 and 2009 had mixed results at best. For instance, performance and revenue generation at the intervened state-owned enterprises increased substantially during GEMAP, but international controllers were unable to get their Liberian counterparts fully invested in proper monitoring and oversight, and the mindset of subordinate public servants seemed to change little beyond the offices of the finance departments where the expatriates sat. As a USAID mid-term review found: 'In other departments that are in less frequent contact with the Controller, old habits have reportedly been slow to change'[27]. For instance, whereas the finance and marketing units at the Liberia Petroleum Refining Company had incorporated modern accounting standards, other departments persisted in producing false receipts. Indeed, evaluators recurrently found that technical assistance was successful only where organisational leadership was aligned with GEMAP objectives[28]. That is, the programme was able to garner support from public officials who were sympathetic, but it was largely incapable of swaying the stance of those who were not.

Across state-owned enterprises, reform efforts made progress under the direct supervision of GEMAP controllers, but they tended to fail when led by local counterparts. In other administrative organisations covered by the programme, the results were equally mixed. Whereas, at one end of the spectrum, the General Auditing Commission was becoming so effective as to elicit political backlash, at the other end, support for the General Services Agency, the centralised supplier of government goods, had been 'irrelevant' or 'scarcely effective'[29]. Local officials shared contrasting evaluations of GEMAP with me. One legislator opined that the right systems had been put in place, but some auditing officials considered that cosignatory powers did not entail a sustainable change in customary practices. For a senior governance coordination official, GEMAP had been, if not a failure, then not as much of a success as its backers claimed. Another governance official agreed with this view. The concept was great, they said, and the aims laudable, but once it was completed the government had nothing in place: no checks and balances, and no systems built. With such major gaps inherited from the design phase, the programme had simply been 'a waste of time, a waste of money'.

Even more interesting is the fact that GEMAP's achievements were actually impossible to properly assess. First, it was really difficult to define the boundaries of the programme. The imperfect aggregation of pre-existing programs under the same label, as well as the presence of similar interventions outside the formal agreement, made it hard for donors to isolate a coherent set of interventions for the purposes of monitoring[30]. According to a researcher who conducted interviews at the time, 'none of the centrally placed persons had an overview of "basic facts" concerning the size and scope of GEMAP activities'. For instance, whereas USAID claimed tax reform as a GEMAP success, those actually carrying out the reform – the IMF and Ministry of Finance – claimed that project was outside the programme[31].

Second, even when one knew where to look, it was not clear what to look for. Initially, GEMAP relied on a quarterly reporting system that emphasised narration over indicators, which had 'proved relatively unsuccessful in providing stakeholders with consistent and meaningful information on programme progress and impact'[32]. It was only after a retreat in August 2008 that a set of empirically verifiable benchmarks was agreed on. Even then, indicators often related to outputs and deliverables instead of impact; annual targets and project targets were confused, with instances of multiple counting; and ultimately 'all targets were so low that life of project goals were achieved every year'[33]. For the drafters of the final USAID review, the unfortunate implication was that 'people who read the history and accomplishments of GEMAP will not have the proof as to accomplishments or impact, just number of people trained and offices assisted'[34].

The pursuit of harmony?

GEMAP was engineered to behave as a true embodiment of the principles dominating aid doctrine at the time, chief among them ownership and harmonisation. I have already discussed the former, and the GEMAP case perfectly highlights the contradictions intrinsic to getting nondevelopmental elites to try to work towards developmental goals. At best, as in Liberia, the international community effectively takes the reins, trading ownership for effectiveness. At worst, as in Sierra Leone, a smart enough government can spend five or six years effectively biting the hand that feeds it. The problem underlying ownership is what economists call a principal–agent problem[35]. Donors behave as a principal delegating a difficult task (reform) to an agent (the local government), whose real preferences they cannot entirely predict; this is further complicated because the task in question is so tricky that it is very hard to disentangle lack of commitment by the agent from totally innocent mistakes or structural constraints. Many in the aid industry will shy away from this characterisation, taking refuge in buzzwords such as 'partnership' and 'alignment'. But the contractual nature of most aid makes the principal–agent problem almost inevitable. In Sierra Leone, the Kabbah government managed to preserve its *bona fides* up to the point where donors were forced to react to blatant clientelism and mismanagement. In Liberia, in contrast, the GEMAP mechanism had a strong element of conditionality and strong-arming built into it, which indicates a group of donors much more comfortable with the idea of disciplining an irresponsible agent.

However, GEMAP faced one additional problem. After all, the government in Freetown had to deal with a single major development partner, the United Kingdom: even if the High Commission and DFID may not have seen eye to eye all the time, the State House in Freetown could be reasonably certain that the buck stopped at Whitehall. Liberia's transitional government, and later President Ellen Johnson Sirleaf, however, did not experience the same advantage (or disadvantage): the end of civil war brought to Monrovia a veritable cornucopia of donors, both multilateral and bilateral, all of them ready to step in and help out. Hence the need to coordinate – or harmonise, in Paris Declaration parlance – aid efforts in the country. Scholars have argued for a while now about the need to harmonise. For starters, when multiple donors get involved in the business of institutional change, they may actually undermine each other by following different agendas[36].

Even on those rare occasions when they agree on everything, there are some surprising transaction costs to having a large family of development partners. The unintended consequences of donor proliferation have long plagued the uneasy sleep of the aid community: in principle, it is better to have as many contributions to development as possible; in practice, a 'too many cooks' kind of problem emerges when each donor has an independent relationship with the recipient government. The local ills of aid fragmentation – overwhelmed public organisations, civil servants serving donors and not citizens – are well established in the 'aid-institutions paradox' and aid dependence scholarship[37]. But there are also consequences for donors themselves: confusion of messages and incentives can enable rent-seeking public actors; competing or contradictory objectives may undermine reform agendas and encourage 'donor shopping'; and a large number of donors may create collective action problems when dealing with the government[38].

Collective action is precisely the problem faced by aid harmonisation efforts such as GEMAP. In Mancur Olson's classic formulation, a collective action problem arises when the benefits of an activity are enjoyed collectively, while the costs of participating in that activity are borne individually[39]. The greatest example of our time is climate change regulations. Every country on Earth benefits from cleaner air, because of its stubborn tendency to flow across lines drawn on a map; however, the cost of reducing emissions is borne by each country individually. Hence the difficulty of getting the entire world to agree on climate change policies, and the constant accusations that one country or another is shirking responsibility by not contributing to the effort. Collective action problems abound in development. Corruption is often seen as a basic collective action problem, as it makes little sense to be the only honest public servant in an organisation full of crooks, where high-minded idealism only leads to a lower income when you discount bribes and kickbacks. Donors, too, are prone to collective action problems: a better institutional environment is likely to improve the effectiveness of every agency's programmes, but not all of them have the appetite to lock horns with the government in order to exact the necessary reforms. In Sierra Leone, for instance, all donors benefited from a relatively strong ACC between 2007 and 2012, but it was Britain alone that would be forever tainted by the suspicion of electoral interference.

It would be nice to imagine that Liberia's international partners built GEMAP precisely to overcome their collective action problems, but the tragic truth behind that story is GEMAP was never fully coordinated: it was, as a multilateral donor official put it, 'a child of the immediate post-conflict moment', beyond which every donor went its own way. Despite its name, GEMAP was not, in fact, a programme, but an umbrella term for a plethora of separate donor projects. There was no shared programming cycle, no pooling of funds, and no integrated reporting lines. The question of resource-sharing and joint disbursement, for instance, did not appear in the agreement, and it had never been a central point of discussion among donors. Instead, at the time the text was drafted, the understanding was that specific GEMAP tasks would be divided between international actors, with funds for them being diverted from pre-existing and mutually disconnected aid streams[40]. What donors had agreed to was a set of common aims, as specified in the programme document, as well as a formal information-sharing mechanism. From the standpoint of the Paris principle of harmonisation, therefore, GEMAP was not so much a realisation as a shared hope. Hence its motley shopping list of objectives, reflecting executive, institutional, and technical components drawn from each donor's objectives and programming preferences.

It is unsurprising, then, that on the odd occasion politics did emerge from beneath layers upon layers of managerial timidity, international backers shied away from an overly and overtly confrontational relationship.

Before I turn the page on the GEMAP narrative, it is worth looking back at one of its constituent interventions to fully understand what happens when aid donors are incapable – or unwilling – to overcome their principal–agent and collective action problems.

An orphan of international aid

The Liberian General Auditing Commission (GAC) was one of the key components of reform mobilisation under GEMAP. As the Bureau of Audits since 1956, and then the General Auditing Office since 1972, the organisation had historically been subordinated to the office of the president, both informally and legally, even after the 1986 Constitution had defined it as an autonomous commission. Part of the GEMAP deal had been to establish a truly apolitical Auditor General, and, in June 2005, the National Transitional Legislative Assembly complied by adopting the General Auditing Commission Act, under which it granted the GAC greater independence and made it report directly to the legislature. When Ellen Johnson Sirleaf assumed office, she invited the European Commission to manage the recruitment of a new Auditor General, and to provide support for the office over the next four years. The job went to John S. Morlu, a young, American-trained Liberian auditor with experience in the financial consulting sector. The new

Auditor General immediately revealed himself to be an energetic leader for the Commission, drafting a sixty-five-page-long organisational blueprint that was part strategic vision, part management plan, and part legal review of the Liberian public audit system[41]. He also took the Commission out of the civil service recruitment system after confronting and winning a challenge from legislators at the supreme court. The way Morlu saw it, the GAC was 'the first line of defence for promoting integrity, transparency and accountability throughout the public sector'[42].

Barely a year after it started receiving European support, the GAC was already considered 'one of the success stories of GEMAP': 127 auditors trained, 11 audits completed, recommendations formulated for the new Public Finance Management Act and financial regulations, and an internal audit strategy drafted for the Ministry of Finance[43]. In what was ultimately a politically charged mission, Morlu could rely on the umbrella of support from the European Delegation in Monrovia, which oversaw the Auditor General's office under a 'Special Dispensation' with the government. Morlu lost no time in trying to broker a broader coalition to supplement its chief donor. He sought the support of peer audit institutions in Ghana and Zambia, adopted the standards and code of ethics designed by the International Organisation of Supreme Audit Institutions (INTOSAI), and courted public support by establishing strong links with civil society organisations and the media. By 2010, the Commission had become the most salient success story of GEMAP, far outpacing other governmental organisations[44]. Strengthened by the links and legitimation coming from different actors, Morlu oversaw the elaboration and publication of over forty reports on Liberian public organisations, many of which had not been audited for over two decades.

In all of these efforts, the GAC served as a lone local champion in the broader anticorruption fight. The two main stakeholders in the auditing system offered little support: the legislature was considered by GAC officials to be 'the weakest link in the process', with legislators rarely acting upon recommendations, and sometimes being named in the reports themselves; and the executive did not enforce the implementation of systems and procedures, even when the recommendations were explicit. According to some public servants, at times the government appeared not to know what to do with the recommendations, simply passing the buck to a separate Governance Commission for policy suggestions. Nor did it pressure ministers and agency chiefs to ensure the independence of internal audit units, or even to have them produce any kind of report. The Liberian ACC, for its part, was emerging only very slowly, under the leadership of the same woman who had adjudicated the 2005 election in favour of Johnson Sirleaf as head of the Electoral Commission, and who had later served as her Attorney General. Frustrated and politically isolated, the GAC took to using its reports as a way of spurring public debate on corruption, publishing every audit and report on its website and stoking the fires of controversy between the Auditor General and the executive.

The role of President Johnson Sirleaf was crucial. In her prior capacity as chairperson of the Governance Reform Commission, she had been a vocal proponent of reform, advocating a strong and independent GAC. When she became president, her priorities changed, however, and she instead sought to ensure that Morlu's challenge would not destabilise her fragile ruling coalition. Indeed, the revolutionary Auditor General himself had quickly become a political thorn in the executive's side. In June 2007, Morlu criticised the omission of part of government revenues from the national budget, and declared that the current administration was 'three times as corrupt as its predecessor'[45]. He shared his concern about 'parallel budgets' with the house speaker in a letter that was subsequently leaked to the press by a senator. In response, Johnson Sirleaf attacked him publicly for exceeding his legal responsibilities[46]. In April 2008, the government appointed two deputy Auditors General without prior consultation with Morlu's office, which made everyone view them as political appointments. It was assumed at the time that their hiring anticipated the eventual departure of the EU's technical assistance in 2008, and of the Auditor General himself in 2009, but an official review found 'no concrete evidence' to support that interpretation[47].

In early 2011, the open confrontation between Morlu and Johnson Sirleaf was the talk of the town. Report by report, the Auditor General had undermined the political coalition sustaining the president's Unity Party, publishing claims against the managing director of the Liberia Petroleum Refining Company, the minister for gender and development, the inspector general of police, the minister of finance, and the minister of internal affairs[48]. The GAC's findings forced Johnson Sirleaf to fire a number of high-profile supporters. At the same time, however, international support for Morlu's quest was beginning to wane: the Europeans had been reluctant to take sides in the clash between president and Auditor General, much less in an election year, and key donors abstained from voicing their concerns. For such an openly interventionist programme, GEMAP's silence was deafening.

Having renewed Morlu's contract in 2009, it was not clear whether the president would keep tolerating him or appoint a friendlier face instead. Senior GAC officials were concerned that a new Auditor General 'without vision and political aspirations' would undo the achievements of the past few years; continued independence, they believed, was predicated on strong support from the Liberian people and international partners. The conflict between Morlu and Johnson Sirleaf escalated to open hostility throughout 2011, with the Auditor General responding to pressure by telling the president to 'call off the dogs' and 'take the darn job'[49]. In March of that year, Ellen Johnson Sirleaf announced her decision not to renew John Morlu as Auditor General.

What followed was a clear effort to defang the GAC. The president's designated successor, Robert Kilby, took the opportunity of his Senate confirmation hearing to accuse Morlu of breaching professional auditing principles by using legal terms and politicising his reports. Kilby claimed that an auditor should be careful about releasing information, much less before the legislature can review it, and that in fact the GAC should 'protect its findings from the public'[50]. His nomination turned into a public scandal when it was revealed during his confirmation hearings that part of his educational resume had been falsified. With the appointment temporarily stalled, the GAC continued operations under an acting Auditor General from the Morlu era. In August 2012, however, Johnson Sirleaf decided to renominate Robert Kilby, reportedly due to a 'reconsideration of the factors that prompted his earlier withdrawal'. Despite concerns about transparency and competition in the process, the Senate quickly confirmed him, and he became Auditor General in September 2012. His tenure was widely regarded as one of paralysis and waste. The GAC did not produce a single report under his leadership. Faced with internal challenges, he forced all personnel to reapply for their positions, eventually firing over forty people who had been at the Commission since Morlu's days[51]. Absent a strong coalition of donors and civil society and a persuasive champion who could broker new alliances, the GAC was effectively subverted.

President Johnson Sirleaf was forced to fire Kilby in July 2013, less than a year into his appointment, when it was revealed that a private accounting firm he owned had signed a contract with the General Service Agency: a conflict of interest that violated Liberia's public procurement legislation[52]. After Kilby's departure in July 2013, the deputy Auditor General once again took over as interim head of GAC until the appointment in September 2013 and confirmation in February 2014 of Yusador Gaye. She had previously served as foreign service inspector general at the Ministry of Foreign Affairs. In her first annual report, Gaye highlighted her desire to 'restore the trust and confidence of all stakeholders'[53]. The GAC completed four reports in 2013, and twenty-two in 2014. A new act was submitted to the legislature that granted 'full financial and operational autonomy' to the Commission[54]. However, in her ninth state of the union address the year before, President Johnson Sirleaf had explicitly called for a 'media-shy' GAC, clearly nipping in the bud any suspicion that the Commission would once again behave as a public challenger to her government.

Between a rock and a hard place

The aspirations of the international aid community in Liberia were decidedly ambitious. Too ambitious, perhaps, but worthy nonetheless. It is impossible to overstate the utter decay and collapse of the Liberian state after a decade with two civil wars and the intervening reign of warlord-turned-president Charles Taylor. The country still bears the physical and psychological scars of war, and its politics are still tainted by the compromises that were necessary to get it away from violence. The international intervention in Liberia effectively secured the country, preventing any backsliding into conflict and instability. However, the task of building the post-conflict state turned out to be more challenging than initially anticipated. Over a decade of bogged-down state building in Afghanistan and Iraq may have soured the donor publics' attitudes towards humanitarianism and internationalism. But the Liberian case is interesting because of the relatively benign environment in which such state building was taking place: no insurgency, no continuing war, small size, relatively stable neighbourhood. Rebuilding a tiny state in West Africa should have been relatively easy. Yet the politics of reform reared its ugly head to spit in donors' faces time and again. They were the same challenges as in Sierra Leone, only supercharged. And, in that sense, they are not too different from the kinds of political dilemmas faced by donors elsewhere in the developing world.

For all its limitations and contradictions, GEMAP was a bold idea, and one that came really close to succeeding. It was designed to tackle the basic politics of change and bring institutional change where it was most sorely needed. It was an example of what development assistance can, and maybe even should, be: an alliance between external sponsors and local reformers to push forward an agenda for change. It was GEMAP that gave wings to Ellen Johnson Sirleaf's early reform agenda and emboldened John Morlu to single-handedly take on a government. How sad, then, that GEMAP would be all but impossible in the current political environment in donor countries. Constricted as they are by the relentless demands for certainty I discussed in Chapter 2, today's donors would shrink away from governance and economic management due to the difficulty of accurately measuring results and impact. Instead, they would likely fund vaccination campaigns and the construction of new rural schools, goals that can more or less deter the worst attacks from aid hawks while retaining a veneer of solidarity. If this had been the case back then, Liberians would not have gotten a reformer like Morlu, and a less-than-honest government would have ruled without challenge. To expand on Andrew Natsios's words, transformational change would have been sacrificed in the altar of measurability.

Even if I strongly believe that intervening in places like Liberia is the right thing to do, this chapter has amply demonstrated that doing so means addressing important challenges about the nature of development assistance. From the Sierra Leonean case, we have learned about the messy politics of institutional change. From the Liberian case, we have learned about donors themselves, and the many ways in which they tend to shoot themselves in the foot in order to comply with the rhetoric of grandiose global goals such as the Paris Declaration principles of ownership and harmonisation. The sweet, sweet irony in all this is that it is often reformers and other local actors who are most likely to challenge the declaration by asking donors to intervene. This begs the question: whose ownership is being served by the development community? And at what point does an aid agency become a diplomatic actor? Those are the main questions of the following chapter.

FIVE | The paradoxes of development diplomacy

The year 1998 had an unusually strong hurricane season in the Northern Atlantic, with the month of October seeing two named storms: Lisa and Mitch. Lisa eventually became a minimum-strength tropical system that veered north and never touched land, but Mitch evolved from tropical storm to hurricane, moving to land with winds of up to 290 kilometres per hour. Over the course of six days, 26 to 31 October 1998, Mitch ravaged large swaths of Central America, wreaking havoc on such a scale that the Economic Commission for Latin America and the Caribbean (CEPAL) called it the greatest natural disaster in the region in two centuries. In Honduras, a small country of six million people, Mitch left in its wake 7,000 dead, 12,000 injured, and 8,000 missing; up to 1.5 million people affected with 85,000 homes partially or totally destroyed; and damaged crops, infrastructure and public utilities. According to CEPAL's calculations, the total cost of destruction reached US$3.7 billion: this was equivalent to 70% of the country's GDP[1].

The international response to the catastrophe was quick. In December 1998, the Inter-American Development Bank hosted a meeting of the Consultative Group for the Reconstruction and Transformation of Central America in Washington, DC, at which US$3.6 billion in aid was committed to the subregion.

The affected countries' presidents argued in that meeting that the Mitch disaster presented a unique opportunity, not just for restoring the region to its pre-hurricane state, but for building a better Central America. Based on the discussions in Washington, the government of Honduras set out to draft a Master Plan for National Reconstruction and Transformation (PMRTN, to use its Spanish acronym), which it presented at a second gathering of the Consultative Group in Stockholm, Sweden, on 25–8 May 1999. The PMRTN's chief aim was to recover the losses caused by Mitch by 2001, while still focusing on the processes of economic and institutional transformation that Honduras had undergone in the 1990s. To that end, the government offered not merely a comprehensive listing of damages, but also a '[s]trategy for accelerated, equitable, sustainable, and participatory development' that transcended the needs of short-term reconstruction and set the foundations for transformation beyond the government's mandate[2].

The Stockholm meeting brought together 400 delegates from fifty donor countries and international organisations. Their discussions centred around a premise clearly formulated by Central American heads of state and the Inter-American Development Bank president, Enrique V. Iglesias: reconstruction would not come at the expense of transformation. The Consultative Group's second meeting resulted in the Stockholm Declaration, a general framework for national reconstruction and international assistance in Central America. For the governments of countries affected by Mitch, the declaration was a means to secure commitments for much-needed relief; for donors, it was an opportunity to take aid and humanitarianism back to the drawing board[3]. That is why, amongst its six principles, the declaration included institutional objectives as well as aid-effectiveness ones. Recipients such as Honduras agreed to the idea of '[c]onsolidating democracy and governance, [and] strengthening government decentralisation, with active participation from civil society', while international sponsors committed to '[c]oordinating donor efforts, guided by the priorities formulated by recipient countries'. In many ways, Stockholm was a precursor of the Paris Declaration and the ensuing decade of global debates about aid effectiveness. What makes Honduras special compared with so many other aid recipients, however, is the fact that it had an enduring donor coordination group.

Canada, Germany, Spain, Sweden, and the United States emerged in Stockholm as the country's chief development partners, a role that was formalised in Madrid in October 1999 with the creation of the Follow-Up Group to the Stockholm Declaration, or G-5. These donors would monitor progress towards the objectives of the Plan Maestro, while also providing assistance in the formulation and implementation of a new Poverty Reduction Strategy (PRS). The strategy was a condition for Honduras's participation in the Heavily Indebted Poor Country Initiative (HIPC) launched by the IMF and World Bank. Debt relief was seen at the time as an essential component of reconstruction, but, in order to qualify, the government would have to prove that it had a clear plan for using the resources freed up by it. In particular, the IMF and World Bank wanted governments to earmark funds for poverty reduction, and they thought that the best way to do so would be to have the PRS process be as open and participatory as possible. With civil society representation, donor support, and financial relief, there was no reason why the government of Honduras could not get the country back on its feet after the devastation of Mitch.

In the previous two chapters, I have sketched out some of the challenges of donor support for reform. In Sierra Leone, the apparent commitment of the government of Ahmad Tejan Kabbah was undermined by clientelist politics, forcing the United Kingdom into the tricky dilemma of either supporting a blatantly corrupt regime or destabilising a fragile post-conflict state. The subversion of the ACC was one of the final straws that broke the aid camel's back. In Liberia, in turn, donors arrived primed for a difficult political relationship with the transitional government, and their strategy was to push forward a slightly coercive reform mechanism that would give them veto power over some government decisions. Despite GEMAP, however, and despite having a sympathetic president in office, donors were unable to sustain their reform agenda due to their own collective action problems.

Honduras was supposed to be different, for several reasons. First, the challenge was to reconstruct after a natural disaster, which is a less politically charged event than a civil war. Second, reconstruction was a basic enough agenda that donors and governments could agree on a long list of objectives and priorities. Third, donors started the process with a formal coordination mechanism, the G-5. Over the following decade, this mechanism would prove so effective that it would draw others in, turning into a G-10, a G-12, a G-15, and eventually a G-16, with dedicated political and technical levels and a growing role in the country as a de facto representative of the international community. With some key obstacles overcome by design, Honduras would be no Sierra Leone or Liberia. Yet the politics of reform has a funny way of derailing donor plans.

This chapter deals with a third major challenge in foreign aid: the blurring of developmental and diplomatic roles and priorities.

It is by now a common element of development criticism that donor motivations are not always innocent or pristine. After all, aid agencies are merely the humanitarian arms of governments with much more pressing and mundane objectives. However, there is another side to this issue of problematic preferences, one that is less well known. By virtue of their very presence in a country, donors can sometime become sources of legitimation in the eyes of local actors, whether they want that responsibility or not. That is exactly what happened in Honduras: in the ten years after Mitch, the G-16 was forced to deal with two electoral turnovers, a Chávez-leaning populist government, a coup d'état (or a 'constitutional crisis', depending on whom you ask), and a less-than-seamless transition back into democracy. That was Honduras for them: come for the poverty-reduction strategy, stay for the political upheaval.

Donor identity and aid diplomacy

For the longest time, the foreign aid system was not really about development. The Cold War mediated almost every form of assistance to what was then called the Third World, which was apportioned between the Soviet and Western spheres of influence[4]. Economists have taken the trouble of going through the numbers to determine whether and how realpolitik affected aid flows, and they have found all manner of interesting – though not too surprising – correlations. Big, bilateral donors tend to send aid to countries that are closely aligned with their foreign policy objectives, whether they are military allies, former colonies, or countries that vote along the same lines in the UN Security Council[5]. Multilateral donors talk the talk of principles, but they seldom walk the walk: neither regional banks nor UN agencies channel their aid primarily to countries where good governance and political freedom prevail[6]. As to small donor countries, their foreign aid has traditionally been tied to the procurement of goods and services provided by their own companies, which is a nifty way of boosting exports under the mantle of humanitarianism. Trade, finance, diplomacy, and security have always been inextricably linked with development assistance.

The end of the Cold War relieved a lot of the diplomatic pressure that was on the aid community, which now found itself able to chart its own path and remedy some of the mistakes of the past. Much of the intellectual debate about aid since 1991 has focused on how to best overcome the abuses and misuses of aid relationships, including the discredited agenda of structural adjustment, which instead of lifting poor countries out of debt managed to impoverish them even further[7]. The reaction to the debacle of the 1980s led to two contradictory pushes within the community. The first push occurred in the 1990s, which saw the rise of the 'good governance' agenda. Over time, this recognised the importance of getting the right institutions for economic growth, service delivery, and sustainable development[8]. Though its aspirations may have been too ambitious[9], at the time it served the purpose of legitimating a political understanding of development, something that I will discuss in greater detail in the next chapter. It was also a very prescriptive agenda, almost to the point of interference with issues that are usually considered to be the monopoly of sovereign nations. For classical theorists of the state and international affairs, the cases of Sierra Leone and Liberia that I have presented would reflect an alarming lack of respect for sovereignty, demonstrating the ease with which the desires of state authorities can be overridden – albeit temporarily – by aid donors.

The second and opposing push in development debates culminated in the 2005 Paris Declaration. The aid effectiveness agenda that began to form in the late 1990s and matured throughout the 2000s was an explicit denunciation of donor overreach and interference. The principle of ownership can be construed as a restatement of national sovereignty for the aid community. The call to align with national priorities, use of country systems, and development of mutual accountability can be interpreted in a managerial sense, but it is not hard to see how 'aid effectiveness' is a polite way of talking about power relations between donors and recipients. Many donors and aid critics subscribe vehemently to the Paris principles, perhaps because they sought to empower recipients; in a way, they represent a happy marriage between Northern self-criticism and Southern resentment. The agenda is periodically reinforced by high-level dialogues and new alliances of donors and recipients. As I explained in the previous chapter, two decades after the end of Cold War, aid agencies have found themselves trapped between the contradictory objectives of improving local institutions and working with governments who may have zero interest in doing so[10].

Not all donors react equally to this apparent paradox of development diplomacy. Each development agency has a unique mandate and identity, which it then has to reconcile with realities on the ground. Some donors have more or less explicit political objectives. USAID, for instance, is known for its democracy promotion efforts, which are only a fraction of all the activities that American agencies, foundations, and NGOs carry out around the world. Sweden, like its Nordic neighbours, places a high premium on human rights and citizen voice, to the extent that its aid agency, SIDA, is barred from working with some recipient governments that are known for their human rights violations. The United Kingdom tries to square the circle of humanitarianism, military cooperation, and trade with Commonwealth nations. Other former colonial powers such as France and Spain tend to use aid to maintain cultural spheres of influence in Francophone Africa or Latin America. Yet other bilaterals are famously technocratic and incapable of working politically, as is the case in Japan. Multilateral donors, as a general rule, tend to be more focused on development assistance, but the devil is in the details. The World Bank is constitutionally barred from interfering in the domestic affairs of member states, a constraint that plagues any efforts to engage in meaningful institutional reform. The UN system is particularly ill-equipped to challenge a recipient government: a UNDP head of office once told me that they did not see themselves as donors so much as mediators between government and donors. And the regional development banks rarely – if ever – question recipient plans on anything but the most technical grounds.

The identity issues of aid agencies have to be understood in light of their bureaucratic environment. Multilaterals have clear roles as semi-autonomous agencies, such as the UNDP, or international financial institutions, such the Inter-American Development Bank. Bilaterals, however, are a tougher nut to crack. A lot of my research over the years has focused on DFID, which was elevated to the rank of independent department with a cabinet-level minister in 1997. DFID's autonomy remains a rarity and source of much envy in the aid community. I discussed in Chapter 2 the decision by conservative governments in Canada and Australia to fold their own agencies back into foreign affairs ministries. However much I may dislike that choice, it is actually the most common arrangement out there.

Spanish development cooperation, for instance, operates under the authority of ambassadors whose approach to aid ranges from benign neglect to total override. USAID is particularly interesting in that regard, with a lot of its clout depending on the interest that ambassadors take in development: an energetic humanitarian can make a USAID mission the centrepiece of American diplomacy in a developing country, but in so doing she can drastically influence the range of interventions that USAID practitioners can and cannot pursue.

In most developing countries, these tricky relationships between aid and diplomatic offices are kept behind closed doors, unfolding in a realm of administrative politics that has little to do with development and much to do with bureaucratic power plays back home. What makes the case of Honduras unique is the fact that the political–technical divide was formally institutionalised within donor coordination. From its earliest days, what would become the G-16 was structured as three levels of operations: a Group of Ambassadors and Representatives (GER in its Spanish acronym) at the very top, a Technical Follow-up Group in the middle, and an array of Sector Working Groups at the bottom. On paper, the arrangement makes perfect sense. Donors needed to be able to speak with interlocutors at the highest levels, including with the president himself, and they needed to have a forum where they could agree on key strategic principles for the entire group. That is what the GER provided. Technical development issues were beyond the remit (and comprehension) of ambassadors, however, so the Technical Follow-up Group brought together heads of cooperation that were able to talk aid strategy and effectiveness. Lastly, the Sector Working Groups appeared as a logical tool for sharing information and debating interventions at the policy level, and would bring together different actors on a sector-by-sector basis.

The G-16's three levels represented a triumph of aid coordination even before it became fashionable to pretend that donors speak with one voice. It also served the purpose of mirroring the array of counterparts that would be involved in implementing and monitoring Honduras's PRS.

Mediating Honduras's Poverty Reduction Strategy

The PRS of Honduras was presented in August 2001 after a participatory drafting process between January 2000 and March 2001 involving 3,500 civil society representatives[11]. Much like the Plan Maestro after Mitch, the PRS aspired to become a 'state policy' rooted in a 'historic commitment by Honduran society'. Its five broad themes resembled to a large extent those of Stockholm: reducing poverty sustainably; benefiting the less-favoured groups and regions; strengthening civil society participation and decentralisation; strengthening governance and democracy; and reducing environmental vulnerability. PRS implementation would be financed chiefly with funds released by debt relief, channelled through a government-run Poverty Reduction Fund. Monitoring would be led by a Poverty Reduction Consultative Council, chaired by the government's Social Cabinet and representing the Department of Finance, civil society and municipalities, with two observers from the donor community. The PRS supplied international assistance with a more detailed and widely known alignment instrument than the Stockholm principles or Master Plan had ever been. There was one wrinkle, though: the strategy was adopted just as the country was getting ready to hold elections. When Hondurans went to the polls on 25 November 2001 they chose a political transition not just between leaders, but also between parties: Liberal Party incumbent Carlos Roberto Flores was replaced by National Party leader Ricardo Maduro.

Honduras has a fairly run-of-the-mill liberal constitution, par for the course in Latin America, with one small but consequential distinction: it does not allow a president to serve for more than a single mandate. In theory, this sounds like a great idea, because it eliminates the distraction of running for re-election while in office. In practice, however, this provision undermines the sustainability of any public policy. The problem of corruption in places such as Honduras is not that politicians are thinking about staying in office: we suffer through that in all democracies, corrupt or not. The real issue is that the state is the main source of enrichment for many in society, whether through jobs, contracts, or bribes. Imagine living in a country where your only real shot at wealth and welfare for you and your family is having a public job. Now imagine being told that in four years you are constitutionally obligated to vacate your office. The constitutional limitation to one mandate does not curb the incentive for corruption in Honduras; it increases it exponentially. The political cycle precludes any kind of policy sustainability. The year before the election, all governing grinds to a halt, and the year after the election, thousands of posts have to be filled through more or less clientelistic means[12]. Both the left-leaning Liberal Party and the right-leaning National Party engage in the same kind of patronage-fuelled recruitment. So, effectively, there are only two years of continued policymaking, and transitions, even within the same party, ensure discontinuity every four years.

Civil society could have been the key to ensuring continuity between the Flores and Maduro administrations. However, the relationship between civil society groups and the Honduran government was at best one of mutual suspicion. Even though the Stockholm Declaration incorporated activists and NGOs, these never fully subscribed to the government's reconstruction agenda. In particular, they worried that a focus on material reconstruction – with an official emphasis on infrastructure rehabilitation – would mean little for the sustainable development of the country without broader social, political and economic reforms[13]. As part of the follow-up to Stockholm, the government had set up a Civil Society Participation Commission, which met regularly and was supposed to play an advisory role. However, the commission was never given the technical or administrative support needed to fulfil its objectives. The G-15 met regularly with this group, and under the leadership of Sweden it began pressuring the government to make it more open to civil society[14]. The donor group already had routine contacts with NGOs through its technical-level working groups, which covered a range of sectors including education, health, disaster prevention, macroeconomic policy, and transparency. The G-15's structure effectively allowed it to engage independently with the government, through ambassadors and heads of cooperation, and with civil society, through working groups. This put it in the unique position of being the only neutral actor able to mediate between the two. While some bilaterals, such as Spain, were hesitant to ruffle the government's feathers, others, such as Sweden, considered civil society participation a non-negotiable part of national reconstruction and development.

Honduras's PRS of 2001 fitted perfectly with Sweden's vision of citizen–government collaboration[15]. After all, the strategy did come out of a wide-ranging participatory process that had brought together thousands of civil society representatives from all over the country. By design, NGOs were supposed to play an active role in the PRS implementation process as members of the Poverty Reduction Consultative Council, which also included government, municipalities, and donors. In addition, donors fostered the creation of a system of *mesas sectoriales*, tripartite sector groups that brought together government and civil society at the sector level. The *mesas* had been part of the national reconstruction process and follow-up to the Stockholm Declaration, covering fourteen different issue areas, although they were later consolidated into seven groups. On top of all this, the donor–civil society–government trifecta was also realised through periodic high-level tripartite dialogues[16]. In principle, the dialogues resulted from a government request for help in monitoring the PRS. In practice, the administration had clear reservations about civil society's capacity or the pertinence of its participation at the sector level, going so far as to delegate management of the *mesas* to the G-15. Civil society, for its part, considered that real participation was missing[17].

By mid-2002, the implementation of the strategy was significantly delayed due to a lack of funding and capacity problems. Much of the staff trained by donors before the elections had been let go after the transition, and their replacements rarely had any knowledge of agreed-upon targets or the capacity to meet them. The government established an Inter-Institutional Technical Group, which brought together vice-ministers, the central planning unit, and sector planning units; but, in practice, the different government bodies were unable to comply with all the tasks they had assumed. There was a clear risk of losing the momentum achieved in the two previous years during the PRS process. The second tripartite dialogue, in December 2002, offered those in attendance a clear disparity between the views of government and those of donors. While the authorities reaffirmed their commitment to the PRS and presented a detailed government plan for 2002–2006, donors voiced their disappointment at what they saw as a slow and laborious process of reform and poverty reduction.

The truth was that the PRS had lost its central role in development policy after being approved as a prerequisite for debt relief. Reaching the HIPC completion point was – predictably – the real priority for the government[18]. In February 2004, the IMF approved a Poverty Reduction and Growth Facility, with the purpose of reactivating the PRS and containing the fiscal deterioration afflicting Honduras. The fourth Consultative Group meeting of 10–11 June 2004 resulted in the Tegucigalpa Declaration: a new attempt at promoting a joint agenda between government, donors, and civil society. Through this agreement, the government committed to lead and coordinate the transformation process in Honduras with higher civil society participation and the strategic support of international assistance. The declaration closed with an explicit acknowledgment of the G-15 and the tripartite dialogue mechanisms that it had spent five years promoting:

> the parts reaffirm the importance of the Follow-Up Group, known today as the G-15, as a monitoring mechanism by the donor community of the transformation process in Honduras. Likewise, they commit to continue developing and strengthening the tripartite mechanisms that enable a continued follow-up of the agreements of this Consultative Group meeting, which will constitute an invaluable guideline for poverty reduction and transformation in Honduras.

Despite all these attempts to relaunch the PRS process, the Second Progress Report published in late 2004 aroused in donors the same kind of reservations they had expressed for years: there was a need to strengthen participatory planning processes and the tripartite fora, in particular, the PRS Consultative Council and the sectoral working groups, that supported the strategy's implementation[19]. However, two new concerns had emerged in addition to these known problems. First, there was an evident disconnect between the executive and the legislature, which limited the degree of ownership and sustainability of the PRS. Second, there was still no clear articulation between pro-poor policies and those public investments categorised by the government as poverty reduction. In the Consultative Group meeting of May 2005 donors lamented the lack of consensus surrounding strategies and action plans for the sector groups[20]. However, in the bigger scheme of things, these complaints mattered little, because on 9 March 2005 the staff of the IMF and World Bank recommended that Honduras reach the HIPC debt relief completion point. As a result, on 5 April the country was able to access US$1 billion in multilateral debt relief, which opened the door to further bilateral relief. Whoever won the upcoming elections of November 2005, the next government of Honduras would encounter a more relaxed fiscal environment and a significant amount of new funds with which to carry out public investments. Once the HIPC completion point had been reached, however, it was difficult to anticipate what role the PRS would play in the new development planning phase, if it was to play any role at all.

The reds are coming

Until 2005, the G-15 had dealt with relatively predictable presidents, representative of the powerful elites at the centre of

Honduran politics. Carlos Roberto Flores, who was president when Hurricane Mitch hit the country, had attended the American School of Tegucigalpa and then Louisiana State University. Ricardo Maduro, his successor from January 2002, had graduated from the posh Lawrenceville preparatory school in New Jersey before going to Stanford. The elections of 27 November 2005 brought Flores's Liberal Party back to power, but the man who assumed the presidency favoured looking South, not North, for political inspiration. Manuel 'Mel' Zelaya was heir to a successful family business, and a career politician of the Liberal Party: in theory, just another member of the country's elite. He had even run for party leader under a relatively centre-right platform called *Movimiento Esperanza Liberal* (MEL, which stands for Liberal Hope Movement). Once in office, however, he confronted internal challenges to his power by aligning himself with Venezuela's Hugo Chávez in a remarkable 'right-to-left switch'[21].

Consistent with his peers within the Bolivarian Alternative for the Americas (ALBA in its Spanish acronym), Zelaya started to espouse a more participatory and direct form of policymaking that put social development at the centre. He had at best a limited commitment to and understanding of the PRS he had inherited, and the people he brought in had limited experience dealing with international assistance. All of this left G-15 donors dismayed[22]. Under Zelaya's presidency, the National Congress of Honduras passed an unprecedented amendment to the national budget, mandating that part of the PRS funds of each government department be executed through municipalities. The decision could have been easily construed as either high-minded decentralisation or flagrant patronage. It put donors in a difficult position, because many of their bilateral aid agreements were predicated on the objectives and processes covered by the PRS. It also caused civil society to walk out of the PRS Consultative Council, forcing the G-15 to once again assume a mediating role between Congress, the government, and NGOs. This task was further hindered by the fact that the sector-level *mesas* had stopped working as a deliberation mechanism since the arrival of the new government[23].

In late 2006, SIDA commissioned a report titled 'Honduras: what happened to the ERP?', which described the 'slow and tortuous pace' with which the new administration was implementing and updating the PRS[24]. Part of the explanation lies with the fact that Zelaya was more interested in policy programmes that were more clearly aligned with his party's poverty reduction philosophy, such as a free tuition programme, which ensured access to education for 200,000 youths; the PRS Decentralization Fund, which transferred funds to local councils; and the Red Solidaria, a cash transfer programme that targeted families and individuals afflicted by extreme poverty, and was headed by the First Lady. In October 2008, Zelaya sought to formally institutionalise these programmes through the creation of a new Social Development Department. By that time, the government had belatedly agreed to update the original PRS, but without really committing to it through clear budgetary priorities. Any kind of international reflection on the effects of the new agenda on the PRS process was abruptly cut short, however, by the arrival of Tropical Depression 16 on 13 October 2008, with floods affecting over 270,000 people and leaving 58,000 homeless. This natural catastrophe was, in turn, overshadowed by the political storm that battered the country in 2009.

Most countries around the world have constitutionally mandated limits on how many terms a president may serve. Few leaders face constitutions as stringent as Honduras's in that regard, but that does not dissuade them from trying to remove term limits altogether[25]. In 2006, Nigerian president Olusegun Obasanjo tried to pass a constitutional bill that would have allowed him to run for a third mandate. In Uganda, Yoweri Museveni achieved that same goal the year before. Much closer to Honduras, both geographically and ideologically, Hugo Chávez's ALBA started toying with the same idea around 2008. The discourse surrounding the abolition of term limits was built upon anti-elite sentiment: Latin America's liberal constitutions were the product of a narrow elite that was usually close – too close for comfort – with industry, the media, and the military. For competing elite factions, limits introduce a certain predictability in politics, allowing parties to alternate in power with enough frequency to share the spoils of power. However, the new populist left in Latin America was not a traditional elite faction: its claim to legitimacy was derived from the people, not formal institutions; its agenda was societal transformation towards social justice, not the temporary stewardship of state and market; and its charismatic leaders were seen as saviours by many among the poor and disenfranchised. It would only be a matter of time before this unique political wave rose against term limits as an arbitrary constraint on the will of the people. The logical result was a series of popular referenda introducing constitutional amendments or entirely new constitutions. Ecuador's Rafael Correa removed term limits in September 2008; Bolivia's Evo Morales and Chávez himself achieved the same in February 2009. That was the regional context in which Mel

Zelaya began to flirt with the idea of abolishing Honduras's single-term limit.

In 2008, a year before his term was supposed to end, Zelaya began paving the way for a constitutional assembly that would reform the constitution, including an amendment to term limits. On November 2008, he issued an executive decree calling for a nonbinding referendum to determine whether the November 2009 elections would include a fourth ballot box (*cuarta urna*) on whether to convene a constitutional assembly. In March 2009, Zelaya announced that the referendum would take place in June; two months later, he issued a second executive decree instructing the National Statistical Institute to hold the poll by 28 June. Opponents saw in the referendum a move to stay beyond his constitutionally limited terms. Supporters, and Zelaya himself, argued that the decision would not affect him, as any constitutional change would happen after he left office. Regardless of motive, the decree arrived at a difficult political time for Zelaya, who had spent years clashing with the media and wealthier corners of the private sector, and who did not have the kind of backing from his own Liberal Party that Morales and Chávez enjoyed in Bolivia and Venezuela. One of his key opponents came from within his own party: Roberto Micheletti, president of the Honduran Congress and presumptive presidential candidate. Arguing on the finer points of the constitution, which precluded reform of key articles such as presidential succession, Micheletti publicly warned that convening the referendum would be illegal, a warning that Zelaya received from the Attorney General's office the day after he announced the June date. In the weeks after the president's second decree, the proposed poll was also deemed illegal by an administrative court, the Supreme Electoral Tribunal, Congress, and the Bar Association.

Seeing his support dwindle in Congress and within his own government, Zelaya turned to the military, who were usually tasked with election logistics; but the head of military command, General Velásquez, refused to release the poll materials that had just arrived from Venezuela. When Zelaya fired the general, the minister of defence and senior military leadership resigned in protest. Things escalated quickly from that moment on: the Supreme Tribunal reinstated Velásquez to his position in an unanimous decision; Micheletti asked him to use the military to protect the constitution; thousands of people marched around the country to protest Zelaya's perceived re-election plans; Zelaya's supporters among labour unions, farmers, and civil society began mobilising themselves; and the president issued a new decree compelling all public institutions to support the poll. Congress began discussing legal means for impeaching Zelaya, but it was the Supreme Tribunal that dealt the critical blow when on 28 June 2009 it issued an arrest warrant for the president. The warrant was swiftly executed by the military, who moved Zelaya to a military airbase before flying him out to Costa Rica.

Aid as legitimation

The events leading up to and following the 2009 constitutional crisis are documented in the final report of Honduras's Truth and Reconciliation Commission[26]. The country eventually returned to relative institutional stability through elections held in November of that year, although the political repercussions would be felt in years to come. For the aid community in Tegucigalpa, the Honduran political crisis of 2009 posed unforeseen questions.

The international community was swift and more or less united in its denunciation of the constitutional crisis. For many, the word 'crisis' itself was a misnomer: what the Supreme Tribunal had done, in cahoots with Congress and the military, was an outright coup d'état. It was this interpretation that led the Organization of American States to temporarily expel Honduras, and to begin a diplomatic effort that saw the crisis not as an internal matter for the government to figure out, but as a conflict situation that could only be solved through international arbitration of a formal agreement between the parties. The United States was much more ambivalent, betraying a certain relief that Honduras – key for its anti-narcotic and immigration operations – would remain safely away from Hugo Chávez's influence.

Doing its best to uphold the principles of aid effectiveness, Honduras's donor partners had spent the better part of a decade working towards better aid harmonisation, more responsiveness to local priorities, and alignment with country strategies. The years of the PRS process may have proved difficult, but they had not brought about particularly unique challenges: real participation and ownership were often missing from PRS processes around the developing world[27]. But Zelaya's rise to power and his gradual alignment with the political ideology behind ALBA forced donor missions to question whose ownership they were supposed to honour. The G-16's first reaction to the arrest and expulsion of President Manuel Zelaya was a press statement issued on 29 June and signed by all bilateral members, the European Commission, and the UN (the Inter-American Development Bank, Central American Bank for Economic

Integration, World Bank, and IMF abstained):

> we express our wish that constitutional order and rule of law are immediately restored, so that the country can return to normalcy … We deplore any attempt to violate the democratic constitutional order and we call for fundamental freedoms, including that of the press, to be upheld … international assistance requires compliance with democratic laws and institutions as well as the respect for Human Rights.

Despite echoes of official diplomatic positions, the donor group faced a very particular kind of challenge. The high political profile that the G-16 had acquired in the decade since Mitch had turned it into a focal point for Honduran society and international actors, who saw in it a source of support for international negotiations as well as political analysis of the crisis. The two main dilemmas were determining what role the G-16 should play vis-à-vis the international negotiations brokered by Costa Rica and the Organization of American States, and what support it should give to the 2009 general elections in an environment of constitutional fracture. The search for solutions to both problems was complicated by the fact that many Honduran interlocutors considered the president's expulsion an act of legitimate constitutional self-defence, while a significant part of the international community had categorised it as a coup d'état. As a collective international actor deeply intertwined in Honduran politics, the G-16 found itself trapped between two sets of completely opposing demands: one asking for institutional continuity and respect for the electoral calendar, the other for the restoration of the status quo ante 28 June in order to bring the emergency to a close.

Analytically, what the G-16 faced in Honduras was the fact that aid, by its very existence, produces a number of political effects. I have called this the 'Aid Interference Principle': a donor cannot enter a political context without altering it[28]. Despite apolitical mandates and protestations to the contrary, donor missions are very much a part of the political landscape of the countries in which they operate. Aid always benefits someone, and whenever local politics is seen as a zero-sum game, it is by definition undermining someone else. I have said this to donors many times in public presentations: an aid project can be a highly subversive thing. Support for NGOs and advocacy groups is an explicit attack on established institutions and elites. Support for technocratic reformers is an implicit attack on politics as usual and the players who benefit from limited rule enforcement. Likewise, budget support to a government represents a consolidation of centralised power by giving regime leaders new resources to distribute how they see fit. Money, ideas, and people: whatever form aid takes, it will always have a profound effect on local actors, legitimising some and delegitimising others; sanctioning existing coalitions or brokering new ones; and diffusing new models and techniques for control or contestation.

There are two kinds of actors who are particularly aware of the Aid Interference Principle. First, donor governments sometimes use foreign aid as an explicit diplomatic incentive. The suspension of development assistance is usually a soft way of responding to violations of domestic or international principles. When it was revealed that Rwanda had provided military support to the M23 rebels in the Democratic Republic of Congo, for instance, many bilateral donors withheld aid disbursements in protest. In contrast, diplomats that I spoke to in Liberia appeared willing to tolerate a certain level of mismanagement and corruption in the interest of securing the country's stability; as one of them said to me, Ellen Johnson Sirleaf could have 'a capable government, or an honest one, but not both'. Second, recipient governments are acutely aware of this instrumental use of foreign aid, and usually work hard to retain donor support or play off donors against one another so as to minimise the chances of coordinated suspension. In Sierra Leone, one of the arguments wielded by parliamentarians alarmed by Valentine Collier's criticisms was that the anti-corruption commissioner's words would be read by international peers and partners: they feared a reputational cost from having such an outspoken individual in such a high-profile position. It was also the fear of delegitimising a post-conflict government that stayed Britain's conditionality for so long, despite numerous concerns and allegations of political interference with the ACC's work.

In contrast to diplomats and political leaders, aid officials and practitioners have a much messier understanding of their role as legitimators of local actors. That is because their projects depend on their ability to work with reluctant reformers in government, often in collaboration with their perceived political enemies in civil society. Some of the professionals I have known throughout the years are astute political observers, players who can read their environment and find the most productive way forward. I will mention some of their stories in the next chapter. Others are mostly clueless, benign but ignorant, ready to be taken advantage of by smarter and cannier local partners.

What gives aid its legitimising power? Some scholars call it 'certification', the mechanism whereby an actor's legitimacy increases through the backing of external, authoritative actors[29].

While this is definitely part of the story, I favour a more mundane explanation. Donor monitoring and reporting is a mostly credible source of information in what are basically information-scarce political environments. Weak states are often home to an information-starved citizenry: papers have limited circulation, radios often follow clear political lines, and television is sometimes government owned. This makes it remarkably easy for governments to increase 'noise' in order to mask their own shortcomings, whether by denouncing the many external constraints they face and circumstances beyond their control, or by celebrating a multiplicity of cosmetic and basically irrelevant reform efforts. That was clearly the case in Sierra Leone, for instance: the outright politicisation of anticorruption efforts by successive government and opposition parties in the past made it almost impossible to objectively determine the government's true preferences. It was also the case in Liberia, where President Johnson Sirleaf and Auditor General Morlu basically presented two mutually exclusive narratives about the government's willingness to carry out reforms. And it was obviously the case in Honduras, where politicisation of every issue by competing elites and a growing clash between government and civil society put donors in the unenviable position of neutral arbiters of truth, asked to take sides as a way to signal who was right in the constitutional crisis: Zelaya or Micheletti, democratic will or institutional stability, popular mobilisation or elite restraint.

After the crisis: 'Regreso al futuro'

With the elections two months away, in September 2009 Manuel Zelaya returned to Tegucigalpa and took refuge at the Embassy of Brazil. Meanwhile, continuing attempts by the

Organization of American States to find an exit to the crisis through negotiations with the de facto government of Roberto Micheletti appeared to be leading nowhere. The main political party candidates repeatedly stated their intention to stand in the November elections, encouraging the international community to 'support the path of democracy' as the only possible way out of the crisis. Some in the media and the government itself publicly accused donors of showing too little flexibility, paying no heed to the true feelings of Hondurans, and supporting the restitution of a president who had squandered aid funds by veering so far away from the PRS. Nevertheless, the G-16 stood firm in its resolve not to provide open support for the elections unless it was under the umbrella of an internationally sanctioned agreement. At last, on 30 October 2009, representatives of Manuel Zelaya and Roberto Micheletti handed over to the Honduran Congress the Tegucigalpa–San José–Diálogo Guaymuras Agreement, leaving the decision to reinstate the president (or not) up to the legislature, and opening up the space for international involvement to resume.

When Porfirio Lobo Sosa was elected president in November 2009, the international community breathed a sigh of relief. Whether it was a 'coup' or a 'constitutional crisis', the removal of president Zelaya had deprived donors of their legitimate contractual partner. Aid projects were effectively suspended as donors struggled to figure out a way to reconcile diplomatic and humanitarian goals, supporting institutional stability without alienating the entire sector of civil society that was aligned with Zelaya's movement. Even after the agreement of late October, the G-16 was faced with the difficult decision of whether to support the electoral process or not. Some donors, such as Japan, were ready to give assistance to guarantee the capacity to hold free and fair elections; others were much less willing to associate with what could be interpreted as a way to legitimise the coup. Once Lobo took office, however, the group once more faced an internationally recognised government, and the diplomacy of aid could finally give way to the actual practice of development assistance.

A key task in aid reactivation was re-establishing links with the national planning system, which the new government was restructuring in pursuit of greater consistency. The focal point of the new blueprint was the Technical Planning Department (SEPLAN in its Spanish acronym), whose main responsibility was to ensure that the operations of line ministries and donors were aligned with a new Nation Plan 2010–2022 and Country Vision 2010–2038. To demonstrate its *bona fides*, SEPLAN confirmed that all PRS indicators were incorporated under the plan, while the PRS Consultative Council was integrated into the Nation Plan Council; it even expressed interest in re-establishing the tripartite dialogue on sectoral issues. SEPLAN also showed significant interest in the aid harmonisation principles coming out of the Paris Declaration (2005) and Accra Agenda for Action (2008), which were to be discussed yet again during a High Level Forum to be convened in Busan, South Korea, in 2011. In March 2010, SEPLAN established the Honduras Foreign Aid Effectiveness Forum to bring together government, G-16, other donors, academic experts, and civil society.

This reinvigorated aid relationship took some time to reach fruition as an overzealous SEPLAN underwent growing pains. Finally, on 29 August 2012, the G-16 and government of Honduras gathered to sign a Joint Declaration that would shape their partnership in the years to come[30]. The key themes were familiar but nonetheless reassuring after the demise of the PRS process:

1. the political process leading up to the 2012–2013 elections;
2. citizen security;
3. human rights;
4. socially inclusive growth; and
5. fiscal governance and transparency in public administration.

The Joint Declaration promised what had not been possible since the 2002 tripartite dialogue, or even – in a stricter sense – since Stockholm: a mutual accountability framework for the transformation of Honduras based on an alignment of donor and recipient priorities. For the government, the declaration supported SEPLAN's efforts to systematise and organise sector policymaking into a single planning framework. For the G-16, it promised to link the political level to the technical work at the *mesas* and working groups, as well as focus work around issues that were crucial for the institutional and political transition. Unfortunately, the new government–donor partnership had little to say about relationships with the third pillar of the original tripartite system: civil society trust in policy processes had been gradually eroded during the PRS fiasco, and the coup had left it so polarised as to make any kind of coherent approach impossible. Deprived of a real voice in the aid contract, those speaking for the majority of Hondurans ended up being the unintended casualties of the return to normality.

Damned if you, damned if you don't

SEPLAN was eventually disbanded as an autonomous agency in the spring of 2014, joining the long list of short-lived Honduran interlocutors that donors had dealt with since Mitch: the Department of the Presidency's Technical Assistance Unit, Technical Department of International Cooperation, Inter-Institutional Technical Group, Reconstruction Cabinet, Social Cabinet, Department of Finance, Department of Social Development, and the Presidential Technical Support Unit. With SEPLAN's demise, the international community learned once more that Honduras was not a predictable recipient country. It had not been so in the unstable days after Mitch, despite the promise of holistic and inclusive reconstruction efforts. Successive political swings undermined the joint agenda that had come out of Stockholm, gradually turning the PRS into an aspirational waste of paper. The administration of Manuel Zelaya proved how easy it was for a recipient government to roll back inherited commitments.

The constitutional crisis of 2009 and its reverberations demonstrate how hard it is for donors, even when united through a strong coordination mechanism, to carry out their programmes in a difficult political environment. I would be hard-pressed to find a country where donors were as influential or as guided by the harmonisation and alignment principles of the Paris Declaration, even before the declaration itself existed. One has to commend the international community in Honduras for their commitment to participatory development and sound national policy. Many individual projects were actually successful, and the involvement of senior diplomats and heads of office protected the G-16 from the worst attempts at manipulation by some local leaders. It was because the political dimension was incorporated into the reconstruction process from the beginning that donors were able to stick together and endure the pendulum swings of elite politics in Tegucigalpa. However, it was also this diplomatic layer that created problems for the G-16 when the coup took place, bringing with it competing demands for recognition and legitimation.

Honduras demonstrates the 'damned if you do, damned if you don't' nature of development assistance as well as the schizophrenia that sometimes plagues donors simultaneously interested in humanitarianism, regional stability, and transnational security. Politics is intrinsic to these aid dilemmas, no matter how much we try to bury it underneath layers upon layers of technical gibberish and accounting requirements. However, that does not mean politics can be easily recognised and integrated into the organisations tasked with managing aid.

SIX | The struggle of thinking politically

'Politics matters.' That is the phrase I kept hearing when I joined the British development studies community in 2013. And I could not have been any more puzzled by it. What did they mean 'politics matters'? Of course it does! What an obvious and banal thing to say, I thought to myself. While it took a while for my puzzlement and – let us be frank – smugness to go away, to this day I can hardly find a more succinct expression of the tragic constraints that we impose on foreign aid agencies and practitioners. What I did not understand at the time was the revolutionary implications of that simple sentence, the subtle ways in which it challenged business as usual in the aid industry. To a recent PhD in political science, 'politics matters' is not so much a revelation as it is an assumption: the really interesting questions are why and how it matters, not whether it does. To aid practitioners and development scholars in the United Kingdom, in contrast, uttering that sentence is a way of subverting a whole host of foundational assumptions about aid policy. In the four years since my introduction to this community, I have been an observer, then a critic, and finally a participant in the 'politics matters' insurgency.

In order to fully understand what this chapter is about, it is important to begin with the many divides between academia and development policy. In the United States, where I pursued my graduate studies, complaining about policymakers was a comfortable trope among political scientists. 'Why don't they listen to us?', we would ask all the time. 'How can they be so ignorant?' Everybody likes to be an underdog, and in the seemingly unbridgeable gap between academia and policy we found a convenient way to study politics without actually having to practice it. For those of us studying the political economy of development, the divide was much wider: some of my professors had worked as consultants, or provided advice to government officials interested in particular countries, but by and large they did so from the comfort of private universities with philanthropist-endowed professorships. Economics was different. While most undergraduates saw it as a step into finance, and many professors considered themselves pure scientists, a PhD in economics was your ticket to the IMF, the Inter-American Development Bank, or the World Bank. The assumptions and models of economics run through the veins of international financial institutions, providing a level of access and influence that we political scientists could only dream about.

Compared to with divide I had seen in the United States, the British development studies community seemed like some sort of promised land. The government provided substantial grants to fund primary research on development issues, and communication and uptake of findings was included as a sine qua non of those grants. Professors everywhere were able to work with DFID projects as external advisors or consultants. The idea of the scholar practitioner was not anathema in the United Kingdom like it was in American academia: it was a badge of honour. Even without the rose-tinted glasses I was wearing at the time, there was something fascinating about what I began calling the 'DFID ecosystem': an interconnected and somewhat incestuous group of university departments, publicly funded programmes, aid units and missions, NGOs, provider firms, and individual consultants. As I will discuss below, it was a classic example of an 'epistemic community': a network of experts and practitioners working together to develop a particular policy agenda[1].

The potential for academic influence seemed so much greater than in the United States that I wondered why statements such as 'politics matters' would even be a thing in this community. However, over time, I learned that there were a least two complementary answers to that question. On the one hand, not all development scholars and researchers are concerned with the politics of development as I have framed it in Chapters 3 through 5. Development studies is not so much a discipline as a collection of like-minded individuals, who share a broad concern about social justice in developing countries. Intellectually, they come from all walks of life, chiefly from economics, geography, anthropology, planning, and sociology. They do study politics, but their understanding of it is largely removed from the theories and debates of political science. So, while an American political scientist might respond to 'politics matters' by asking 'how and why?', a development studies scholar is likely to ask 'what do you mean by politics?'. That's the first part of the explanation. On the other hand, the aid community exhibits an even greater diversity of backgrounds than academia, with an emphasis on the kinds of technical knowledge that are considered part and parcel of development: engineering, planning, medicine, statistics, management, and so on. There appear to be remarkably few political science types in the aid business, especially compared with economists. That is the even simpler second part of the explanation.

This chapter is about the epistemic community that has spent decades repeating the 'politics matters' mantra: the eclectic group of practitioners and intellectuals who have tried to persuade aid agencies time and again of the need to think politically in order to manage the challenges I have documented in Sierra Leone, Liberia, and Honduras. However, this chapter is also about how their efforts are undermined time and again by the dysfunctional politics of aid that result from the home environment described in Chapters 1 and 2.

The almost revolution

The post-World War II international aid system has had a contentious relationship with politics, very nearly culminating in but never quite reaching a resolution. Thomas Carothers and Diane de Gramont have elegantly termed this trajectory 'the almost revolution'[2].

Carothers and de Gramont make a very useful distinction between political goals and politically smart methods: the former refers to objectives such as democratisation, human rights, and gender empowerment, whereas the latter refers to ways of providing assistance that take into account the complex political nature of development challenges. Strangely enough, explicitly controversial political goals have traditionally had a bigger influence in foreign aid than more explicitly technical political methods. As I discussed in the previous chapter, bilateral donors such as the United States or the Nordic countries are known for advancing political agendas side by side with their more humanitarian interventions. The diversity in donor identity makes political goals a fixture of the community, and thus easy to identify and debate. In contrast, politically smart methods are more difficult to define, apply, and evaluate. This often leads to a conflation of the two. This point was made abundantly clear to me as I prepared to give a talk on political analysis to Spanish aid agency personnel in Madrid. 'You have to make sure that you clarify what you mean', my contact there told me, 'because for most people in the room the word "political" means "partisan"'.

The confusion between political goals and politically smart methods is frequent among donors. It is rooted in the technocratic history of the aid system as well as in the tenuous links between academic political science and the policy world. For decades, the leading theories and paradigms in development emerged from economics. Modernisation theory rests on an assumption of growing economic diversification based on technological advancement and urbanisation. At the time, some of the most progressive economists even thought that economic backwardness could be seen as an advantage: by borrowing innovations that had taken centuries to develop in Europe, less developed countries could perhaps leapfrog over whole stages of modernisation. Development was considered first and foremost a liquidity problem, leading to a 'big push' mentality that saw aid as an injection of capital and ideas that would propel countries out of poverty spirals and into self-sustaining development. When this somewhat optimistic idea was debunked, the combination of new strands of economic theory – transaction costs and organisations – and 1980s neoliberal politics nurtured the paradigm of structural adjustment: liberalisation, privatisation, deregulation and rationalisation of the state appeared to be the logical way to reduce rents and improve economic incentives.

It would not be until the 1990s that politics was finally allowed into the development agenda, and that was only after the debacle of external debt and structural adjustment had left many developing countries worse off. With international financial institutions under attack for their blind adherence to neoliberal tenets, new institutional economics provided a legitimate entry point for questions about the politics of change. The World Bank's *World Development Report 1997* remains a marquee achievement in that regard, mainstreaming the idea that the state could serve as a facilitator – and not just an obstacle – for development objectives. That being said, the increased attention to institutions did not immediately translate into more politically astute aid. Instead, the 1990s are associated with the rise of the 'good governance' agenda, a nebulous and worryingly normative term that encompasses a whole raft of intermediate political objectives such as democratisation, decentralisation, rule of law, or public sector reform. This ambitious but ill-defined agenda would inevitably fail, for two reasons. First, many of these political goals are incredibly difficult to achieve, often taking decades or even centuries. Second, their knock-on effects on other developmental goals such as economic growth and human development are easier to state in theory than to demonstrate in practice.

The 1990s turn towards institutions was hampered by a growing chasm between academic political science and the practical politics of development. Scholars who study institutions are remarkably bad at explaining why things change. If we focus on individual actors and incentives, we tend to model their decisions and interactions as mostly stable equilibria, to use a term from game theory. If we look at the evolution of organisations instead, historical paths loom large in explanations for divergence between more and less developed countries. Finally, analysts that pay attention to culture and ideas are more likely to see them as ingrained and deeply rooted determinants of behaviour than tools to be manipulated by actors. Political scientists are at their strongest when they study stable differences and at their weakest when they try to explain change. Yet change is what development is about, which means that politics as an academic discipline is ill-equipped to supply useful models to development practitioners, who are left to their own devices. It is unsurprising, therefore, that what amounts to political analysis in aid programming bears little resemblance to what political scientists do.

Politically smart methods began to be articulated by a few brave souls in the aid community around the turn of the century. The genealogy of what has come to be known as political economy analysis (PEA) is particularly narrow, relying on the outsized influence of a handful of key individuals who were curious and courageous enough to push against a system designed to leave politics out of the equation. These influential thinkers and practitioners have tended to cluster around DFID, which has acted as a de facto leader in politically smart aid. Over time, many donors and international financial institutions have come to develop their own frameworks and tools for political analysis, to the extent that we can now speak of an intellectual agenda spanning most of the aid system. But it is a testament to DFID's leadership and investments that a lot of the work of this community tends to centre around the United Kingdom.

Within DFID, serious work on political analysis began in the early 2000s through the commissioning of Drivers of Change (DoC) reports. Relying on a partnership with consultants from firms such as Oxford Policy Management and think tanks such as the Overseas Development Institute (ODI), the DoC reports sought to understand 'the underlying political system and the mechanics of pro-poor change', asking 'a structured set of questions' for each country office[3]. Over twenty DoC studies were conducted between 2002 and 2004, with direct encouragement and support from Secretary of State for International Development Clare Short. However, by late 2004 the momentum had stalled, and the dedicated DoC team was disbanded due to insufficient demand[4]. One explanation for the decline was the difficulty of translating broad country analysis into practical recommendations, with little attention to 'levers of change'[5]. This prompted a turn within DFID from institutions and structures towards 'the politics of decision-making'[6], which crystallised in a 2009 'How to note', which clearly outlined how PEA could inform the formulation of country plans, choice of aid modalities and partners, project design, and any dialogue with potential partners[7].

The World Bank was another pioneer in political analysis, despite all of its institutional constraints on doing overtly political work. Its PEA trajectory is pretty similar to DFID's. In 1999, Bank offices starting commissioning institutional and governance reviews that identified 'performance failures' in public institutions, deployed standardised methods to assess them, and analysed 'the feasibility of reform recommendations with a rigorous assessment of political realities and constraints'[8]. Despite putting PEA on the agenda, the reviews stopped short of making it mainstream, partly because of a 'growing recognition that many desirable policies [were] just not feasible', and partly due to 'scepticism about how to move from high level analysis to specific operational recommendations'[9]. Throughout the 2000s, the Bank's Social Development department produced a number of toolkits on institutional analysis and policy reform, with limited impact[10]. However, the real consolidation of PEA as a legitimate operational tool came with the adoption in 2007 of an organisation-wide Governance and Anti-Corruption Strategy (GAC), and particularly with the release in 2009 of a framework on 'problem-driven political-economy analysis', which managed to translate the abstract ideas behind the politics of change into a more practical lexicon understood by Bank personnel[11].

DFID and the World Bank were not alone in pursuing the practical analysis of politics. In the Netherlands, one of the key initiators of PEA in the United Kingdom designed a 'strategic governance and anti-corruption assessment framework' in 2005. This reads like an evolved version of DoC, and later inspired other donor toolkits[12]. Sweden's aid agency, SIDA, also developed its own variety of 'power analysis', with a greater emphasis on accountability, rights, and inequality[13]. In December 2013, I attended a meeting of the OECD Development Assistance Committee (OECD–DAC) Network on Governance in Paris, at which most of the two dozen donors present had developed some form of political analysis (including, much to my surprise, the IMF). Throughout the community, proponents have struggled with the challenge of reconciling academic political analysis with practical operational implications, prompting a generational shift from PEA as a product to be commissioned at specific points in time to PEA as a process to be integrated into day-to-day management[14]. To an optimistic observer, this may have signalled the triumph of the new agenda, and the beginning of the end of conventional, politically blind aid. Being a contrarian, however, I had a number of questions about how prevalent the agenda really was.

Fractured bureaucracies

In January 2013, I took up a new job at DFID-funded Effective States and Inclusive Development Research Project (ESID); the 'DFID-funded' part is not gratuitous, and will become relevant later. My first project with ESID was researching the extent to which political economy analysis was shaping donor practice. We decided to focus on what we considered to be the leaders in this kind of work – DFID and the World Bank – reasoning that if this new trend was going to have an impact, it would do so first in these two places. The pair under study also presented an interesting contrast between bilateral and multilateral, as well as between different aid cultures: more technocratic in the Bank's case, and more political in DFID's. Our plan was to sift through public and internal documentation as well as conduct a number of interviews with personnel in both agencies. These interviews would take place across their headquarters and three country offices that were relevant for ESID's broader research: Ghana, Uganda, and Bangladesh. ESID had already looked into the broader trend of PEA in the donor community[15]; we were looking for evidence of impact.

As we carried out our field visits, it became increasingly clear that the task at hand would not be easy. For all of the reasons covered in Chapter 2, aid professionals are often reluctant to share information that can be considered sensitive or could be used against their agencies. As it turned out, political analyses of the kind we were interested in fell squarely into that category. 'Studies are generally not disseminated due to their sensitive nature', DFID advisors told us, before adding the caveat that 'sometimes findings are dropped in meetings when it is deemed that the government needs to take action'. Or, as a World Bank task team leader in Uganda put it: '[y]ou only share what you think is not going to damage your working relationship, not discussions of clientelism or regime maintenance'. Interestingly, and resonating with the challenges of aid coordination discussed in the previous two chapters, the limited circulation of political analysis applies to other donors, too. No matter how close the official relationship, no matter how many sector working groups are created, aid practitioners who conduct or commission PEAs tend not to share the reports themselves, and certainly not without edits. Instead, the usual practice is to invite colleagues in other agencies to presentations, where the key findings are distilled into less incriminating PowerPoint slides. For a DFID advisor, this turned political analysis into the 'unstructured sharing of gossip'.

'Lack of sharing lowers the incentives of staff to invest a lot in it', a World Bank PEA expert told me, 'so a lot of the work is left unfinished'. Because of their preliminary nature, and also as an extension of the sensitivity concern, in many cases PEA reports were never properly archived, leaving current staff with only the vaguest notion of the kinds of assumptions or analysis that fed into the programmes they inherited. For instance, when asked about past analyses, a DFID advisor in Bangladesh responded by asking us – in an ironic twist – whether we could do the work of compiling past reports to give the office a better sense of what they had commissioned. Interestingly, we encountered these two obstacles to a similar extent in both the World Bank and DFID, despite the fact that the latter was our own funder: receiving funds from the same department was apparently not enough to earn the requisite trust to access most of the relevant material. When we managed to engage in honest conversation with DFID advisors or

World Bank specialists, it became clear that PEA as an acronym meant very different things to them.

The more people we talked to, and the more documents we asked for, the more we realised that PEA was not a donor-wide agenda but a dedicated effort by key individuals, often in isolation, to make particular aid programmes more attuned to the reality of the politics of change. Even though we often speak about donors as monolithic entities, they are in fact fairly decentralised organisations, with a lot of discretionary power resting with the heads of country offices. In our research, this manifested in two clear findings: there was no consistency across country offices, or between them and headquarters; and there was no consistency between successive generations of managers, whose personalities and proclivities could shape the entire mission's political outlook. We found that donors' approach to PEA consisted of short-lived, isolated bursts of activity that migrated from one office to the next as key individuals changed jobs. A few of our observations can illustrate this pattern.

Ghana's World Bank office seemed like one of the most prominent places to ask about political analysis, having commissioned a number of studies into political economy and developed a politically informed country assistance strategy. However, when we arrived in Accra in 2013, we were warned by DFID advisors that the office was not a good research site for our project. Likewise, our first meeting with some Bank specialists there confirmed the sense that not much was happening. Undeterred by the appearance of a negative case, we decided to probe a little deeper into how the World Bank in Accra had transitioned from a politically informed aid mission into a fairly technocratic one. As it turned out, it could all be explained by a simple change in senior staff. 'The desire to work on PEA is likely driven by the leadership of the country team', the team told us. 'The Country Director leads these initiatives. With the exception of two or three country directors, PEA has not become mainstream in operational terms.'

Up until 2012, the Accra office had been headed by a country director with a PhD in political science and an appetite for difficult questions. His leadership in turn empowered an energetic governance specialist, who decided to experiment with new approaches to tackling development challenges. For instance, with the prospect of windfall profits from oil on the horizon, the Bank team facilitated the creation of a network of experts, civil society advocates, and policymakers concerned with the development of adequate legislation to curtail abuse of power and corruption. This was not a conventional aid project but something more akin to an advocacy campaign: instead of replicating best practices and propping them up with personnel and financial assistance, the World Bank decided to shape the foundations that would enable Ghanaians to demand more accountable natural resource management.

As innovative as this strategy was, and as celebrated as it is to this day by some of the local players who took part in it, the overtly political approach inevitably ruffled feathers in the Ghanaian government, who saw an entrepreneurial country director overstepping his mandate and interfering in domestic affairs. When a new government took office in 2012, the president reportedly asked the World Bank to install a more traditional head of office, and the Bank complied. By the time we visited Accra in 2013, under the aegis of a new and classically technocratic development manager, PEA had largely disappeared from the radar, and the office had ceased any kind of follow-up on the considerable political investments that had been made before. The two key actors had moved on by then – one into academia, the other into a different African country – and there was no one with the necessary skill or inclination to continue the challenge. As we learned later, the World Bank's burst of politically smart work in Ghana had been fuelled not just by personality, but by funds and support coming from headquarters in Washington, DC.

The World Bank is famously reluctant to employ political scientists, tending to cover political economy issues under the much safer rubric of 'governance', which is further disguised as an appendix to 'public sector'. Resistance stems partly from the two conflicting understandings of 'political': good governance policy goals on the one hand, and politically smart methods on the other. So, it came as a bit of a surprise when, in 2007, the Bank adopted an organisation-wide Governance and Anti-Corruption Strategy. The GAC, as it was known, was supposed to help the Bank transition towards a more systematic and analytically sound incorporation of governance and anticorruption issues across its country portfolios. The money to pay for all of this, however, would not come from its own budget. Instead, in 2008, three donors – the United Kingdom, Norway, and the Netherlands – set up a trust fund to finance the strategy's implementation. The Governance Partnership Facility (GPF) covered support for better country strategies, new analytical work, and innovative governance interventions. Crucially, the facility would finance 'a portion of Bank staff and operating costs for the implementation in selected countries of CGAC business plans that rigorously and systematically address the governance impediments to development'[16].

The donors behind GPF were acutely aware of the risks of doing governance work within the World Bank, which they saw:

> constrained by inadequate resources, partly because some governments are reluctant to borrow for governance reforms, because teams are already committed to supporting other partner government priorities, and because there is a shortage of credible governance advisors with broad development knowledge and hands-on experience[17].

By injecting external funds into the Bank's internal environment, they were hoping to change the incentive structure. At first, the bet seemed to be paying off. In countries such as Ghana, country management units suddenly found themselves with new funds earmarked for GAC work, which enabled them to commission PEAs and recruit much-needed governance specialists. In its first year alone, the GPF funded twenty-eight new studies[18]. At headquarters, the facility provided the resources and impetus behind the creation of a PEA Community of Practice, which facilitated learning and crafted new analytical toolkits for Bank personnel. Some of the most recent PEA frameworks that I mentioned in the previous section were in fact GPF products[19].

Despite those early successes, the GPF's impact was never that great to begin with, as it was built upon the same fragmented foundations that plague all aid bureaucracies. Although it aimed to mainstream governance across the entirety of World Bank operations, the facility remained very much a product by and for governance types, as did the GAC. By the end of 2010, GPF grants totalled $65 million, and a sizeable chunk of this went to the Poverty Reduction and Economic Management Network housing public sector specialists; this raised eyebrows among members of rival networks[20]. In addition, the facility did not increase the quality of political economy work in sector operations, which 'seldom discussed political incentives to implement governance reforms'[21]. Only 63% of Bank staff were 'fully familiar' with the GAC strategy, and many of those did not think they had the requisite skills to manage governance challenges[22]. Tragically, even when studies were conducted, 'the solutions proposed to address political-economic constraints were more or less conventional and technocratic', similar to those suggested a decade earlier during the PRS fad[23]. As to the Community of Practice, much of it circled around the personality and commitment of a couple of key individuals: when one of them retired and the other moved to a different part of the Bank, much of its coordinating and knowledge-sharing work ground to a halt. This had repercussions in country work. As one PEA expert told me, not having clear PEA guidance for country teams and managers left them in a vulnerable position. This explains the turn of events in Ghana.

As the main financial backer of GAC, DFID's PEA proponents were effectively outsourcing a lot of the work they could not carry out themselves. By funding an ambitious strategy within a large and central development player, they could indirectly influence their own operating environment. I can just imagine them saying 'our minister won't listen, but if he sees the World Bank doing governance, then he will want to look smart by doing it too'. But advocates stumbled time after time over the myriad routines, requirements, and cultures that dominate aid bureaucracies. This research project into PEA had unveiled the administrative barriers that prevent donors from thinking politically: the apolitical nature of programming requirements and processes; the considerable discretion enjoyed by managers, who are rewarded on the basis of disbursement; and the deep rifts between different sectors of development assistance, as manifested in the different professions[24]. Organisational barriers such as these, together with the contradictory incentives I discussed in earlier chapters, have come to be identified as the key impediments in the march towards more politically informed aid[25].

The inability of PEA proponents to grapple with their own organisations is perhaps the most fascinating paradox that I have encountered in my work on this topic. But don't take my word for it. As a GAC evaluation put it, 'PEA reports largely ignored the political economy of aid itself and, in particular, the reputational risks for the Bank as a major donor in aid-dependent countries'[26]. This was just a repetition of the demise of DFID's DoC approach, which 'triggered debate within DFID about how far internal, organisational incentives support continued development and implementation' of analytical work[27]. In particular, PEA 'may not be well aligned with donor incentives to demonstrate short-term impact, respond to their own taxpayers and lobby groups, and to spend allocated aid resources'[28]. The World Bank's reports also tended to ignore 'how donor decisions – including Bank lending decisions – influenced the decisions of country decision-makers to improve (or neglect) governance'[29]. One only has to reflect on the cases of Sierra Leone, Liberia, or Honduras to see how easy it is for recipient governments to toy with donors, playing to their worst incentives while continuing the 'ritual dances of reform'. If the reality is so obvious, and if the warnings were so clearly stated over a decade ago, why did PEA proponents fail to incorporate the political economy of aid into their strategies? Answering that question requires us to turn our gaze away from operations and back towards the home donor environment.

Politics, results, adaptation

It has been almost twenty years since the development industry began talking about adopting more politically informed approaches to aid programmes. That is two decades' worth of proposals; organisational battles; international workshops; intellectual controversies; false starts; fleeting victories, frameworks and toolkits; resentment towards doubters; and overall disappointment with the challenge of overcoming the deeply rooted assumptions and institutionalised practices of the international development community. The struggle of 'politics' in development becomes an interesting sociological puzzle when one considers the parallel rise and relative success of alternative norms such as 'results-based programming' or 'adaptive learning', which have managed to outpace politics in both public appeal and organisational change in a fraction of the time. What makes this puzzle all the more interesting is the fact that these three cognitive maps – politics, experiments, and results – have competed for the same policy space in the wake of a major austerity crisis in donor countries, coupled with increased criticism about the ineffectiveness of foreign aid. In a way, they are all solutions to the same problem, and understanding why some fared better than others can enhance our understanding of the messy politics of promoting development.

The rise of results-oriented aid has taken the industry by storm since 2010, with many donors adopting various forms of payment-by-results or results-based financing in their aid portfolios[30]. These approaches follow a diagnosis that points to the principal–agent problem at the centre of foreign aid; the same problem, it must be remembered, that conditionality sought to address. Results-oriented aid is designed to overcome conventional barriers by establishing a contractual agreement on what is to be achieved. The recipient actor then has absolute freedom to pursue these objectives in whatever way it sees fit, and the actual outcome is measured by an independent third-party evaluator[31]. Instead of installing a costly project implementation unit on the ground or disbursing large sums of money in exchange for an unenforceable commitment, results-based aid dangles a juicy carrot in front of recipients as a way to incentivise action. The focus on results also resonates with the rise of 'delivery units' around the developing world, modelled after Tony Blair's own unit while he was Britain's prime minister. Indeed, Blair's Africa Governance Initiative has worked with countries throughout Africa to bring precisely this kind of results-oriented management to the centre of government[32].

There are some pretty significant limitations to these kinds of results-based approaches, but also a very obvious strength. First, contractual approaches such as cash-on-delivery assume that governments have the capacity – financial, technical, or otherwise – to actually implement the desired programmes, but they may lack the willingness or immediate funds to do so. This is somewhat true in countries such as Ethiopia and Rwanda, where semi-authoritarian developmental regimes are aggressively pursuing poverty reduction and economic transformation. However, it is not clear that the specific modality of aid is doing anything there that a conventional grant would not achieve. Second, many sectors of development are not particularly quantifiable, as I discussed in Chapter 2. This creates a bias towards service delivery issues where outputs are tangible, meaning less attention is paid to transformational interventions. Third, aid that overwhelmingly supports the centre of government can have a detrimental effect on what are often weak democracies with limited checks on the executive, which puts a not inconsiderable amount of trust on individual leaders[33]. Despite all of this, results-based approaches are eminently consistent with the warped politics of aid under austerity that prevail in donor countries, creating a semblance of evidence-based policymaking with zero risk to taxpayer money. That, by itself, is probably what keeps the entire agenda afloat.

The second big competitor with the politics agenda is the growing movement seeking to redefine development policy around ideas such as adaptation and experimentation[34]. In September 2014, there was a big meeting in London cohosted by the World Bank's GPF and the ODI. The event was attended by World Bank personnel, consultants, researchers, and a few representatives from other aid agencies such as DFID and DFAT. It was a strange affair: a mixture of public relations and stock-taking. On the one hand, the World Bank used the event to launch its new Governance Global Practice, one of fourteen issue-based units resulting from a lengthy and controversial internal restructuring process. On the other, some of the panels were devoted to the question of integrating governance broadly speaking, and political analysis more specifically, into aid programming. The result was a blend of repetition and platitude that left many participants unsatisfied. I distinctly remember wandering the venue after a few useless sessions and coming across a discussion about the possibility of moving things beyond the stale PEA agenda. It was in that side conversation that a new aid movement was born.

One month later I attended another meeting, this time in Boston: this was smaller, more targeted, and managed in a much more disciplined and constructive way. The invitation-only event gathered consultants, academics, representatives from foundations, staffers from small development organisations, and aid professionals. Hosted by Harvard University's Building State Capability Project and ODI's Politics and Governance team, the meeting produced the 'Doing Development Differently' (DDD) manifesto, a collective call for reinventing development interventions according to some intuitive but subversive principles. These included focusing on problem solving; building on local ownership; brokering coalitions for change; blending design and implementation; managing risk through many small bets; and delivering results that empower, are sustainable, and build trust. The proponents and early signatories of the DDD manifesto were a self-described 'emerging community of development practitioners and observers', a list which would eventually comprise several hundred individuals as well as a dozen small organisations. Over the following years, DDD proponents and sympathisers would meet regularly, in different venues and multiple countries, to further document cases and instances of adaptive, iterative, and innovative development interventions. The general contours of the approach were even published in an ODI report, *Adapting Development*, which called for 'a radically different approach to development'[35]. The team at Harvard started offering online courses to practitioners and experts, and released a fully-fledged handbook on how to do development in a flexible, iterative and problem-oriented manner[36]. In less than three years, DDD events began attracting hundreds of participants to swanky venues, hosting vibrant exchanges and even artists-in-residence.

Many of those who currently participate claim that they are Doing Development Differently, even if at times they are just doing solid development management or good political-analysis work. It is a testament to the success of DDD that it has lured in so many practitioners, even before the actual practicalities of the agenda were fleshed out.

While the results-based approach tends to bring in money, and the adaptive approach brings in all the cool kids, the politics approach appears to be stuck in a rut. There is a Thinking and Working Politically Community of Practice that, for years, stayed well clear of any limelight, operating more as a therapy group where PEA types could share war stories about their ignorant and recalcitrant organisations. It was only in 2016 that the Community secured funding to establish a secretariat and gradually develop a public profile. There have also been publications upon publications explaining the need to think politically, and what this actually entails[37]. Yet some of the key experts who kept the Community alive through its early years eventually moved on to the greener pastures of Doing Development Differently[38]. Why the failure to launch?

The politics, results, and adaptation networks are all examples of what some theorists would call an 'epistemic community', that is, 'a network of professionals with recognised expertise and competence in a particular domain and an authoritative claim to policy-relevant knowledge within that domain or issue-area'[39]. Four key ingredients are necessary for an epistemic community: a shared normative goal, shared causal or explanatory beliefs, shared notions of what is valid proof, and a common set of policy practices. The results network clearly ticks all four boxes, and so does the DDD network. Both approaches were designed with specific practices in mind, based on very particular theoretical interpretations (respectively, principal–agent and institutional failure) and a relatively solid quantitative analysis of what did not work. Having leading scholars and think tanks among its core proponents – the Center for Global Development and the ODI/ Kennedy School of Government, respectively – ensured a modicum of methodological rigour and intellectual respectability.

In contrast, the politics group remains at best an incipient epistemic community. For most of its existence, it has not had a clear intellectual basis that could anchor it rigorously. Most of its members are practitioners or development studies scholars, with only limited engagement with the political science literature. Many of the Thinking and Working Politically workshops I have attended included a variation on a recurrent polemic about whether 'incentives' as a concept can encompass all the ways in which power operates[40], which seems a rather basic and arcane discussion to have when there are bigger fish to fry. Its basic claim to relevance rests on a wealth of presumed 'negative' evidence: interventions that failed because of their inattention to politics. Unfortunately, compiling this kind of evidence is difficult for two reasons, which have already been covered in previous chapters. First, donors are not likely to capture what they actually do. Second, stories of failure can endanger practitioners' career prospects. A subgroup within the Thinking and Working Politically community has spent the last few years frantically chasing whatever evidence they could find to support their case[41]. This is despite the astute warning from a senior member of the network in that ill-fated September 2014 event that a persuasive anecdote in the ears of a minister may do more to advance an agenda than all the evidence in the world.

What future for politically smart programming?

By the time we finished our field research into the mysteri-
ous turnaround of the World Bank's politically savvy office
in Ghana, one of the key players there had already moved on
to Nigeria. Emboldened by a fearless country director and a
respected minister of finance, as well as a couple of effective
governors, she was planning to develop a politically informed
portfolio approach built on the lessons from Accra while her
window of opportunity remained open. For a time, I was privy
to this process of building an adaptive, learning programme of
activities: using PEA by world-renowned experts on Nigerian
politics to get everybody on the same page; conducting case
studies on failed interventions to understand what could have
been done better; integrating a governance filter at the country
level so that all project proposals were made as politically smart
as possible; engaging the services of third-party researchers to
monitor and evaluate the learning side of the programme; and
building a joint high-level team of Nigerian and international
scholars to oversee the approach. In a rare example of actual
learning and sharing, the approach was summarised and disseminated through a public report branded as a case of Doing
Development Differently (although when I was involved it was
still a politically smart approach)[42].

A year after my participation in this particular effort stopped, I
received a rather terse e-mail from the senior World Bank specialist in charge, asking for a phone call. 'I have a problem', she said.
'The programme has worked so well that our dissemination of
the experience has created demand within the World Bank Africa
region, with other country offices asking whether we can replicate
our approach there. The problem is, I don't have any people with

the skills to manage this kind of programme the way I have in Nigeria'. I gave her some feedback and recommendations, and, honestly, I do not know to this day what came of this curious case of demand outpacing supply. Such is the bane of the innovator in the aid world: there are only so many people with the inclination, intellectual curiosity, and – to put it bluntly – guts to stake their careers on new ways of doing things. I can count on the fingers of two hands the names of influential individuals whose personalities have impacted the politics agenda in DFID, the World Bank, and the OECD. It is on their shoulders that the current crop of PEA proponents is somewhat precariously perched. When some of them shifted to Doing Development Differently, so did their institutional affiliations, contact networks, name recognition, and reputational investments. Like a swarm of fireflies in the night, donor offices light up and vanish as they move from one job to another.

There is a very real question about the sustainability of these efforts. Political science began studying the politics of development decades ago, and it will continue to do so for the foreseeable future; it has the intellectual freedom of academia, and its agenda is not driven by VfM considerations (at least for now). But the fragile epistemic community of political analysis is a small player within a big aid community that is largely impervious to its complaints. As a result of the hostile political environment in donor countries (Chapters 1 and 2); the intrinsic challenge of the politics of change (Chapter 3); the limitations of donor interventions (Chapters 4 and 5); and the community's own inability to agree on a clear, simple message, such as 'results' or 'adaptation', political analysis remains a minority aspirational goal within the broader foreign aid system, outspent and outshouted by cleverer, more charismatic advocates. It is with this history of failure in mind that I move on to the next chapter, towards an alternative model for understanding development assistance across the entire chain from donor public to embattled reformer.

SEVEN | Understanding the messy politics of change

Can we move beyond the theatrics of aid budgets and the banality of certainty? Is there a way to work through the ugly politics of change, the limits of donor influence, and the paradox of development diplomacy? Are we doomed to a never-ending struggle to think politically? Political analysis may be helpful in understanding the limits of aid, but it has rarely been reassuring or encouraging when it comes to charting the way forward. Development, from a political perspective, seems just too complex, too contextual, and too morally ambiguous to model with any kind of certainty. Is there any way to wade through the politics swamp without falling into the usual platitudes such as 'politics matters'? Based on everything that I have studied and seen over the years, and despite all the personal stories of strife and insurmountable odds, I believe that there is. Call me an optimist, but in the cases of the Sierra Leone ACC, the Honduran *mesas sectoriales*, and the GPF, what I see is an unquenchable thirst for development assistance as a moral and worthwhile endeavour. However, in order to understand the puzzling appetite for fights that reformers and their supporters share, we need a different outlook on how development assistance works.

Before we begin, let us decidedly step away from the straw men that all too often grab the spotlight in development debates:

managerialism and critical approaches. As the cases of Sierra Leone, Liberia, and Honduras demonstrate, managerialism in development is at best a fanciful illusion, and at worst a deceptive mirage. The kinds of institutional change processes that most development interventions embody or require cannot be neatly captured by modelling measurable risks and outputs. It is an inescapable conundrum of aid, as Andrew Natsios wrote, that quantifiable interventions tend to be the least transformational, and vice versa. That the community is so deeply submerged in managerial discourse and requirements is a testament to the combined loudness of aid sceptics and austerity hawks, coupled with the baffling inability of aid practitioners to mount a challenge. We use managerial tools not because they are best for the job at hand, but because they are best for keeping our jobs. To dismiss anything that does not fit these tools is to restrict the richness of development to a tiny subset of comparatively irrelevant interventions. Asking for evidence-based interventions and VfM may seem like the responsible thing to do with taxpayer money, but, in reality, it is a Trojan horse for a particular interpretation of development that has nothing to do with poverty and reform, and everything to do with partisan squabbles.

The polar opposite of managerialism is what could be labelled critical approaches to development. Instead of managers and economists, this corner of the ring is populated by anthropologists and self-styled critical scholars, who use foreign aid as a convenient punching bag for decrying the evils of colonialism and capitalism. There is nothing wrong with analysing the history of power relations that has led to current underdevelopment, or the fundamentally troubled relationship between donors and recipients; I have written about precisely that topic in this very

book. However, critical approaches often go a step further, imbu-
ing development practitioners with a mix of emotional blindness
and neglectful abuse of power that can only be redeemed by withdrawing from the planning enterprise altogether. Contrary to the
image of development as an engineering task to be managed, critical scholars often consider it an inescapably violent process, in
which the wills and desires of the global proletariat are once again
subordinated to the capricious schemes of NGOs and corporation neocolonialism. Once more, this is not a real exploration of
development, but a Trojan horse for waging political and intellectual battles against the system of neoliberal capitalism.

Moving away from this surrogate confrontation between neoliberal and anti-system factions requires us to also jettison some
of the inherited assumptions about what development assistance
is or how it works. In the preceding chapters, I have laid down
the foundations of such an effort, introducing relatively basic
concepts and analytical models from various social sciences to
explain the multiple layers of development politics. In this chapter, I build on those foundations, sketching out the four conceptual shifts involved in an alternative way of understanding the
messy politics of aid. I call this approach 'contentious development politics'.

Moving beyond conventional wisdom on aid

Many scholars and practitioners have sought to make sense of
foreign aid, but they have often done so in a piecemeal manner. It
is not enough to establish the presence of diverse donor motivations, because even identical motivations can lead to very different aid dynamics[1]. It is also conceptually suspect to make blanket
statements about the shortcomings of donor interventions and

plans. This approach not only dismisses the possibility of variation in donor–recipient relations, but also deprives recipient actors of any agency by placing an inordinate causal weight on donor organisations[2]. At the same time, focusing almost exclusively on recipient politics also neglects the conceptual and practical possibility that the interaction with donors has the potential to alter local conditions for change[3]. Instead, I would like to recover the more analytically sophisticated approach to aid that developed out of the days of structural adjustment: a pragmatic emphasis on the incentives and ideas surrounding decision-makers in recipient countries as well as the impact that external actors had on them, with the clear goal of understanding the problems of aid dependence and reform failure[4].

It is important to take the assessment of foreign aid away from purely technical and economistic conceptions and into the realm of political analysis. Recent surveys of the problem of effectiveness extensively discuss the difficulties of foreign aid programming and evaluation in light of donor and recipient shortcomings[5]. Such an emphasis on the minutiae of project design, implementation, and performance monitoring is also evident in the current trend of field experiments and randomised trials[6]. Against the problem of aid ineffectiveness, it seems that both scholars and practitioners have responded with a critique of instruments, modalities, and methodologies; however, in so doing they have obscured the political realities of aid, the contentious space of interaction in which donors and recipients attempt to reconcile divergent interests and conflicting incentives. I believe the object of analysis should not simply be the input or output of foreign aid, but rather the political process that links them together[7].

What I propose is an analytical rethinking of the politics of aid, a framework that I am calling 'contentious development politics'. I am convinced that this is a productive lens through which to understand how aid projects and initiatives unfold on the ground, why they so often fail, and why their real impact is unlikely to be captured by a constricting political environment in donor countries. It resonates with the research and policy advice that I have done and given over a decade, in countries such as Sierra Leone, Liberia, and Honduras. It is also consistent with the latest practitioner trends, such as 'adaptive development', with its focus on brokers, dynamics, and coalition-building[8]. It can be summarised thus: incumbents and challengers, advancing processes of mobilisation and demobilisation, leading to episodes of reform across the many fields of development assistance.

The many fields of development assistance

I begin from the assumption that 'foreign aid' is not a unified policy, system, or – for lack of a better word – thing. Throughout the book, I have introduced many different aid relationships, each operating in its own space: the interaction between publics and pundits, politicians and bureaucrats, headquarters and country offices, country offices and recipient governments, aid officials and reformers, practitioners and scholars. Development assistance is best understood, not as a unified issue area, but as a patchwork of nested and overlapping fields. I borrow the word 'field' from organisation theorists, who have spent decades thinking about how firms and other types of organisations tend to congregate around specific markets or policies, always keeping an eye on one another and competing or cooperating to influence their environment[9]. Social and organisational fields are a useful

concept for understanding stability and change. Their boundaries are stable but porous; their membership is fluid; and their
goals and regulations are subject to reinterpretation and contestation. Fields tend to have incumbents, who are invested in
business as usual, and challengers, who seek to establish a new
status quo; I will return to this point in the next section. Most
importantly, organisational fields are connected to one another,
whether it is by way of smaller fields aggregating into a larger one,
or neighbouring fields influencing one another[10].

There is such a thing as a broad international aid field, which,
taken as a whole, includes all funders, implementers, consultants,
NGOs, and researchers working on development issues, from the
World Bank to Oxfam to the Institute of Development Studies to
Crown Agents. But then development organisations – large and
small, governmental and nongovernmental – comprise multiple
smaller fields representing individual administrative units such as
evaluation departments, research units, or country offices. The
nested and overlapping fields of international development, in
which aid donors have traditionally been the centre of gravity, are
also permeated by less formal and transorganisational epistemic
fields in the form of professions and communities of practice. Just
as development actors locate themselves in organisational hier-
archies, they also tend to identify with professional or scientific
communities that cut across organisational boundaries; economists, managers, or health specialists tend to keep in touch with
colleagues elsewhere, including peer organisations, consulting
firms, and academia. This kind of cross-organisational, knowl-
edge-based field is exemplified by such initiatives as the Paris
Declaration on Aid Effectiveness or the Doing Development Differently community.

Goals, relationships, and legitimate forms of action vary as one moves from higher- to lower-level fields, as well as between formal and informal ones. The broad development level, for instance, is mainly focused on goals and operating principles, such as the SDGs. The national level is slightly less abstract and more consequential, with discussions about the role of development assistance relative to diplomatic or economic concerns, as well as the relative power of different traditional and nontraditional donors. The organisational level is focused on defining results and the managerial structures and processes for financing, pursuing, and evaluating them. Most debates circle around budgetary allocation and the effectiveness of overall assistance policy, but inter-organisational debates on topics such as the aid effectiveness agenda also get a look-in. Lastly, at the operational level, one encounters debates about the merits of programming and evaluation tools, as well as about the role of new forms of knowledge in shaping these tools.

Even without going any further, a field approach to development assistance immediately brings to light the challenges and contradictions of various policy agendas that are ostensibly focused on aid. For example, polemics by public intellectuals such as William Easterly and Jeffrey Sachs usually take place at the broadest possible level, with little repercussion in lower levels. In turn, conversations about the 0.7% and global goals are primarily political-level phenomena, with only general implications for management and operations. Increases in aid budgets do not automatically translate into greater effectiveness on the ground, nor do clear-cut, measurable targets tell us much about how to achieve them. Such transnational policy agendas as the Thinking and Working Politically Community of Practice and

Doing Development Differently find it hard to match rhetoric with reality due to the challenge of translating debates into organisational changes.

Incumbents and challengers

In any particular field of development assistance, some actors will be relatively powerful and satisfied, while others will be relatively powerless and dissatisfied. Academic work on social movements has generated a simple yet intuitive distinction that is useful for our purposes: incumbents and challengers[11]. Incumbents tend to be the actors who benefit most from the status quo, either because it resonates with their beliefs and goals and serves their interests, or because they have invested a lot of time and resources in adapting to it[12]. Incumbents tend to be wary of change or outright hostile towards it. Challengers, in contrast, seek to upend the established order of things, advancing new policy objectives, new forms of decision-making, or new normative goals[13]. Challengers are agents of change, which they pursue by familiar means: lobbying, scheming, advocating, coordinating, framing. Again, this is a simplified conceptual distinction, but one that I have found tremendously useful in my own work.

Reformers are the ultimate challengers, because reform – and development in that sense – is the ultimate challenge to political incumbents. In Sierra Leone in the early 2000s, Valentine Collier was an obvious, if unexpected, challenger to the incumbent regime of the Sierra Leone People's Party and President Kabbah. He did not play by the usual rules of the game; he built his own parallel organisation based on the idea of integrity; and he dared to investigate sitting ministers, despite all manner of political interference. By and large, reformers mount challenges and politicians oppose them; but sometimes it is not so clear cut. Part of what stifled donor coordination in Liberia was the rise to power in 2006 of a president who had acted as a challenger when she was out of office. As long as Ellen Johnson Sirleaf sat outside government she was a vocal advocate of governance reform; the minute she stepped into the Executive Mansion, however, she began acting as an incumbent wary of rocking the boat. Hence her conflict with Auditor General Morlu. Contrast this with the case of Mel Zelaya in Honduras, the man who became president as a run-of-the-mill elite incumbent but then turned his allegiance towards Chávez and Venezuela, launching a direct challenge to Honduran political elites and donors alike.

Aid practitioners are not so easy to classify. That is because the same individuals may feel powerful or powerless depending on the level they inhabit on any given day. Consider three weeks in the life of a World Bank senior manager. In week one, discussions about potential interventions with local partners feel lopsided, due to the intrinsically unequal aid relationship: the manager usually holds the power of the purse as well the legitimacy of a major international donor. In week two, the same manager shifts to a much more passive and even vulnerable position when advocating the introduction of politically smart methods in Bank interventions: faced with a massive, unwieldy, eminently technocratic bureaucracy, the impact of a single advocate can feel utterly irrelevant. Then again, in week three, the manager attends a meeting of the Thinking and Working Politically Community of Practice, where she feels like a coconspirator in a bigger agenda for influencing aid debates. The level of engagement, which is to say the field of engagement, shapes her experience as an actor.

Incumbents and challengers across the different fields of aid tend to form alliances that bolster their own internal struggles. The Sierra Leone ACC staff pleaded with Clare Short in 2002 to combat the government's political interference. In time, Collier came to rely on the British High Commission in Freetown to act as an intermediary between his office and Kabbah's. In Liberia, GEMAP was an attempt to strengthen individual donor programmes by presenting a united front against the corrupt transitional government, linking efforts across ministries and departments to a higher political objective with buy-in from the president. Facing neglect from their own governments, both Collier and Morlu appealed to donors and the media to marshal support for reform. The Thinking and Working Politically community was born out of challengers' desire to join efforts in different development agencies. Doing Development Differently was an even clearer and stronger expression of this kind of alliance, using the strength of numbers, visibility, and legitimacy to effectively challenge incumbents across aid fields.

Reform mobilisation and demobilisation

How does a new agenda become the incumbent idea? What are the mechanisms by which challengers usurp power? What are the strategies that incumbents use to deter and contain projects of change? In a general sense, change is often the result of exogenous shocks coming from neighbouring fields, and less often the result of accumulated incremental changes within the field itself. External ideas – such as 'good governance', 'participation', and 'adaptation' – are used by challengers as a springboard for initiating processes of change; external allies – incumbents in neighbouring fields – buttress and nurture these reform efforts.

However, incumbents also use their political, organisational, and economic resources to resist such pressures for change. In practice, development is not a single process of change, but a tug-of-war between reform mobilisation and demobilisation. These are competing processes in which challengers and incumbents, respectively, work to organise coordinated action for change or pre-empt and minimise the success of such action[14].

Every aid intervention can, and, to my mind, should, be seen as a process of mobilisation. Corruption and governance interventions, such as the ACC in Sierra Leone and GEMAP in Liberia, represented a clear and present danger to the clientelism underlying those countries' political systems. Had these two projects worked as intended, many politicians in Freetown and Monrovia would have found themselves much poorer and either out of office or indicted. These are just very obvious examples: the many fields of aid are chock-full of this kind of threat to the status quo. The participatory requirements of the poverty reduction strategy papers in the early 2000s were a clear threat to elite politics[15]. When donors asked the government in Tegucigalpa to sit at the *mesas tripartitas* with civil society representatives, they were implicitly telling political leaders that their policies were not inclusive, that their electoral victories did not really represent the will of the people, and that sovereignty did not give them carte blanche over the country's long-term development.

However, every aid intervention is likely to be met with a proportional push-back in order to safeguard the institutional status quo. Kabbah's appointment of Henry Joko-Smart as anti-corruption commissioner was a very effective demobilisation tactic, plunging the ACC into the inaction of the 'dark ages'. Johnson Sirleaf's choice of Auditor General, Robert Kilby – a man who told the legislature that the Commission should 'protect its findings from the public' – had the same impact. The abandonment of the tripartite system and the PRS by successive Honduran governments was a not-so-subtle means of disempowering civil society, sending them back to a subordinate role away from any decision-making power. Sometimes demobilisation does not work, or it backfires: the 2007 elections in Sierra Leone are a testament to the dangers of going too far, or too visible, in counter-reform efforts. Other times demobilisation does work, through less purposive but more insidious means: challengers get burnt out, informal politics is too hard to uproot, donor attention eventually shifts elsewhere. To paraphrase the *Rolling Stones*, time is on the incumbent's side, yes it is.

Mobilisation and demobilisation are also present inside donor fields, and most crucially in the agendas I introduced in the last chapter. Thinking and Working Politically, Doing Development Differently, and the results agenda are all competing narratives advanced by epistemic communities seeking to reform aid organisations. Their chief struggle is not against one another, however, but against the incumbents back home: those aid hawks and deniers I covered in Chapters 1 and 2, who have managed to take over much of the public debate about aid, pre-empting and sabotaging any attempt to make it more transformational. And reform mobilisation and demobilisation are not exclusive to development intervention on the ground: the very organisational soul of aid is being fought over in the pages of *The Daily Mail* and William Easterly's books.

Scholars of social movements and contentious politics have fleshed out these two broad and rather abstract processes with a number of concrete mechanisms[16]. I will only highlight three of them here, which I find particularly relevant for understanding the politics of development.

Organisational appropriation. One of the first steps in mobilisation is for challengers to appropriate key organisations as the core of a potential reform coalition. Whether we talk about the World Bank country office in Nigeria, the Liberian GAC, or the ODI in London, challengers need the legitimacy, name recognition, financial means, and technical know-how that an organisation brings with it. In some contexts, appropriation means designing a new mandate and vision for the organisation, while in others it simply involves enforcing what regulations already exist in the books (sometimes the most subversive act is just to apply the rules). In response, incumbents will seek to appropriate key organisations for the purposes of forestalling challenges and destabilising emergent reform coalitions. Kabbah's re-appropriation of the ACC in 2005 and the arrival of a technocratic World Bank country director in Accra in 2012 are just two examples of this kind of response.

Brokerage. A key part of building a reform coalition is attracting the political support of sympathetic incumbents and challengers in neighbouring fields. Development coalitions, as I have shown, often rely on bringing together public servants, civil society organisations, media organisations, and international actors. Brokerage makes distant fields more proximate. Donors, in particular, are in a privileged position to participate in brokerage, sometimes arbitrating between incumbents and challengers, as they did in Sierra Leone, and at other times strengthening reformers by funding and organising support coalitions around them, as they did in Liberia. Incumbents are also likely to seek allies in proximate public sector fields, for instance, in ministries of justice and parliaments, brokering a coalition that isolates reformers in their organisations.

Legitimation. Legitimacy is a precious commodity in contentious development processes, and both challengers and incumbents often seek validation from external actors who can buttress them ideationally or materially. This mechanism is key for the stabilisation of reform coalitions, and it can either reinforce or pave the way for the previous two mechanisms. In a globalised policy landscape, international actors are the most likely to serve as agents of legitimation for institutional change. For two decades now, DFID has served as funder but also legitimator of many reform efforts; so has the World Bank, when led by enlightened managers. However, domestic social fields may be equally relevant or more so in other contexts. The Honduran Congress played a huge role in delegitimising Mel Zelaya in 2009, with the backing of the Supreme Tribunal, the military, and segments of civil society; in contrast, the international community was almost powerless throughout the constitutional crisis, and ultimately incapable of restoring Zelaya back to power.

Development episodes, not outcomes

My characterisation of development interventions – and arguably all reforms across aid fields – as competing political processes has implications for determining success and failure. Anyone familiar with public policy knows that definitive results are rare. Over the years, there is an ebb and flow to priorities, budgets, and targets, a constantly moving bar that makes assessments of impact difficult. A new results-oriented agenda has taken over foreign aid in the last decade, chiefly as a by-product of austerity programmes. I devoted most of Chapter 2 to critiquing the assumptions and implications of this agenda, questioning whether outputs can be easily identified for the most challenging types of intervention. I have also introduced an understanding of development as institutional change, which is by definition a slow and bumpy road, full of twists and turns, and prone to reversals. For all these reasons, it seems to me that determining the success of aid by what can be accurately measured in a two-to-five-year timeframe is a fool's errand. I will go further than that: it is methodologically questionable, organisationally self-defeating, and morally suspect.

But what is the alternative? My catalogue of reformer struggles and donor misadventures in Sierra Leone, Liberia, and Honduras could easily be construed as an exercise in conventional aid criticism: projects did not work as intended and money was wasted, end of story. However, I would consider this a myopic and cheap reading of the evidence. What aid achieved in those countries may not have looked like much according to the most reductive of quantitative indicators, but it amounted to much more than what donors themselves probably expected. Those interventions launched entire processes of reform mobilisation and demobilisation, prompting a re-examination of political norms, legitimate representation, and development objectives. They empowered some key local actors, giving them funds and skills that would allow them to continue fighting even after donors left. They delegitimised corrupt incumbents, and in some instances effectively toppled presidents who preyed on their own countries. They gave reformers hope.

Even if one does not trust my reading of the evidence, it is obvious that simplistic result assessments cannot tell the whole story. This is why I propose that we discuss development assistance not in terms of 'more or less spurious numbers', but in terms of the episodes of reform that they launch and sustain. In Sierra Leone, we can clearly see an episode of strong mobilisation from 2000 to 2005, an equally strong episode of demobilisation in 2005–7, and a return to reform mobilisation from 2008 onwards. Three distinct episodes of developmental change or continuity, fuelled by international interventions. We can argue that the first episode was unsuccessful to the extent that it did not prevent a strong reversal. However, it did plant the seeds for Abdul Tejan-Cole to take over as anti-corruption commissioner in 2008, revising the ACC Act and securing prosecutorial autonomy for the Commission. In that light, the Collier years were far from a total waste of aid money. However, understanding the secondary impact of the early years of DFID support to the ACC requires looking beyond the life of the project itself, and certainly beyond its cancellation after 2006. It also requires a more qualitative approach to the evidence, tracing the causal steps that led from the ACC Act of 2000 to the ACC Act of 2008[17].

A similar logic applies to the ongoing processes of change within the aid industry itself. I may have questioned PEA's lack of impact within DFID or the World Bank after fifteen years of advocacy, just as others have studied the surprisingly short lifespan of other PEA frameworks[18]. Indeed, looking at the implementation of the World Bank's 2007 GAC in isolation may yield a poignant story of good intentions crashing into the rocky shore of organisational reality. But it was that same strategy that enabled innovation in Ghana, which in turn led to a ground-breaking approach to politically smart and adaptive aid in Nigeria[19]. The GPF that supported the strategy's implementation between 2008 and 2014 may be seen as an episode of lukewarm impact, but its secondary effects – the repercussions of getting new blood and ideas into the World Bank – may be felt for decades to come.

In defence of eclecticism

The theoretical snippets peppered throughout these chapters come from various corners of the social sciences. My reading of institutions is mostly derived from new institutional economics. The collective action and principal–agent models originate in microeconomic and game theory. I looked to international relations and policy studies for the concept of epistemic communities and the diffusion of ideas. My take on organisations and fields comes from economic and organisation sociology. The concepts introduced in this chapter are borrowed quite liberally from the literature on contentious politics. This particular mix of analytical ingredients is, in a sense, a reflection of my own journey as a researcher, grounded in political science but dabbling in a few neighbouring disciplines. It also grows out of a conviction that social science is a toolkit, full of different implements that we can employ depending on the problem we want to investigate. Some very smart people have called this approach 'analytic eclecticism': a pragmatist intellectual ethos combined with an appetite for messy problems that can be explained through complex causal stories[20]. It is an outlook that seeks to make sense of the world with a very specific, often practical purpose. In that sense, it relies on what Max Weber called the 'capacity and the will to deliberately take up a stance towards the world and lend it meaning'[21].

Yet I harbour doubts regarding the feasibility of this kind of agenda, given that eclecticism and pragmatism do not necessarily sit well with the academic and practitioner fields of development. In a mostly but not entirely tongue-in-cheek manner, I often tell my students that development studies is a made-up discipline; and I say that as someone trained in the made-up discipline par excellence: political science. The academic study of development is full of selective remembering; creative borrowing; and a bit of sneaky stealing from economics, sociology, geography, politics, and/or anthropology. Even so, the discipline has not managed to translate this diversity of influences into an eclectic corpus of research. Instead, it has subdivided into its own little factions, with battle lines largely drawn according to how close to economics or anthropology one is.

Nowhere did I see this more clearly than at the 2016 Development Studies Association meeting in Oxford, where two keynote speeches were scheduled: one by famous economist Daron Acemoglu, and the other by famous anthropologist Tania Li. Acemoglu's claim to fame is the study of institutional history through game theory logic[22]; Li's is her critique of the development industry as a violent exercise of imposition[23]. Their presentations did not disappoint: the economist offered a formal model of democratisation throughout history, while the anthropologist questioned the very understanding of development as a discourse and agenda complicit with neoliberal capitalism. There was some overlap in audience, though Li's talk was better attended and appeared to be received with enthusiasm, at least compared with the lukewarm scepticism afforded to Acemoglu. The organisers had somehow managed to – wittingly or unwittingly – stage a perfect physical representation of the split within development studies, between critical approaches on the one hand and positivist researchers on the other.

The coda to these two presentations – funny or tragic, depending on your outlook – is how unrelated they were to actual development practice. Neither of the speakers had anything to say about ongoing processes of reform around the world, which are clearly too messy for elegant criticism or elegant formal modelling. In a discipline haunted for too long by the suspicion of collusion with practitioners, the keynotes signalled perhaps a certain intellectual maturity and autonomy. For me, however, they represented an abdication of the legitimate role that development scholars can play in advising officials or engaging in public debate on aid. It is precisely that connection between scholarship and practice, however messy and incestuous, that had attracted me to development studies in the United Kingdom in the first place. How sad, then, to see the conventional split between 'social sciences' and 'humanities' replicate itself within the microcosm of development.

Is there room for contentious development politics in this broken community? I certainly hope so. But it demands that scholars step out of their comfort zones, and, unfortunately, academia is currently dominated by powerful incentives against dabbling of any kind. It is precisely that weariness and boredom with paradigms and hyper-specialisation that led to the development of 'analytic eclecticism' as a new intellectual agenda. However, there are few financial or career incentives for doing cross-disciplinary work, and most of us default instead to the kind of safe but ultimately mundane replication that Thomas Kuhn called 'normal science'[24].

Even if the academic side suddenly congealed into an eclectic but coherent approach to the politics of aid and development, there is no guarantee that the policy side would welcome it. As I pointed out in the previous chapter, academic boundaries are mirrored in the professional boundaries of the aid industry. DFID's advisor cadres and the World Bank's global practices are separate professional categories with distinct skill sets and analytical requirements. Politics and governance are at best allocated their own silo, and at worst diluted through their incorporation into the broader, more nebulous category of public sector management, which is mostly populated by public administration experts, auditors, and evaluators. Who is interested in contentious development as a framework for understanding the politics of aid? Governance practitioners and consultants, hopefully; going much further than that is probably a stretch.

The missing piece of the discourse puzzle

There is one pretty substantial problem with contentious development politics as an approach: it is not compatible with public narratives about aid and development in donor countries. As I discussed in Chapter 1, few people really care about aid to begin with, and those that do are either hawkish conservatives or the very practitioners whose livelihoods depends on aid. There is a good reason why managerialist and critical discourses are so prevalent: they speak to bigger, more complex political battles unfolding in the West. On one side is the hyper-conservative movement that took advantage of the financial crisis to impose a questionable austerity agenda, and on the other side is the anti-capitalist and anti-globalisation movement that reads Piketty and participates in 'occupy'-style movements. Foreign aid features in this battle of narratives in one of two ways, either as a compliant bureaucracy that can 'prove' its results or as an instrument of neoliberalism that is inimical to human dignity. In between these two poles, the believers are few and far between, and for every pragmatic internationalist like Paul Collier there is a messianic salesman like Jeff Sachs. When it comes to foreign aid, the political centre has become a rather lonely space.

Many foreign aid projects do not work as intended. Sometimes they struggle with structural constraints or demobilisation efforts.

At other times, funds are wasted with incapable or unwilling implementation partners. And in more cases than practitioners would willingly acknowledge, projects are just badly designed, lazily reproducing the best-practice flavour of the day with little attention to actual problem-solving. However, there are also countless aid projects that do work as intended. Moreover, aid projects often have positive unintended consequences that are impossible to foresee, such as empowering erstwhile partners or diffusing new ideas about integrity, inclusion, and deservingness. Aid can train future challengers. It can generate useful information and policy models that bring together reform coalitions. It can even sway the minds of the most dominant of leaders. But of course, none of this usually makes it into project evaluations, much less aggregate reports by aid agencies.

What bothers me about our silly aid debates is that they demean the work of people like Valentine Collier and John Morlu. People like them risk their careers, reputations, and in some cases even their livelihoods to achieve the kinds of reforms that will make their states more effective, their politics more accountable, and their economies more vibrant. They challenge and get beaten down for it. It is not their fault that their struggles do not fit predictable results frameworks or the superficial rhetoric of partisan politics. Reformers will continue to do the messier jobs of development long after donors lose their patience or shift their attention to the crisis du jour. It is bad enough that aid interventions offer them lukewarm support in their uphill battles; but then their work is erased from official record, their names sacrificed at the altar of quantifiable evidence.

It bothers me also because what we ask them to do is basically everything that our modern Western societies stand for.

Transplanting our partisan debates to development assistance is utterly pointless. Sierra Leoneans and Hondurans do not have bloated welfare states that need more efficient management, nor do they have neoliberal markets that need to be reined in through government regulation. The challenge of development is not too much state or too much market: it is not enough of either. Informal institutions undermine attempts to build an efficient private sector, due to the lack of impartial judiciaries, public procurement systems, and sector regulation. The game is usually rigged in favour of cronies and allies of the president and his party. Similarly, informal institutions undermine attempts to build an effective public bureaucracy, due to the lack of meritocratic recruitment, autonomy from political interference, and objective evaluation; the system is designed to enrich political clients through cushy public sector jobs. No reasonable citizen of a donor country could disagree with the notion that Liberians deserve better markets and states. Left–right dichotomies simply do not travel well once we move into low-income countries and fragile states.

Whenever I explain these things to friends, family, or colleagues who are not too familiar with aid, it appears to make sense to them. And yet every time I do so, I am forced to start from scratch, just because there is no public narrative about development as a political process. At best, in countries such as Spain, aid is seen as a humanitarian imperative that all too easily devolves into naïve volunteerism. At worst, in countries such as the United States, libertarians and Trump voters display a belligerent disdain for anything foreign, especially if it is related to welfare. This undermines any attempt to add nuance to the mix: the contentious politics of development are just too complex, too ugly, too unseemly. They are an object of scorn for those who decry aid, and a liability for those who support it. As our public debates become ever more Manichean and post-truth, the messy politics of change become harder to justify.

So, what are we to do? Should we just forget about Collier? Pretend that the G-16 was never asked to take sides after a palace coup? Hope for the best when dealing with leaders like Museveni and Johnson Sirleaf? Erase and forget every single innovation and reform effort by aid practitioners around the world? What a boring world that would be. If the analytical toolkit that I have presented here teaches us anything, it is that change is won, never given. It is up to the various reform coalitions within development – Thinking and Working Politically, Doing Development Differently, and others – to 'come out' and develop a public narrative that can begin to counteract decades of misinformation and manipulation. Perhaps then insiders will feel more comfortable reporting what really goes on in the field: the ups and downs, the heroes and villains, the victories and defeats.

Reformers and their supporters desperately need a new vision for aid that recognises their work. Contentious development politics is just a framework: a toolkit, as I have said. It is messy and eclectic, but also problem- and action-oriented. It goes against the hyper-specialisation of development studies, but it has roots across the social sciences. Hopefully it can supply an alternative set of assumptions and expectations for a counter-narrative of aid.

Conclusion

Why do we lie about aid? Because it is very hard not to.

Donor publics cover the gamut from misinformed to suspicious about foreign aid. Debates about budgets have less to do with development than the age-old competition between fiscal hawks and welfare-state defenders. The fight over aid expenditures is peripheral to the overall war, but no less useful to both sides. For progressives, it is a quick and cheap way to demonstrate humanitarianism and solidarity, definitely quicker and cheaper than any kind of reform of domestic services and benefits. For conservatives, it is a convenient target of opportunity for cuts, yielding headlines and attention without actually endangering any established interest groups. The public is by and large left out of these conversations, limiting any kind of restraint on viciousness or silliness.

The aid constituency, in the meantime, is so dependent on the development budget for its own survival that its views are automatically compromised. However, it is also so relatively tiny that it cannot have a major influence outside aid departments and agencies. This leaves practitioners at the mercy of politicians when it comes to ideological agendas such as the VfM craze that has taken the industry by storm since the financial crisis. The elusive quest for certainty is one that all aid professionals must undertake; they ignore it at their own peril. But that does not lead to increased accountability to taxpayers.

Instead, what we end up with is a fiction, a flawed evidence base that perpetuates misunderstandings about aid, while redirecting money and effort away from the truly transformational and towards the banal. Donor publics are largely oblivious to this usurpation of the aid system by false narratives, which undermines their ability to have an informed debate about development assistance.

The fiction of aid as a technical, accounting process crumbles upon contact with reality. Development is not a series of fixes to be measured but of battles to be fought. Transformational change is predicated on institutional change, which is bound to create winners and losers. There is really no other way to look at it: most aid projects are institutional interventions seeking to uproot pervasive informal institutions such as clientelism and exclusion, and the local partners they rely on are often the very representatives of the political elites that benefit from the status quo. When donors support reformers, as they did in Sierra Leone with the ACC, they set themselves up for lengthy, intractable fights, often taking two steps back for every step forward. Conditionality is a difficult tool to use, and it is often more tempting to pretend that reform is happening in order to retain access to leaders and keep the aid flowing.

Some donors will always side with local leaders, no matter what, effectively becoming spoilers for any process of institutional reform. Even when all donors agree on overarching goals, their organisational systems and priorities may make them incapable of actually coordinating to secure development objectives. In Liberia, GEMAP was an innovative mechanism for getting all international actors on the same page. However, when a president who said all the right things came into office, GEMAP revealed its true colours: a patchwork of disconnected interventions that could easily be controlled by local elites as donor attention waxed and waned. The limits to donor influence become particularly obvious when diplomacy seeps into development relationships. Originally built as a reconstruction mechanism after Hurricane Mitch, the G-16 donor group in Honduras evolved into the de facto representative of the international community, which put it in the uncomfortable role of mediator. Donors were forced to mediate between civil society groups and successive elite governments that had little appetite for participatory initiatives. When the government of Mel Zelaya was overturned via a palace coup bringing together congress, the judiciary, and the military, the G-16 was effectively paralysed, incapable of reconciling the legitimating effect of aid partnerships with the local demand for political support.

It is easy to see that the messy politics of institutional change, conditionality, donor collective action, and international mediation are a nonstarter for a donor environment obsessed with budgets, VfM, and certainty. No wonder most aid practitioners and organisations choose to obfuscate this reality, if only to survive and continue providing assistance to whatever local processes appear sensible at the time. Epistemic communities of scholars and practitioners have sought to advance alternative understandings of development, broadening the space for uncertainty and flexibility, but their impact has been limited. The Thinking and Working Politically community remains isolated and inchoate, hampered by a messy academic subdiscipline – development politics – that cannot even agree on fundamentals. The DDD community has had much more success, comparatively, attracting participants from all corners of the aid system; yet, there is a real risk that management buzzwords have outpaced substance.

Understanding aid politics may require a different kind of analytical approach, one that focuses on episodes of mobilisation and demobilisation by incumbents and challengers across multiple reform fields. This will necessitate the crafting of an alternative public narrative that can gradually push against the worst excesses of proxy managerialism and criticism. A key element of this narrative has to be a moral vision for where to go next.

Intricate ethics in Kampala

I began this book with an example of faux donor outrage at corruption in Uganda, so it is only fitting that I return to that country in my conclusion. One of the most interesting interventions I have encountered over the years is a DFID-funded project in Uganda called Expanding Social Protection (ESP). Social protection programmes have diffused around the developing world since the poverty-reduction success stories of Brazil's *Bolsa Familia* and Mexico's *Progresa/Oportunidades*: conditional cash transfer schemes in which families were given money in exchange for sending their kids to school. Inspired by their example – or simply seeking quick wins – policymakers across Latin America and Africa tried to create their own conditional cash transfer programmes, grant schemes, and other forms of social assistance and social protection. This does not mean that the transplant works automatically. A defining feature of *Oportunidades* and *Bolsa Familia* was objective monitoring for the purposes of registering beneficiaries and documenting the impact of the programmes. This kind of data collection is more political than it sounds, as it curtails opportunities for discretionary allocation and clientelism. At a more basic level, the programmes rest on notions of deservingness and entitlement, which define who should benefit from public assistance[1].

Uganda has neither the kind of regime that likes to curtail clientelism, nor the basic social norms that make some particular social groups more deserving of government handouts. Instead, the National Resistance Movement regime can probably be described as a clientelist dominant-party system, in which formal institutions are just a façade for more insidious forms of informal politics[2]. As to social norms, there is a strong sense among Ugandans that able-bodied individuals ought to sustain themselves through work, no matter their age. It was in this unwelcoming context that DFID partnered with the Ugandan Ministry of Gender and Social Development to create a new unit – staffed with a mix of expatriate consultants and local bureaucrats – tasked with gradually building the demand for social protection.

During repeated visits to Kampala, I had a chance to speak with some of the practitioners working on ESP, who shared with me the story behind what a public DFID evaluation called rather obliquely 'an influencing programme'. Following emerging good practices, the ESP team began by conducting a political-economy analysis to figure out the best way forward. Two lessons quickly emerged. First, in contrast with more open societies, NGOs and communities had little actual impact on Uganda's policymaking, and therefore the 'voices of the poor' were effectively useless in the process of creating the space for social protection. Second, in contrast with more rational governments, whatever social protection scheme was designed could not be based on fixed criteria or a piloting logic that would privilege some districts over others. So, while the logical approach would be to trial a new grant in a few districts, gather data, and then roll it out, the ESP team determined that social protection in Uganda would be an all or nothing bet.

With these parameters in mind, the unit set out to overcome its chief political obstacles: a hostile Ministry of Finance wary of mounting costs for an untested intervention, and a disinterested political regime that saw no immediate gain in a Brazil-style social protection programme. The ESP team decided that working on the latter would naturally help them overcome the former, so they focused their efforts on capturing the imagination of Uganda's political elites. They directed their advocacy towards key potential champions within Parliament, sending them on study tours to other countries in the region, where they could meet with peers and bureaucrats who had already launched social protection programmes. They made sure that MPs saw the potential electoral benefits of social protection transfers, which were sure to earn them the gratitude of constituents. This was coupled with a public communication campaign targeting the talk radio shows most popular among Kampala elites, who were most likely to influence the government's thinking.

Over time, a critical mass of politicians, bureaucrats and influential players coalesced around the idea of a new social grant to the elderly, to be piloted in a limited number of districts. In order to ensure the appearance of fair distribution, the grant was not based on absolute but relative criteria: it would target the 100 oldest citizens in each constituency. The pilot was so successful that other MPs began to clamour for a national roll-out. Finance officials were livid at this blatant bypass of their role as policy gatekeepers, but by then the cat was out of the bag: the space for social protection had been effectively expanded.

I asked two ESP team members whether they worried that by appealing to electoral gains they might have inadvertently reinforced the clientelist undercurrents of Ugandan politics, entrenching the very practices that fuel patronage and corruption. They readily admitted it was a legitimate concern, but it seemed like the only way to achieve their goals. In order to bring social protection into Ugandan national policy, they had to work with the political system, however ugly it might seem.

I use this stylised narrative as an example with students and aid practitioners when I speak to them about working politically. It is a way of making tangible the inescapable trade-offs of aid in countries with strong informal institutions, like Uganda. Over time, however, I have realised that what keeps bringing my thoughts back to that conversation in Kampala are the ethical implications. Was the ESP team wrong to bypass civil society and the poor, directing all their efforts to receptive politicians instead? Were they too Machiavellian in their decision to work with clientelist politics instead of against it, as so many donors officially claim to do?

The ESP case is a clear example of what moral philosopher Frances Kamm calls 'intricate ethics'[3]. The public discourse of aid in donor countries has no place for this kind of moral messiness. The VfM imperative, the results agenda, and, indeed, most conversations about aid follow a quintessentially utilitarian logic: the value of aid has to be calculated with reference to its demonstrable effects on the ground relative to the cost that it brings to taxpayers. Explicitly, if aid interventions do not – or cannot – show enough results, the greater good is achieved by cutting aid budgets and redirecting them to worthier, more impactful goals. This utilitarianism is predicated on the assumption of risk, not the kind of uncertainty I discussed in Chapter 2 based on the works of Frank Knight[4]. Yet there are obvious questions to be raised here. At the most basic level, what are we to do when reality does not lend itself to this kind of actuarial exercise? What moral logic should guide our assistance 'when evidence, data and calculations (not to mention units of account) are all hazy'[5]?

The alternative to consequentialism (the broader approach to which utilitarianism belongs) is what Kamm and other moral philosophers call non-consequentialism, 'a type of normative ethical theory that denies that the rightness or wrongness of our conduct is determined *solely* by the goodness or badness of the consequences of our acts or of the rules to which those acts conform'[6]. Non-consequentialists believe that all moral calculations are based on some kind of value system, and that the means need to be evaluated separately from the ends. If a utilitarian would ask of foreign aid whether it works, a non-consequentialist might ask whether it is the right thing to do.

It should be apparent by now which side I take in this philosophical debate. Supporting Valentine Collier was the right thing to do at the time. The consequences of doing so were beyond DFID's control: Kabbah's transition from vocal support to open hostility, the public sector's reaction to an entrepreneurial ACC, the decisions of the Attorney General to stall prosecutions, and the lack of guidance and oversight from Parliament. There was just too much uncertainty. However, there were also unforeseen achievements: the recruitment and training of an entirely new cadre of ethical public servants, the introduction of a certain fear of committing corrupt offences, the creation of new public expectations about the government's behaviour, and the ultimate commitment of the next president to creating one of the most autonomous anticorruption bodies in Africa. Clearly uncertainty alone is not a reason to dismiss any of these positive externalities. Supporting the ACC was, by my value-based calculation, the right thing to do.

The system of *mesas tripartitas* in Honduras, bringing together donors, government, and civil society, was also the expression of a particular set of values. Participation and human rights are key elements of the Swedish aid agenda, so it comes as no surprise that Sweden was one of the chief proponents of the PRS process and the most outspoken donor among the G-16. Jettisoning utilitarianism does not mean embracing blindness, however; it was SIDA that commissioned and released a number of studies on the PRS process and its impact on issues such as gender. In an uncertain policy world, political analysis becomes almost a moral imperative for a donor who wants to actually navigate the messy politics of change[7]. Value-based interventions have challenges of their own, certainly, but these are not necessarily worse than the contradictions and pathologies of spurious utilitarianism.

The question is not whether a rights- or inclusion-centred approach can function as an alternative to VfM calculations. It is whether our Western societies can provide the moral foundations for such an alternative value system.

A new moral vision?

A contentious understanding of development has difficult practical implications. Instead of placing ownership in elite-controlled governments and aligning with disingenuous policy proposals, aid donors can choose to support budding pro-poor elites or develop the capacity of the poor to speak for themselves. This is not an unrealistic proposition: with their focus on human rights, Nordic aid donors have been doing it for years. In fact, that is how grassroots and advocacy organisations themselves work to create political spaces for pro-poor reform. Aid can serve as an asset for those seeking to disrupt entrenched elites. Many conventional donor projects already have this disruptive quality. DFID has funded efforts by bureaucrats in Uganda to create the space for a social protection system, or programmes to expand political knowledge and policy coordination by civil society organisations in Ghana. These are not interventions geared towards short-term incremental results; they are long-term investments in transformational change. They work against the grain of the political-economy of development so that the elites of tomorrow may be a tiny bit weaker than those of today.

The process of making aid useful starts at home, with taxpayers and politicians in developed countries. We should actually try to make aid debates be about development for a change, by rethinking our misconceptions and asking our leaders to stop using aid budgets for political theatre. The key here is to realise that this is not an issue of left versus right, conservative versus progressive. Our partisan politics have evolved over centuries of institutional development and economic transformation to the point that no reasonable politician would make the case for abolishing the public service or establishing a totalitarian controlled economy. We inhabit a political world characterised by strong markets and strong states. Parties and ideologues may differ regarding the extent to which we should rely more on one or the other, but we operate under the assumption that both markets and states are important. We do not know how lucky we are: in many developing countries, both markets and states are open to predation and unchecked exploitation. That is why our domestic political labels mean nothing for development. Who would want to expand public programmes when the civil service is corrupt and unprofessional? Who would want to privatise health care when people cannot afford even basic medicine? The moral case for aid depends on our understanding of this very fact: the terms of political debate in London or Washington are not really applicable in Kampala or Monrovia. Development is the process of building both stronger states and stronger markets, and that is why foreign aid should be a cause that both economic liberals and social democrats can get behind.

Twenty-five years ago, David H. Lumsdaine published a book called *Moral Vision in International Politics*, in which he documented the rise of the foreign aid regime during the Cold War[8]. I was introduced to this book as part of my training in international relations theory, where Lumsdaine features as one of the early proponents of the study of ideas as an alternative to sheer material interests. However, it is only now that I fully understand what the book was really about. In retrospect, the message was crystal clear, but that does not make it any less subversive. The central argument was that 'efforts to build a better world can effect significant change in international politics: vision, hope, commitment, conviction sometimes make a big difference'[9]. Does that hold true for our post-austerity, post-truth, post-internationalist times?

Lumsdaine's book is particularly powerful in that he took the most obviously interest-driven period of international politics – the Cold War – and demonstrated that security concerns and economic interests alone simply could not explain the rise of the foreign aid regime. He charted new analytical territory, challenging a bipolar conventional wisdom so familiar that it undermines any claim of originality from a Tania Li or a William Easterly:

> Critics on the left have assailed foreign aid as simply a tool of cold-war interests and as a way of promoting the destructive inroads of capitalism in the Third World. Critics on the right have assailed foreign aid as a boondoggle, an inappropriate use of tax dollars, an instrument that props up inefficient socialist regimes and encourages state planning, and the tool of self-serving bureaucrats[10].

Lumsdaine did not deny the roles that self-interest and diplomacy play, acknowledging that up to a third of all aid responds to security concerns, commercial strategy, and post-colonial relations. But while transient self-interest can easily justify ad hoc aid transfers, it cannot explain sustained commitments, much less their expansion over time. Instead, the aid system was born out of a very particular world view: 'an inclusive, humane internationalism, which perceived a responsibility on the part of the developed countries to help fight poverty in the less developed, and which conceived of the world as an interdependent whole whose problems were the concern of all peoples'[11]. This may sound terribly naïve to a twenty-first-century audience, but the humane internationalism that Lumsdaine wrote about was a foundational element of our modern liberal democracies, as expressed by Winston Churchill and Franklin D. Roosevelt in the Atlantic Charter.

The distance between those leaders and the current crop of nativists and isolationists is nowhere clearer than it is in foreign aid. Self-defeating donor politics are clearly an expression of a degrading commitment to internationalism. Sustainability is the key dilemma going forward. Is the moral vision that expanded the foreign aid regime gone? Can it survive without an equal commitment to domestic welfare states? Is the humane internationalism underpinning development assistance a relic of a more civilised age?

The world is now more interconnected than it ever was, and yet the core system of values that underpinned foreign aid has gone the way of embedded liberalism, the welfare state, and most of the Western post-World War II order[12]. Almost three decades since the end of the Cold War, the early optimism of multilateralism and human rights has been eroded by a string of failures that began in Rwanda in 1994 and reaches all the way to the intractable Syrian conflict. All we have to guide aid now is a group of seventeen SDGs that the entire international community has nominally agreed to pursue: a kitchen sink covering every conceivable aspect of liberal development[13]. Somehow Roosevelt's four freedoms – speech, worship, want, and fear – have become our 169 targets and 230 indicators. You would be hard pressed to find a more apt metaphor for the transition from a principled to a utilitarian vision of internationalism.

There is perhaps room for hope behind the scenes, in the small changes taking place within the aid community itself. The 2017 *World Development Report* is a strong statement in favour of understanding how power relations influence institutional trajectories and, through them, developmental outcomes[14]. It is also a welcome update of the 1997 *World Development Report* that brought institutional analysis into the development mainstream. DFID's new 'smart rules' are legitimating an entirely new generation of aid interventions more concerned with transformational change than mere accounting, empowering advisors to really engage with the politics of development in recipient countries. The adaptive development agenda is galvanising hundreds of practitioners and public servants around the world, who otherwise would have remained isolated and embattled. Donor politics may be the most noxious that we have probably seen, but that has not stopped challengers from launching agenda after agenda to make aid smarter, more flexible and adaptive, and better matched to political context. That may be an encouraging thought. Without visionary leaders who are unafraid to defend the value of humane internationalism, it is up to practitioners, scholars, consultants, students, and concerned citizens to voice, argue, advocate, lobby, and demand a new moral vision for foreign aid. It is certain to be an uphill struggle, but nothing that local reformers and aid innovators do not face on a daily basis.

In the meantime, challengers will continue to work, away from the limelight, in the cracks of the system, without hope of reward or recognition, just because of the values they hold. This leads me to one final point: the values of development reformers are not partisan, they are human. Individuals cannot exercise self-reliance and personal responsibility in a system that stifles expression and punishes dissent. Societies cannot exercise solidarity and equity in a system that the powerful can stack in their favour. The very human values we associate with donor countries are up for grabs in those developing countries with the weakest public institutions. That is why in the aid world one can easily find religious and civic organisations, businesses and public servants, and elite consultants and poor volunteers all working towards roughly the same end, no matter how uncertain, no matter how hard. This work would be a bit easier if citizens and taxpayers were willing to let go of familiar tropes, convenient fictions, and spurious moral calculations. For aid to continue buttressing reformers in the twenty-first century, our own lies at home need to give way to the messy truth about promoting development.

Notes

INTRODUCTION

1. Irish Aid, 'Audit report into Irish Aid misappropriated funds in Uganda – Department of Foreign Affairs and Trade', accessed 10 April 2017, www. dfa.ie/news-and-media/press-releases/press-release-archive/2012/ november/report-into-misappropriated-aid-funds-uganda/.
2. Aoife Barry, 'Irish Aid: Tánaiste "absolutely disgusted" after alleged Uganda aid fraud', accessed 10 April 2017, www.thejournal.ie/uganda -aid-funds-650192-Oct2012/.
3. 'Ugandan government returns misappropriated funds to Ireland', *BBC News*, 7 January 2013, www.bbc.co.uk/news/world-20935149.
4. Irish Aid, 'Uganda Country Strategy Paper 2016–2020' (Dublin: Irish Aid, 2016).
5. Daron Acemoglu and James A. Robinson, *Why Nations Fail: The Origins of Power, Prosperity, and Poverty* (London: Profile, 2012).
6. James Ferguson, *The Anti-Politics Machine: 'Development', Depoliticization, and Bureaucratic Power in Lesotho* (Minneapolis, MN: University of Minnesota Press, 1990); Tania Li, *The Will to Improve: Governmentality, Development, and the Practice of Politics* (Durham, NC: Duke University Press, 2007), www.loc.gov/catdir/toc/ ecip074/2006035585.html; William Easterly, *The Tyranny of Experts: Economists, Dictators, and the Forgotten Rights of the Poor* (New York: Basic Books, 2014).
7. Dambisa Moyo, *Dead Aid: Why Aid Is Not Working and How There Is Another Way for Africa* (London: Allen Lane, 2009).
8. Derek Fee, *How to Manage an Aid Exit Strategy: The Future of Development Aid* (London: Zed Books Ltd, 2012).
9. World Bank, *World Development Report 1997: The State in a Changing World* (New York: Oxford University Press, 1997).

10. David Hudson and Adriana Leftwich, 'From political economy to political analysis', Research Paper (Birmingham: Developmental Leadership Program, 2014).

11. Jonathan Fisher and Heather Marquette, 'Donors doing political economy analysis™: from process to product (and back again?)', Research Paper (Birmingham: Developmental Leadership Program, 2014).

12. Abdul-Gafaru Abdulai and Sam Hickey, 'The politics of development under competitive clientelism: insights from Ghana's education sector', *African Affairs* 115, no. 458 (1 January 2016): 44–72, doi:10.1093/afraf/adv071.

ONE

1. El País, 'Un ansia infinita de paz, el amor al bien y el mejoramiento social de los humildes', *EL PAÍS*, 16 April 2004, http://elpais.com/diario/2004/04/16/espana/1082066402_850215.html.

2. Ibid.

3. Jose Antonio Sanahuja, '¿Un nuevo ciclo en la política de Cooperación Española? Prestar atención a los actores y los procesos de toma de decisiones' (Madrid: FRIDE, 2009).

4. El País, 'Zapatero promete aumentar la ayuda al desarrollo hasta el 0,7% en ocho años', *EL PAÍS*, 9 February 2004, http://elpais.com/elpais/2004/02/09/actualidad/1076318220_850215.html.

5. Miguel Angel Moratinos, 'Comparecencia del Ministro de Asuntos Exteriores y Cooperación, Miguel Ángel Moratinos' (Madrid: Congreso de los Diputados, June 2004).

6. Jose Antonio Alonso, 'Cooperación Española: desafíos para una nueva legislatura', ICEI Paper (Madrid: Instituto Complutense de Estudios Internacionales, 2008).

7. Sanahuja, '¿Un nuevo ciclo en la política de Cooperación Española? Prestar atención a los actores y los procesos de toma de decisiones'.

8. Manuel de la Iglesia-Caruncho, 'The politics and policy of aid in Spain', IDS Research Report (Brighton: Institute of Development Studies, 2011).

9. David Halloran Lumsdaine, *Moral Vision in International Politics: The Foreign Aid Regime, 1949–1989* (Princeton, NJ: Princeton University Press, 1993).

10. Andreas Fuchs, Axel Dreher, and Peter Nunnenkamp, 'Determinants of donor generosity: a survey of the aid budget literature', *World Development* 56 (April 2014): 172–99, doi:10.1016/j.worlddev.2013.09.004.

11. J. P. Therien and A. Noel, 'Political parties and foreign aid', *American Political Science Review* (2000): 151–62.

12. Dustin Tingley, 'Donors and domestic politics: political influences on foreign aid effort', *The Quarterly Review of Economics and Finance* 50, no. 1 (February 2010): 40–9, doi:10.1016/j.qref.2009.10.003.

13. Rick Travis, 'Problems, politics, and policy streams: a reconsideration US foreign aid behavior toward Africa', *International Studies Quarterly* 54, no. 3 (1 September 2010): 797–821, doi:10.1111/j.1468-2478.2010.00610.x.

14. Pamela Paxton and Stephen Knack, 'Individual and country-level factors affecting support for foreign aid', *International Political Science Review* 33, no. 2 (1 March 2012): 171–92, doi:10.1177/0192512111406095.

15. Bruce Drake, 'Wide partisan gap exists over U.S. aid to world's needy', *Pew Research Center*, 13 March 2013, www.pewresearch.org/fact-tank/2013/03/13/wide-partisan-gap-exists-over-u-s-aid-to-worlds-needy/.

16. Bianca DiJulio and Jamie Firth, 'Data note: Americans' views on the U.S. role in global health', *The Henry J. Kaiser Family Foundation*, accessed 23 January 2015, http://kff.org/global-health-policy/poll-finding/data-note-americans-views-on-the-u-s-role-in-global-health/.

17. Eurobarometer, 'Europeans, development aid and the millennium development goals', Special Eurobarometer (Brussels: Eurobarometer, 2010).

18. Paul Collier, *The Bottom Billion: Why the Poorest Countries Are Failing and What Can Be Done About It* (Oxford: Oxford University Press, 2007): 183.

19. William Easterly, 'The cartel of good intentions: the problem of bureaucracy in foreign aid', *The Journal of Policy Reform* 5, no. 4 (1 December 2002): 223–50, doi:10.1080/1384128032000096823; William Easterly, *The White Man's Burden: Why the West's Efforts to Aid the Rest Have Done So Much Ill and So Little Good* (New York: Penguin Press, 2006).

20. By Priti Patel Secretary Of State For International Development, 'PRITI PATEL Says a Well-Financed Aid Budget Is Just a Means to an End', *Mail Online*, 13 September 2016, www.dailymail.co.uk/~/article-3788169/index.html.

21. By Brendan Carlin for *The Mail on Sunday*, 'MPs ignore petition calling for end to 0.7% foreign aid budget', *Mail Online*, 19 June 2016, www.dailymail.co.uk/news/article-3648701/MPs-ignore-petition -signed-230-000-readers-called-end-government-s-0-7-foreign-aid -budget.html.

22. Michael Rubin, '5 questions every presidential candidate should answer: foreign aid edition', 20 April 2015, www.aei.org/publication/ 5-questions-every-presidential-candidate-should-answer-foreign -aid/.

23. By Ian Birrell for *The Mail on Sunday*, 'SHAMED: foreign aid fat cats who built £1.4billion empire … with YOUR tax money', *Mail Online*, 23 May 2015, www.dailymail.co.uk/news/article-3094436/SHAMED -Foreign-aid-fat-cats-built-1-4billion-empire-tax-money.html.

24. Homi Kharas and Noam Unger, 'Set to lead again? New U.S. engagement on global development', *Brookings*, 28 September 2010, www .brookings.edu/opinions/set-to-lead-again-new-u-s-engagement-on -global-development/.

25. Josh Rogin, '165 House Republicans endorse defunding USAID', *Foreign Policy*, 20 January 2011, http://foreignpolicy.com/2011/ 01/20/165-house-republicans-endorse-defunding-usaid/.

26. Ibid.

27. Brian M. Riedl, 'How to cut $343 billion from the federal budget', The Heritage Foundation, 28 October 2010, www.heritage .org/budget-and-spending/report/how-cut-343-billion-the-federal -budget.

28. Lumsdaine, *Moral Vision in International Politics: The Foreign Aid Regime, 1949–1989*; Therien and Noel, 'Political parties and foreign aid'; A. Maurits van der Veen, *Ideas, Interests and Foreign Aid* (Cambridge: Cambridge University Press, 2011).

29. van der Veen, *Ideas, Interests and Foreign Aid*.

30. de la Iglesia-Caruncho, 'The politics and policy of aid in Spain', p. 43.

31. Ibid., p. 44.

32. Alonso, 'Cooperación Española: desafíos para una nueva legislatura'.

TWO

1. Condoleezza Rice, 'Campaign 2000: Promoting the National Interest', *Foreign Affairs* 79, no. 1 (January/February 2000): 44–62.

2. Carol Lancaster, *George Bush's Foreign Aid: Transformation or Chaos* (Washington, DC: Center for Global Development, 2008).

3. Ben Barber, 'Andrew Natsios: getting USAID on its feet', *Foreign Service Journal*, no. September 2002 (2002): 20–7.

4. Andrew Natsios, 'The clash of the counter-bureaucracy and development', Essay (Washington, DC: Center for Global Development, July 2010).

5. Ibid., p. 3.

6. Moyo, *Dead Aid*.

7. William Easterly, *The Elusive Quest for Growth: Economists' Adventures and Misadventures in the Tropics* (London: The MIT Press, 2001).

8. Easterly, *The White Man's Burden*.

9. Easterly, *The Tyranny of Experts*.

10. Nilima Gulrajani, 'Transcending the great foreign aid debate: managerialism, radicalism and the search for aid effectiveness', *Third World Quarterly* 32, no. 2 (1 March 2011): 199–216, doi:10.1080/01436597.2011.560465.

11. Jeffrey Sachs, *The End of Poverty: How We Can Make It Happen in Our Lifetime* (New York: Penguin, 2005).

12. Nina Munk, *The Idealist: Jeffrey Sachs and the Quest to End Poverty* (New York: Doubleday, 2013).

13. Collier, *The Bottom Billion*.

14. Pete Trolio, 'Inside the takedowns of AusAID and CIDA', *Devex* (19 January 2015), www.devex.com/news/inside-the-takedowns-of-ausaid-and-cida-85278.

15. Michelle Grattan, 'DFAT secretary's tough message about AusAID integration', *The Conversation*, 3 November 2013, http://theconversation.com/dfat-secretarys-tough-message-about-ausaid-integration-19799.

16. Department of Foreign Affairs and Trade, *The New Aid Paradigm*, 2014, www.youtube.com/watch?v=4rSxEj1dT6M.

17. DFID, 'Bilateral aid review technical report' (London: Department for International Development, 2011): 3.

18. Ibid.

19. Treasury Officer of Accounts, 'Regularity, propriety and value for money' (London: HM Treasury, 2004).

20. National Audit Office, 'Value for money', accessed 9 April 2017, www.nao.org.uk/successful-commissioning/general-principles/value-for-money/#notes.

21. DFID, 'DFID's approach to value for money (VfM)' (London: Department for International Development, July 2011).

22. DFID, 'How to note: country governance analysis. A DFID practice paper' (London: Department for International Development, February 2007).

23. DFID, 'How to note: operational plans' (London: Department for International Development, December 2010).

24. DFID, 'Sierra Leone operational plan 2011–2015' (London: Department for International Development, 2012).

25. DFID, 'How to note: writing a business case' (London: Department for International Development, December 2012).

26. Frank H. (Frank Hyneman) Knight, *Risk, Uncertainty and Profit* (Boston; New York: Houghton Mifflin Company, 1921), http://archive.org/details/riskuncertaintyp00knigrich.

27. Mark Blyth, *Great Transformations: Economic Ideas and Institutional Change in the Twentieth Century* (Cambridge: Cambridge University Press, 2002).

28. Pablo Yanguas, 'The role and responsibility of foreign aid in recipient political settlements', *Journal of International Development* 29, no. 2 (1 March 2017): 211–28, doi:10.1002/jid.3269.

29. F. M. Kamm, *Intricate Ethics : Rights, Responsibilities, and Permissible Harm: Rights, Responsibilities, and Permissible Harm* (New York: Oxford University Press, 2006).

THREE

1. David Lappia, 'Survey report: national perceptions and attitudes towards corruption in Sierra Leone' (Freetown: Department for International Development, 2000).

2. 'Sierra Leone's war against corruption', *New African* (January 1999).

3. The corrupt practices included in the Act were corrupt acquisition of wealth; soliciting or accepting an advantage; using influence for contracts; corrupting a public officer; soliciting or accepting advantage for a public officer; misappropriation of public funds or property; misappropriation of donor funds or property; impeding foreign investment; and corrupt transaction with agents.

4. Acemoglu and Robinson, *Why Nations Fail*.

5. Douglass C. North, *Structure and Change in Economic History* (New York: W. W. Norton, 1981); Douglass C. North and Barry R. Weingast, 'Constitutions and commitment: the evolution of institutions governing public choice in 17th century England', *Journal of Economic History* 49, no. 4 (1989): 803–32; Douglass C. North, John Joseph Wallis, and Barry R. Weingast, *Violence and Social Orders: A Conceptual Framework for Interpreting Recorded Human History*, 1st edn (Cambridge: Cambridge University Press, 2009).

6. Douglass C. North, *Institutions, Institutional Change and Economic Performance* (Cambridge: Cambridge University Press, 1990).

7. This definition of institutions is central to a school of thought commonly identified as 'new institutional economics'; it is challenged from various corners of sociology, geography, anthropology, history, and development studies. However, North's conception has found ample purchase in economics, political science, and mainstream development thinking, including the World Bank and DFID. It is also useful for my analytical purposes in this book, and that is why I use it.

8. Peter A. Hall and Rosemary C. R. Taylor, 'Political science and the three new institutionalisms', *Political Studies* 44, no. 5 (1 December 1996): 936–57.

9. Niccolò Machiavelli, *The Prince* (1513). Quentin Skinner and Russell Price, eds., Chapter 6 (Cambridge: Cambridge University Press, 1988)

10. Government of Sierra Leone, 'Anti-Corruption Commission annual report 2001' (2002): 3,4.

11. Ibid., p. 8.

12. 'Heading for the door', *Africa Confidential* (5 April 2002).

13. Government of Sierra Leone, 'Anti-Corruption Commission annual report 2002' (2003): 6, 7, 10.

14. International Crisis Group, 'Sierra Leone after elections: politics as usual?', *Africa Report* (12 July 2002): 16–17.

15. Ibid., p. 16.

16. Ibid., p. 17.

17. 'Kabbah's cabal', *Africa Confidential* (31 May 2002).

18. UNAMSIL, 'Twenty-fifth report of the Secretary-General on the United Nations mission in Sierra Leone, S/2005/273' (26 April 2005): 20.

19. 'Anti-corruption boss condemns MPs', *Concord Times* (7 April 2005).

20. Sierra Leone Parliament, 'Second public sitting of the Committee on Privileges held at Parliament Building, Tower Hill, on Wednesday 22nd June 2005' (22 June 2005).

21. International Crisis Group, 'Sierra Leone: the election opportunity', *Africa Report* (12 July 2007): n. 61.

22. 'President Kabbah's "sack" letter to anti corruption commissioner, Val Collier', *Concord Times* (17 November 2005).

23. International Crisis Group, 'Sierra Leone: the election opportunity', p. 9.

24. Gretchen Helmke and Steven Levitsky, 'Informal institutions and comparative politics: a research agenda', *Perspectives on Politics* 2, no. 4 (2004): 725–40, doi:10.1017/S1537592704040472.

25. Jean-François Médard, 'The underdeveloped state in tropical Africa: political clientelism or neo-patrimonialism?', in *Private Patronage and Public Power: Political Clientelism in the Modern State*, ed. Christopher Clapham (New York: St. Martin's Press, 1982); Thomas M. Callaghy, *The State-Society Struggle: Zaire in Comparative Perspective* (New York: Columbia University Press, 1984); Nicolas van de Walle, *African Economies and the Politics of Permanent Crisis, 1979–1999* (Cambridge: Cambridge University Press, 2001).

26. Lant Pritchett, Michael Woolcock, and Matt Andrews, 'Looking like a state: techniques of persistent failure in state capability for implementation', *Journal of Development Studies* 49, no. 1 (2013): 1–18.

27. William Reno, *Corruption and State Politics in Sierra Leone* (Cambridge: Cambridge University Press, 1995).

28. Lansana Gberie, *A Dirty War in West Africa: The RUF and the Destruction of Sierra Leone* (Bloomington: Indiana University Press, 2005).

29. Max Weber, *Economy and Society: An Outline of Interpretive Sociology* (Berkeley, CA: University of California Press, 1978): 320.

30. North, *Institutions, Institutional Change and Economic Performance*, p. 91.

31. Barbara Geddes, *Politician's Dilemma: Building State Capacity in Latin America* (Berkeley, CA: California University Press, 1994); Anne Mette Kjaer, '"Old brooms can sweep too!" An overview of rulers and public sector reforms in Uganda, Tanzania and Kenya', *Journal of Modern African Studies* 42, no. 3 (2004): 389–413.

32. Pierre Englebert and Denis M. Tull, 'Postconflict reconstruction in Africa: flawed ideas about failed states', *International Security* 32, no. 4 (1 April 2008): 106–39.

33. Charles Tilly and Sidney Tarrow, *Contentious Politics* (New York: Oxford University Press, 2006); Doug McAdam, Sidney Tarrow, and Charles Tilly, *Dynamics of Contention* (Cambridge: Cambridge University Press, 2001).

34. Neil Fligstein and Doug McAdam, *A Theory of Fields* (Oxford: Oxford University Press, 2012).

35. John W. Kingdon, *Agendas, Alternatives, and Public Policies*, 2nd edn (New York: Harper Collins, 1995).

36. Government of Sierra Leone, 'Anti-Corruption Commission annual report 2002'.

37. DFID and Government of Sierra Leone, 'A long-term partnership for development between the Government of the United Kingdom of Great Britain and Northern Ireland and the Government of the Republic of Sierra Leone (Memorandum of Understanding)' (17 November 2002).

38. DFID, 'Annual review of DFID support to the Anti-Corruption Commission phase 2 in Sierra Leone' (25 January 2007).

39. Ibid., p. 29.

40. With no personal stake in the success of the British intervention in Sierra Leone, Benn had written a letter to Kabbah in March 2005 complaining about the government's failure to address the worsening corruption; Kabbah in turn had replied with a twenty-six-page letter complaining about DFID's behaviour in Sierra Leone.

41. DFID, 'EV 690 country programme evaluation: Sierra Leone' (September 2008).

42. 'Britain blacklists Kabbah, SLPP gov't for corruption', *Concord Times* (18 April 2007).

43. 'The first-round fight', *Africa Confidential* (3 August 2007).

44. 'Doing good, not doing well', *Africa Confidential* (24 August 2007).

45. Jimmy D. Kandeh, 'Rogue incumbents, donor assistance and Sierra Leone's second post-conflict elections of 2007', *Journal of Modern African Studies* 46, no. 4 (11 November 2008): 603, doi:10.1017/S0022278X08003509.

46. 'A clean sweep, maybe', *Africa Confidential* (21 September 2007).

47. Government of Sierra Leone, 'Anti-Corruption Commission annual report 2007' (2008): 5–6.
48. International Crisis Group, 'Sierra Leone: a new era of reform', *Africa Report* (31 July 2008): 18.
49. 'Peace and the looming crisis', *Africa Confidential* (20 February 2009).
50. UNIOSIL, 'Sixth report of the Secretary-General on the United Nations Integrated Office in Sierra Leone, S/2008/281' (29 April 2008): para. 37.
51. 'Peace and the looming crisis'.
52. 'We go no tire', *Africa Confidential* (20 November 2009); Government of Sierra Leone, 'Anti-Corruption Commission annual report 2009' (2010).
53. UNIPSIL, 'Fourth report of the Secretary-General on the United Nations Integrated Peacebuilding Office in Sierra Leone, S/2010/135' (15 March 2010): para. 61.
54. Government of Sierra Leone, 'Anti-Corruption Commission annual report 2010' (2011).
55. Government of Sierra Leone, 'National public perception survey on corruption (draft)' (April 2010).
56. 'With a little help from his friends', *Africa Confidential* (14 December 2007).
57. 'The new man picks his team', *Africa Confidential* (19 October 2007); 'Shake-up in Freetown', *Africa Confidential* (5 March 2009); 'More power for Freetown', *Africa Confidential* (9 October 2009).
58. UNIOSIL, 'Fifth report of the Secretary-General on the United Nations Integrated Office in Sierra Leone, S/2007/704' (4 December 2007): para. 15.
59. Government of Sierra Leone, 'Anti-Corruption Commission annual report 2009', p. 7.

FOUR

1. European Commission, 'Liberia Country Strategy Paper and National Indicative Program (period 2004–2007)' (2004): 7.
2. Government of Liberia, 'Republic of Liberia Truth and Reconciliation Commission, volume II: consolidated final report' (30 June 2009): 296–97.
3. US Department of State, 'Liberia 2003', Country Reports on Human Rights Practices, Bureau of Democracy, Human Rights, and Labor (25 February 2004).

4. United Nations and World Bank, 'Joint Needs Assessment – National Transitional Government of Liberia' (February 2004): 12.

5. Ibid., p. 24.

6. Joan M. Nelson, ed., *Economic Crisis and Policy Choice: The Politics of Adjustment in the Third World* (Princeton, NJ: Princeton University Press, 1990); Dani Rodrik, 'How should structural adjustment programs be designed?', *World Development* 18, no. 7 (July 1990): 933–47, doi:10.1016/0305-750X(90)90077-B; Thomas M. Callaghy and John Ravenhill, eds., *Hemmed In: Responses to Africa's Economic Decline* (New York: Columbia University Press, 1993); Tony Killick, 'Principals, agents and the failings of conditionality', *Journal of International Development* 2, no. 4 (1997): 483–95; World Bank, *Assessing Aid: What Works, What Doesn't, and Why* (Washington, DC: Oxford University Press, 1998); Axel Dreher, 'IMF conditionality: theory and evidence', *Public Choice* 141, no. 1–2 (4 August 2009): 233–67, doi:10.1007/s11127-009-9486-z; Joseph Wright and Matthew Winters, 'The politics of effective foreign aid', *Annual Review of Political Science* 13 (2010): 61–80.

7. Callaghy and Ravenhill, *Hemmed In*.

8. Jeffrey Herbst, 'The structural adjustment of politics in Africa', *World Development* 18, no. 7 (1990): 948–58; David Dollar and Jakob Svensson, 'What explains the success or failure of structural adjustment programmes?', *The Economic Journal* 110, no. 466 (2000): 894–917, doi:10.1111/1468-0297.00569; van de Walle, *African Economies and the Politics of Permanent Crisis, 1979–1999*; Joseph Wright, 'Aid effectiveness and the politics of personalism', *Comparative Political Studies* 43, no. 6 (24 February 2010): 735–62, doi:10.1177/0010414009358674.

9. OECD, 'Paris Declaration on Aid Effectiveness' (Paris: OECD Publishing, 2 March 2005).

10. Ibid., para. 16.

11. Simon Chesterman, 'Ownership in theory and in practice: transfer of authority in UN statebuilding operations', *Journal of Intervention and Statebuilding* 1, no. 1 (2007): 3–26, doi:10.1080/17502970601075873.

12. World Bank, 'Reforming public institutions and strengthening governance – a World Bank strategy' (September 2000): 11.

13. Stephen D. Krasner, 'Sharing sovereignty: new institutions for collapsed and failing states', *International Security* 29, no. 2 (2004): 98.

14. National Transitional Government of Liberia, 'Results-Focused Transitional Framework (RFTF)' (7 January 2004).
15. European Commission, 'Liberia Country Strategy Paper and National Indicative Program (period 2004–2007)' (2004): 8, 14.
16. Adedeji Ebo, 'The challenges and opportunities of security sector reform in post-conflict Liberia', Occasional Paper (Geneva: Geneva Centre for the Democratic Control of Armed Forces (DCAF), 2005): 25.
17. Government of Liberia, 'National anti-corruption strategy' (December 2006): 7.
18. US Department of State, 'Liberia 2005', Country Reports on Human Rights Practices, Bureau of Democracy, Human Rights, and Labor (8 March 2006).
19. Government of Liberia, 'Governance and Economic Management Assistance Program' (2005): 13.
20. Renata Dwan and Laura Bailey, 'Liberia's Governance and Economic Management Assistance Program (GEMAP) – a joint review by the Department of Peacekeeping Operations' Peacekeeping Best Practices Section and the World Bank's Fragile States Group' (New York; Washington, DC: United Nations and World Bank, May 2006): 10.
21. Ibid., pp. 13–14.
22. USAID, 'USAID activities under GEMAP in Liberia', Impact Assessment Report (July 2008): 6.
23. European Commission, 'Draft annual report 2007 Liberia' (September 2008).
24. Government of Liberia, 'Governance and Economic Management Assistance Program', pp. 6, 16.
25. Government of Liberia, 'Mid-term evaluation of the Governance and Economic Management Assistance Program (GEMAP)' (15 August 2008): 16.
26. US Department of State, 'Liberia 2006', Country Reports on Human Rights Practices, Bureau of Democracy, Human Rights, and Labor (6 March 2007).
27. USAID, 'USAID activities under GEMAP in Liberia', Impact Assessment Report, p. 10.
28. USAID, 'Governance and Economic Management Assistance Program (GEMAP) – IBI annual report to USAID' (October 2009): 39.
29. USAID, 'USAID activities under GEMAP in Liberia', Impact Assessment Report, p. 19.

30. Government of Liberia, 'Mid-term evaluation of the Governance and Economic Management Assistance Program (GEMAP)', p. 18.

31. Louise Andersen, 'Outsiders inside the state: post-conflict Liberia between trusteeship and partnership', *Journal of Intervention and Statebuilding* 4, no. 2 (June 2010): 131, doi:10.1080/17502970903533660.

32. USAID, 'Governance and Economic Management Assistance Program (GEMAP) – IBI annual report to USAID', p. 40.

33. USAID, 'Final evaluation of USAID GEMAP activities – Sibley International LLC' (June 2010): 28.

34. Ibid., p. 30.

35. Jean-Jacques Laffont and David Martimort, *The Theory of Incentives: The Principal-Agent Model* (Princeton, NJ: Princeton University Press, 2002).

36. Pablo Yanguas, 'Leader, protester, enabler, spoiler: aid strategies and donor politics in institutional assistance', *Development Policy Review* 32, no. 3 (1 May 2014): 299–312.

37. Deborah Bräutigam, 'Aid dependence and governance' (Stockholm: Expert Group on Development Issues, 2000); Deborah Bräutigam and Stephen Knack, 'Foreign aid, institutions, and governance in Sub-Saharan Africa', *Economic Development and Cultural Change* 52, no. 2 (2004): 255–85; Todd Moss, Gunilla Pettersson, and Nicolas van de Walle, 'An aid-institutions paradox? A review essay on aid dependency and state building in Sub-Saharan Africa', Working Paper 74 (Washington, DC: Center for Global Development, 2006).

38. Nicolas van de Walle, *Overcoming Stagnation in Aid-Dependent Countries* (Washington, DC: Center for Global Development, 2005): 47; Stephen Knack and Aminur Rahman, 'Donor fragmentation and bureaucratic quality in aid recipients', *Journal of Development Economics* 83, no. 1 (2007): 177.

39. Mancur Olson, *The Logic of Collective Action; Public Goods and the Theory of Groups*, Harvard Economic Studies, Vol. 124 (Cambridge, MA: Harvard University Press, 1965).

40. Dwan and Bailey, 'Liberia's Governance and Economic Management Assistance Program (GEMAP) – a joint review by the Department of Peacekeeping Operations' Peacekeeping Best Practices Section and the World Bank's Fragile States Group', p. 18.

41. Government of Liberia, 'General Auditing Commission: a blueprint for accountability, transparency, and good governance' (January 2007).
42. Ibid., p. 5.
43. Government of Liberia, 'Mid-term evaluation of the Governance and Economic Management Assistance Program (GEMAP)', pp. 18–19.
44. European Commission, 'Design and formulation mission to EC support to strengthening the General Auditing Commission (GAC) of Liberia', Design Study (Monrovia: European Commission, January 2010): 10–11.
45. European Commission, 'Draft annual report 2007 Liberia', p. 6.
46. 'Rumours and plots: President Johnson-Sirleaf's enemies have come out in the open with a raft of allegations and threats of military action', *Africa Confidential* (3 August 2007).
47. Government of Liberia, 'Mid-term evaluation of the Governance and Economic Management Assistance Program (GEMAP)', pp. 53–4.
48. 'Honesty – not the easiest policy', *Africa Confidential* (22 July 2011).
49. 'Need to review Auditor General's tenure', *The Analyst* (27 April 2011).
50. 'New AG indicts John Morlu', *The New Dawn* (5 September 2011).
51. Moses D. Sandy, 'The rise and fall of Robert Kilby', *Front Page Africa Online* (18 July 2013).
52. Ibid.
53. Government of Liberia, 'General Auditing Commission annual report 2013' (Monrovia: General Auditing Commission, 2014): 5.
54. Government of Liberia, 'General Auditing Commission annual report 2014' (Monrovia: General Auditing Commission, 2015): 5.

FIVE

1. Economic Commission for Latin America and the Caribbean, 'Honduras: assessment of the damage caused by Hurricane Mitch, 1998' (New York: United Nations, 1999).
2. Government of Honduras, 'Plan maestro para la reconstruccion y transformacion nacional' (Tegucigalpa: Government of Honduras, 1999).
3. Joshua Lichtenstein, 'After Hurricane Mitch: United States Agency for International Development Reconstruction and the Stockholm Principles' (Boston, MA: Oxfam America, 2001).

4. Thad Dunning, 'Conditioning the effects of aid: Cold War politics, donor credibility, and democracy in Africa', *International Organization* 58, no. 2 (2004): 409–23.

5. Alberto Alesina and David Dollar, 'Who gives foreign aid to whom and why?', *Journal of Economic Growth* 5, no. 1 (1 March 2000): 33–63, doi:10.1023/A:1009874203400.

6. Eric Neumayer, 'The determinants of aid allocation by regional multilateral development banks and United Nations agencies', *International Studies Quarterly* 47, no. 1 (2003): 101–22.

7. Callaghy and Ravenhill, *Hemmed In*; van de Walle, *African Economies and the Politics of Permanent Crisis, 1979–1999*.

8. World Bank, *World Development Report 1997: The State in a Changing World*; World Bank, *World Development Report 2002: Building Institutions for Markets* (Washington, DC: World Bank, 2002); World Bank, *World Development Report 2003: Sustainable Development in a Dynamic World* (Washington, DC: World Bank, 2003); World Bank, *World Development Report 2004: Making Services Work for Poor People* (Washington, DC: World Bank, 2004).

9. Merilee S. Grindle, 'Good enough governance: poverty reduction and reform in developing countries', *Governance* 17, no. 4 (2004): 525–48.

10. Englebert and Tull, 'Postconflict reconstruction in Africa'.

11. Government of Honduras, 'Estrategia para la reduccion de la pobreza: un compromiso con todos' (Tegucigalpa: Government of Honduras, 2001).

12. Sarah Hunt, 'Breaking the rules, breaking the game: external ideas, politics and inclusive development in Honduras', ESID Working Paper 52 (Manchester: Effective States and Inclusive Development Research Centre, 2015).

13. Lichtenstein, 'After Hurricane Mitch: United States Agency for International Development Reconstruction and the Stockholm Principles', p. 15.

14. Ibid., p. 31.

15. Government of Honduras, 'Estrategia para la reduccion de la pobreza: un compromiso con todos'.

16. Government of Honduras, 'Informe final de la reconstruccion nacional: logros y lecciones del proceso' (Tegucigalpa: Government of Honduras, 2003): 56–7.

17. Government of Honduras, 'Honduras poverty reduction strategy: progress report' (Tegucigalpa: Government of Honduras, 2003): 7.
18. Ibid., p. 5.
19. Government of Honduras, 'Poverty reduction strategy: progress report 2004' (Tegucigalpa: Government of Honduras, 2005).
20. SIDA, 'Honduras: presupuestar la ERP' (The Hague: Institute of Social Studies, 2005): 32; SIDA, 'Honduras: ¿qué pasó con la ERP?' (The Hague: Institute of Social Studies, 2007): 16.
21. Clayton M. Cunha Filho, André Luiz Coelho, and Fidel I. Pérez Flores, 'A right-to-left policy switch? An analysis of the Honduran case under Manuel Zelaya', *International Political Science Review* (4 February 2013), doi:10.1177/0192512112468918.
22. Sarah Hunt, 'Honduras PRSP update July 2006' (Tegucigalpa: Trocaire, 2006).
23. SIDA, 'Honduras: ¿qué pasó con la ERP?', p. 16.
24. SIDA, 'Honduras: ¿qué pasó con la ERP?'
25. John M. Carey, 'The reelection debate in Latin America', *Latin American Politics and Society* 45, no. 1 (1 April 2003): 119–33, doi:10.1111/j.1548-2456.2003.tb00234.x; Daniel N. Posner and Daniel J. Young, 'The institutionalization of political power in Africa', *Journal of Democracy* 18, no. 3 (31 July 2007): 126–40, doi:10.1353/jod.2007.0053.
26. For a thorough account of the events leading to the crisis, see Honduran Truth and Reconciliation Commission, 'Para que los hechos no se repitan: informe de la comision de la verdad y la reconciliacion' (Tegucigalpa: Honduran Truth and Reconciliation Commission, 2011).
27. Jeremy Gould, ed., *The New Conditionality: The Politics of Poverty Reduction Strategies* (London; New York: Zed Books Ltd, 2005).
28. Yanguas, 'The role and responsibility of foreign aid in recipient political settlements'.
29. Tilly and Tarrow, *Contentious Politics*.
30. Government of Honduras, 'Declaración conjunta del gobierno de honduras con el grupo de cooperants G-16' (Tegucigalpa: Government of Honduras, 2012).

SIX

1. Peter M. Haas, 'Introduction: epistemic communities and international policy coordination', *International Organization* 46, no. 1 (1992): 1–35.

2. Thomas Carothers and Diane de Gramont, *Development Aid Confronts Politics: The Almost Revolution* (Washington, DC: Carnegie Endowment for International Peace, 2013).

3. DFID, 'Drivers of change public information note' (London: Department for International Development, September 2004).

4. Tom Dahl-Østergaard *et al*, 'Lessons learned on the use of power and drivers of change analyses in development co-operation' (Paris: OECD, 20 September 2005): 4.

5. DFID, 'Briefing: using drivers of change to improve aid effectiveness. A DFID practice paper' (London: Department for International Development, November 2005): 2.

6. Adrian Leftwich, 'From drivers of change to the politics of development: refining the analytical framework to understand the politics of the places where we work'. Note of Guidance for DFID Offices (London: Department for International Development, 6 February 2007).

7. DFID, 'Political economy analysis how to note' (London: Department for International Development, July 2009).

8. Nick Manning and Laura Bureš, 'Institutional and governance reviews' (Washington, DC: World Bank, 2001): 1.

9. Dahl-Østergaard *et al*, 'Lessons learned on the use of power and drivers of change analyses in development co-operation', p. 17.

10. Social Development Department, 'Tools for institutional, political, and social analysis of policy reform: a sourcebook for development practitioners' (Washington, DC: World Bank, 2007); Social Development Department, 'The political economy of policy reform: issues and implications for policy dialogue and development operations' (Washington, DC: World Bank, November 2008).

11. Verena Fritz, Kai Kaiser, and Brian Levy, 'Problem-driven governance and political economy analysis: good practice framework' (Washington, DC: World Bank, September 2009).

12. Sue Unsworth and Conflict Research Unit, 'Framework for Strategic Governance and Corruption Analysis (SGACA): designing strategic responses towards good governance' (The Hague: Clingendael Institute, Ministry of Foreign Affairs, 2008); Wil Hout and Lydeke Schakel, 'SGACA: The rise and paradoxical demise of a political-economy instrument', *Development Policy Review* 32, no. 5 (1 September 2014): 611–30, doi:10.1111/dpr.12075.

234 NOTES

13. SIDA, 'Power analysis' (Stockholm: SIDA, 2006).

14. Fisher and Marquette, 'Donors doing political economy analysis™: from process to product (and back again?)'; Pablo Yanguas, 'Making political analysis useful: adjusting and scaling', Briefing Paper (Manchester: Effective States and Inclusive Development Research Centre, 2015); David Hudson, Heather Marquette, and Sam Waldock, 'Everyday political analysis', Note (Birmingham: Developmental Leadership Program, 2016).

15. Laura Routley and David Hulme, 'Donors, development agencies and the use of political economic analysis: getting to grips with the politics of development?', ESID Working Paper (Manchester: Effective States and Inclusive Development Research Centre, 2013).

16. GPF Secretariat, 'Governance Partnership Facility: program document (P111816)' (Washington, DC: World Bank, 2008): 3.

17. Ibid., 6.

18. GPF Secretariat, 'Governance Partnership Facility: interim report November 2008–April 2009' (Washington, DC: World Bank, 2009).

19. Fritz, Kaiser, and Levy, 'Problem-driven governance and political economy analysis: good practice framework'.

20. World Bank, 'World Bank country-level engagement on governance and anticorruption: an evaluation of the 2007 strategy and implementation plan' (Washington, DC: World Bank, 2011): 42.

21. Ibid., p. 83.

22. World Bank, 'Strengthening governance: tackling corruption. The World Bank Group's updated strategy and implementation plan' (Washington, DC: World Bank, 6 March 2012): 56.

23. World Bank, 'World Bank country-level engagement on governance and anticorruption: an evaluation of the 2007 strategy and implementation plan', p. 86.

24. Pablo Yanguas and David Hulme, 'Barriers to political analysis in aid bureaucracies: from principle to practice in DFID and the World Bank', *World Development* 74 (October 2015): 209–19, doi:10.1016/j.worlddev.2015.05.009.

25. Sue Unsworth, 'What's politics got to do with it?: Why donors find it so hard to come to terms with politics, and why this matters', *Journal of International Development* 21, no. 6 (2009): 883–94; James Copestake and Richard Williams, 'The evolving art of

political economy analysis: unlocking its practical potential through a more interactive approach', Development Futures Paper (Oxford: Oxford Policy Management, 2012); Wil Hout, 'The anti-politics of development: donor agencies and the political economy of governance', *Third World Quarterly* 33, no. 3 (2012): 405–22; Fisher and Marquette, 'Donors doing political economy analysis™: from process to product (and back again?)'.

26. World Bank, 'World Bank country-level engagement on governance and anticorruption: an evaluation of the 2007 strategy and implementation plan', p. 85.

27. Dahl-Østergaard *et al*, 'Lessons learned on the use of power and drivers of change analyses in development co-operation', p. 19.

28. Ibid., p. 26.

29. World Bank, 'World Bank country-level engagement on governance and anticorruption: an evaluation of the 2007 strategy and implementation plan', p. 85.

30. Stephan Klingebiel and Heiner Janus, 'Results-based aid: potential and limits of an innovative modality in development cooperation', SSRN Scholarly Paper (Rochester, NY: Social Science Research Network, 12 May 2014), https://papers.ssrn.com/abstract=2436625.

31. Nancy Birdsall *et al*, *Cash on Delivery: A New Approach to Foreign Aid* (Washington, DC: CGD Books, 2012).

32. Heidi Tavakoli *et al*, 'Unblocking results: using aid to address governance constraints in public service delivery' (London: Centre for Aid & Public Expenditure/Overseas Development Institute, May 2013), www.odi.org.uk/sites/odi.org.uk/files/odi-assets/publications-opinion-files/8409.pdf.

33. Pablo Yanguas and Badru Bukenya, '"New" approaches confront "old" challenges in African public sector reform', *Third World Quarterly* 37, no. 1 (2016): 6–7, doi:10.1080/01436597.2015.1086635.

34. Matt Andrews, *The Limits of Institutional Reform in Development: Changing Rules for Realistic Solutions* (Cambridge: Cambridge University Press, 2013).

35. Leni Wild *et al*, 'Adapting development: improving services to the poor' (London: Overseas Development Institute, 2015).

36. Matt Andrews, Lant Pritchett, and Michael Woolcock, *Building State Capability: Evidence, Analysis, Action* (Oxford; New York: Oxford University Press, 2017).

37. Leni Wild and Marta Foresti, 'Putting politics into practice: aiming for more politically informed aid programming', *Developing Alternatives* 14, no. 1 (2011): 18–23; Alina Rocha Menocal, 'Getting real about politics: from thinking politically to working differently' (London: Overseas Development Institute, March 2014); David Booth and Sue Unsworth, 'Politically smart, locally led development' (London: Overseas Development Institute, September 2014).

38. David Booth, Daniel Harris, and Leni Wild, 'From political economy analysis to doing development differently: a learning experience' (London: Overseas Development Institute, 2016).

39. Haas, 'Introduction', p. 3.

40. Hudson and Leftwich, 'From political economy to political analysis'.

41. Booth and Unsworth, 'Politically smart, locally led development'; Niheer Dasandi, Heather Marquette, and Mark Robinson, 'Thinking and working politically: from theory building to building an evidence base', Research Paper (Birmingham: Developmental Leadership Program, 2016).

42. Kathy Bain, David Booth, and Leni Wild, 'Doing Development Differently at the World Bank: updating the plumbing to fit the architecture' (London: Overseas Development Institute, 2016).

SEVEN

1. Carol Lancaster, *Foreign Aid: Diplomacy, Development, Domestic Politics* (Chicago, IL: University of Chicago Press, 2008); van der Veen, *Ideas, Interests and Foreign Aid.*

2. Stephen Browne, *Aid and Influence: Do Donors Help or Hinder?* (Abingdon: Taylor & Francis, 2012); Easterly, *The White Man's Burden*; Lindsay Whitfield, *The Politics of Aid : African Strategies for Dealing with Donors* (Oxford: Oxford University Press, 2008); Moyo, *Dead Aid*; Jonathan Glennie, *The Trouble with Aid: Why Less Could Mean More for Africa* (London: Zed Books Ltd, 2010).

3. Robert Calderisi, *The Trouble with Africa: Why Foreign Aid Isn't Working* (New York: St. Martin's Press, 2006).

4. Callaghy and Ravenhill, *Hemmed In*; van de Walle, *African Economies and the Politics of Permanent Crisis, 1979–1999.*

5. Roger Riddell, *Does Foreign Aid Really Work?* (Oxford; New York: Oxford University Press, 2007); George Mavrotas, *Foreign Aid for Development: Issues, Challenges, and the New Agenda* (Oxford: Oxford University Press, 2010).

6. Abhijit V. Banerjee, *Making Aid Work* (Cambridge, MA: The MIT Press, 2007); William Easterly, *Reinventing Foreign Aid* (Cambridge, MA: The MIT Press, 2008).

7. Bertin Martens, *The Institutional Economics of Foreign Aid* (Cambridge: Cambridge University Press, 2002).

8. Wild *et al*, 'Adapting development: improving services to the poor'.

9. Paul DiMaggio and Walter W. Powell, 'The iron cage revisited: institutional isomorphism and collective rationality in organizational fields', *American Sociological Review* 48, no. 2 (1 April 1983): 147–60; W. Richard Scott, *Institutions and Organizations: Ideas and Interests*, 3rd edn. (London: SAGE, 2008).

10. Fligstein and McAdam, *A Theory of Fields*.

11. Ibid.

12. North, *Institutions, Institutional Change and Economic Performance*.

13. Kingdon, *Agendas, Alternatives, and Public Policies*; Neil Fligstein, 'Social skill and the theory of fields', *Sociological Theory* 19, no. 2 (2001): 105–25, doi:10.1111/0735-2751.00132.

14. I borrow these terms and much on what follows from the literature on contentious politics, e.g., Tilly and Tarrow, *Contentious Politics*.

15. Sam Hickey, 'Beyond the poverty agenda? Insights from the new politics of development in Uganda', *World Development* 43 (March 2013): 194–206.

16. McAdam, Tarrow, and Tilly, *Dynamics of Contention*; Tilly and Tarrow, *Contentious Politics*; Sidney Tarrow, *Power in Movement: Social Movements and Contentious Politics*, 3rd edn (Cambridge; New York: Cambridge University Press, 2011).

17. Political scientists would call such an approach 'process tracing'. See Alexander L. George and Andrew Bennett, *Case Studies and Theory Development in the Social Sciences* (London: The MIT Press, 2004); Andrew Bennett and Colin Elman, 'Qualitative research: recent developments in case study methods', *Annual Review of Political Science* 9, no. 1 (2006): 455–76, doi:10.1146/annurev.polisci.8.082103.104918.

18. Hout, 'The anti-politics of development'; Hout and Schakel, 'SGACA'; Yanguas and Hulme, 'Barriers to political analysis in aid bureaucracies'.

19. Bain, Booth, and Wild, 'Doing Development Differently at the World Bank: updating the plumbing to fit the architecture'.

20. Rudra Sil and Peter J. Katzenstein, 'Analytic eclecticism in the study of world politics: reconfiguring problems and mechanisms across research traditions', *Perspectives on Politics* 8, no. 2 (June 2010): 411–31, doi:10.1017/S1537592710001179; Rudra Sil and Peter J. Katzenstein, *Beyond Paradigms: Analytic Eclecticism in the Study of World Politics* (New York: Palgrave Macmillan, 2011), https://he.palgrave.com/page/detail/Beyond-Paradigms/?K=9780230207950.

21. In Patrick Thaddeus Jackson, *The Conduct of Inquiry in International Relations: Philosophy of Science and Its Implications for the Study of World Politics* (London; New York: Routledge, 2011): 143.

22. Daron Acemoglu and James C. Robinson, *Economic Origins of Dictatorship and Democracy* (Cambridge; New York: Cambridge University Press, 2006).

23. Li, *The Will to Improve*.

24. Thomas S. Kuhn, *The Structure of Scientific Revolutions* (Chicago, IL: University of Chicago Press, 1966).

CONCLUSION

1. Armando Barrientos and Juan Miguel Villa, 'Evaluating antipoverty transfer programmes in Latin America and Sub-Saharan Africa. Better policies? Better politics?', *Journal of Globalization and Development* 6, no. 1 (2015): 147–79, doi:10.1515/jgd-2014-0006; Tom Lavers and Sam Hickey, 'Investigating the political economy of social protection expansion in Africa: at the intersection of transnational ideas and domestic politics' (2015), https://papers.ssrn.com/sol3/papers.

2. Sam Hickey *et al*, 'The political settlement and oil in Uganda', ESID Working Paper (Manchester: Social Science Research Network, 31 March 2015), http://papers.ssrn.com/abstract=2587845.

3. Kamm, *Intricate Ethics*.

4. Yanguas, 'The role and responsibility of foreign aid in recipient political settlements'.

5. Onora O'Neill, 'Global justice: whose obligations?', in *The Ethics of Assistance: Morality and the Distant Needy*, by Deen K. Chatterjee (Cambridge: Cambridge University Press, 2004): 245.

6. Kamm, *Intricate Ethics*, p. 11.

7. Yanguas, 'The role and responsibility of foreign aid in recipient political settlements'.

8. Lumsdaine, *Moral Vision in International Politics: The Foreign Aid Regime, 1949–1989*.

9. Ibid., p. 5.

10. Ibid., p. 31.

11. Ibid., p. 32.

12. Blyth, *Great Transformations*.

13. United Nations, 'Transforming our world: the 2030 agenda for sustainable development' (New York: United Nations, 2015).

14. World Bank, *World Development Report 2017: Governance and the Law* (Washington, DC: World Bank Publications, 2017).

Bibliography

Abdulai, Abdul-Gafaru, and Sam Hickey. 'The politics of development under competitive clientelism: insights from Ghana's education sector'. *African Affairs* 115, no. 458 (1 January 2016): 44–72, doi:10.1093/afraf/adv071.

Acemoglu, Daron, and James A. Robinson. *Economic Origins of Dictatorship and Democracy*. Cambridge; New York: Cambridge University Press, 2006.

Acemoglu, Daron, and James A. Robinson. *Why Nations Fail: The Origins of Power, Prosperity, and Poverty*. London: Profile, 2012.

Africa Confidential. 'A clean sweep, maybe', 21 September 2007.

Africa Confidential. 'Doing good, not doing well', 24 August 2007.

Africa Confidential. 'Heading for the door', 5 April 2002.

Africa Confidential. 'Honesty – not the easiest policy', 22 July 2011.

Africa Confidential. 'Kabbah's cabal', 31 May 2002.

Africa Confidential. 'More power for Freetown', 9 October 2009.

Africa Confidential. 'Peace and the looming crisis', 20 February 2009.

Africa Confidential. 'Rumours and plots: President Johnson-Sirleaf's enemies have come out in the open with a raft of allegations and threats of military action', 3 August 2007.

Africa Confidential. 'Shake-up in Freetown', 5 March 2009.

Africa Confidential. 'The first-round fight', 3 August 2007.

Africa Confidential. 'The new man picks his team', 19 October 2007.

Africa Confidential. 'We Go No Tire', 20 November 2009.

Africa Confidential. 'With a little help from his friends', 14 December 2007.

Alesina, Alberto, and David Dollar. 'Who gives foreign aid to whom and why?' *Journal of Economic Growth* 5, no. 1 (1 March 2000): 33–63, doi:10.1023/A:1009874203400.

Alonso, Jose Antonio. 'Cooperación Española: desafíos para una nueva legislatura'. ICEI Paper. Madrid: Instituto Complutense de Estudios Internacionales, 2008.

The Analyst. 'Need to review Auditor General's tenure', 27 April 2011.

Andersen, Louise. 'Outsiders inside the state: post-conflict Liberia between trusteeship and partnership', *Journal of Intervention and Statebuilding* 4, no. 2 (June 2010): 129–52, doi:10.1080/17502970903533660.

Andrews, Matt. *The Limits of Institutional Reform in Development: Changing Rules for Realistic Solutions*. Cambridge, MA: Cambridge University Press, 2013.

Andrews, Matt, Lant Pritchett, and Michael Woolcock. *Building State Capability: Evidence, Analysis, Action*. Oxford; New York: Oxford University Press, 2017.

Bain, Kathy, David Booth, and Leni Wild. 'Doing Development Differently at the World Bank: updating the plumbing to fit the architecture'. London: Overseas Development Institute, 2016.

Banerjee, Abhijit V. *Making Aid Work*. Cambridge, MA: The MIT Press, 2007.

Barber, Ben. 'Andrew Natsios: getting USAID on its feet'. *Foreign Service Journal*, no. September 2002 (2002): 20–7.

Barrientos, Armando, and Juan Miguel Villa. 'Evaluating antipoverty transfer programmes in Latin America and Sub-Saharan Africa. Better policies? Better politics?'. *Journal of Globalization and Development* 6, no. 1 (2015): 147–79, doi:10.1515/jgd-2014-0006.

Barry, Aoife. 'Irish Aid: Tánaiste "absolutely disgusted" after alleged Uganda aid fraud'. Accessed 10 April 2017, www.thejournal.ie/uganda-aid-funds-650192-Oct2012/.

BBC News. 'Ugandan government returns misappropriated funds to Ireland', 7 January 2013, www.bbc.co.uk/news/world-20935149.

Bennett, Andrew, and Colin Elman. 'Qualitative research: recent developments in case study methods'. *Annual Review of Political Science* 9, no. 1 (2006): 455–76. doi:10.1146/annurev.polisci.8.082103.104918.

Birdsall, Nancy, William D. Savedoff, Ayah Mahgoub, and Katherine Vyborny. *Cash on Delivery: A New Approach to Foreign Aid*. Washington, DC: CGD Books, 2012.

Birrell, Ian (for *The Mail on Sunday*). 'SHAMED: foreign aid fat cats who built £1.4billion empire… with YOUR tax money'. *Mail Online*, 23 May 2015, www.dailymail.co.uk/news/article-3094436/SHAMED-Foreign-aid-fat-cats-built-1-4billion-empire-tax-money.html.

Blyth, Mark. *Great Transformations: Economic Ideas and Institutional Change in the Twentieth Century*. Cambridge: Cambridge University Press, 2002.

Booth, David, Daniel Harris, and Leni Wild. 'From political economy analysis to Doing Development Differently: a learning experience'. London: Overseas Development Institute, 2016.

Booth, David, and Sue Unsworth. 'Politically smart, locally led development'. London: Overseas Development Institute, September 2014.

Bräutigam, Deborah. 'Aid dependence and governance'. Stockholm: Expert Group on Development Issues, 2000.

Bräutigam, Deborah, and Stephen Knack. 'Foreign aid, institutions, and governance in Sub-Saharan Africa'. *Economic Development and Cultural Change* 52, no. 2 (2004): 255–85.

Browne, Stephen. *Aid and Influence: Do Donors Help or Hinder?* Abingdon: Taylor & Francis, 2012.

Calderisi, Robert. *The Trouble with Africa: Why Foreign Aid Isn't Working*. New York: St. Martin's Press, 2006.

Callaghy, Thomas M. *The State-Society Struggle: Zaire in Comparative Perspective*. New York: Columbia University Press, 1984.

Callaghy, Thomas M., and John Ravenhill, eds. *Hemmed In: Responses to Africa's Economic Decline*. New York: Columbia University Press, 1993.

Carey, John M. 'The reelection debate in Latin America'. *Latin American Politics and Society* 45, no. 1 (1 April 2003): 119–33, doi:10.1111/j.1548-2456.2003.tb00234.x.

Carlin, Brendan (for *The Mail on Sunday*). 'MPs ignore petition calling for end to 0.7% foreign aid budget'. *Mail Online*, 19 June 2016, www.dailymail.co.uk/news/article-3648701/MPs-ignore-petition-signed-230-000-readers-called-end-government-s-0-7-foreign-aid-budget.html.

Carothers, Thomas, and Diane de Gramont. *Development Aid Confronts Politics: The Almost Revolution*. Washington, DC: Carnegie Endowment for International Peace, 2013.

Chesterman, Simon. 'Ownership in theory and in practice: transfer of authority in UN statebuilding operations'. *Journal of Intervention and Statebuilding* 1, no. 1 (2007): 3–26, doi:10.1080/17502970601075873.

Collier, Paul. *The Bottom Billion: Why the Poorest Countries Are Failing and What Can Be Done About It*. Oxford: Oxford University Press, 2007.

Concord Times. 'Anti-corruption boss condemns MPs', 7 April 2005.

Concord Times. 'Britain blacklists Kabbah, SLPP gov't for corruption', 18 April 2007.

Concord Times. 'President Kabbah's "sack" letter to anti corruption commissioner, Val Collier', 17 November 2005.

Copestake, James, and Richard Williams. 'The evolving art of political economy analysis: unlocking its practical potential through a more interactive approach'. Development Futures Paper. Oxford: Oxford Policy Management, 2012.

Dahl-Østergaard, Tom, Sue Unsworth, Mark Robinson, and Rikke Ingrid Jensen. 'Lessons learned on the use of power and drivers of change analyses in development co-operation'. Paris: OECD, 20 September 2005.

Dasandi, Niheer, Heather Marquette, and Mark Robinson. 'Thinking and working politically: from theory building to building an evidence base'. Research Paper. Birmingham: Developmental Leadership Program, 2016.

Department of Foreign Affairs and Trade. *The New Aid Paradigm*, 2014, www.youtube.com/watch?v=4rSxEj1dT6M.

DFID. 'Annual review of DFID support to the Anti-Corruption Commission phase 2 in Sierra Leone', 25 January 2007.

———. 'Bilateral aid review technical report'. London: Department for International Development, 2011.

———. 'Briefing: using drivers of change to improve aid effectiveness. A DFID practice paper'. London: Department for International Development, November 2005.

———. 'DFID's approach to value for money (VfM)'. London: Department for International Development, July 2011.

———. 'Drivers of change public information note'. London: Department for International Development, September 2004.

DFID. 'EV 690 country programme evaluation: Sierra Leone', London: Department for International Development, September 2008.

DFID. 'How to note: country governance analysis. A DFID practice paper'. London: Department for International Development, February 2007.

———. 'How to note: operational plans'. London: Department for International Development, December 2010.

———. 'How to note: writing a business case'. London: Department for International Development, December 2012.

———. 'Political economy analysis how to note'. London: Department for International Development, July 2009.

———. 'Sierra Leone operational plan 2011–2015'. London: Department for International Development, 2012.

DFID and Government of Sierra Leone. 'A long-term partnership for development between the Government of the United Kingdom of Great Britain and Northern Ireland and the Government of the Republic of Sierra Leone (Memorandum of Understanding)', 17 November 2002.

DiJulio, Bianca, and Jamie Firth. 'Data note: Americans' views on the U.S. role in global health'. *The Henry J. Kaiser Family Foundation*, 23 January 2015, http://kff.org/global-health-policy/poll-finding/data-note-americans-views-on-the-u-s-role-in-global-health/.

DiMaggio, Paul, and Walter W. Powell. 'The iron cage revisited: institutional isomorphism and collective rationality in organizational fields'. *American Sociological Review* 48, no. 2 (1 April 1983): 147–60.

Dollar, David, and Jakob Svensson. 'What explains the success or failure of structural adjustment programmes?' *The Economic Journal* 110, no. 466 (2000): 894–917, doi:10.1111/1468-0297.00569.

Drake, Bruce. 'Wide partisan gap exists over U.S. aid to world's needy'. *Pew Research Center*, 13 March 2013, www.pewresearch.org/fact-tank/2013/03/13/wide-partisan-gap-exists-over-u-s-aid-to-worlds-needy/.

Dreher, Axel. 'IMF conditionality: theory and evidence'. *Public Choice* 141, no. 1–2 (4 August 2009): 233–67, doi:10.1007/s11127-009-9486-z.

Dunning, Thad. 'Conditioning the effects of aid: Cold War politics, donor credibility, and democracy in Africa'. *International Organization* 58, no. 2 (2004): 409–23.

Dwan, Renata, and Laura Bailey. 'Liberia's Governance and Economic Management Assistance Program (GEMAP) – a joint review by the Department of Peacekeeping Operations' Peacekeeping Best Practices Section and the World Bank's Fragile States Group'. New York; Washington, DC: United Nations and World Bank, May 2006.

Easterly, William. *Reinventing Foreign Aid*. Cambridge, MA: The MIT Press, 2008.

———. 'The cartel of good intentions: the problem of bureaucracy in foreign aid'. *The Journal of Policy Reform* 5, no. 4 (1 December 2002): 223–50, doi:10.1080/1384128032000096823.

———. *The Elusive Quest for Growth: Economists' Adventures and Misadventures in the Tropics*. London: The MIT Press, 2001.

———. *The Tyranny of Experts: Economists, Dictators, and the Forgotten Rights of the Poor*. New York: Basic Books, 2014.

———. *The White Man's Burden: Why the West's Efforts to Aid the Rest Have Done So Much Ill and So Little Good*. New York: Penguin Press, 2006.

Ebo, Adedeji. 'The challenges and opportunities of security sector reform in post-conflict Liberia'. Occasional Paper. Geneva: Geneva Centre for the Democratic Control of Armed Forces (DCAF), 2005.

Economic Commission for Latin America and the Caribbean. 'Honduras: assessment of the damage caused by Hurricane Mitch, 1998'. New York: United Nations, 1999.

El País. 'Un ansia infinita de paz, el amor al bien y el mejoramiento social de los humildes'. *EL PAÍS*, 16 April 2004, http://elpais.com/diario/2004/04/16/espana/1082066402_850215.html.

———. 'Zapatero promete aumentar la ayuda al desarrollo hasta el 0,7% en ocho años'. *EL PAÍS*, 9 February 2004, http://elpais.com/elpais/2004/02/09/actualidad/1076318220_850215.html.

Englebert, Pierre, and Denis M. Tull. 'Postconflict reconstruction in Africa: flawed ideas about failed states'. *International Security* 32, no. 4 (1 April 2008): 106–39.

Eurobarometer. 'Europeans, development aid and the millennium development goals'. Special Eurobarometer. Brussels: Eurobarometer, 2010.

European Commission. 'Design and formulation mission to EC support to strengthening the General Auditing Commission (GAC) of Liberia', Design Study (Monrovia: European Commission, January 2010).

———. 'Draft annual report 2007 Liberia', September 2008.

———. 'Liberia Country Strategy Paper and National Indicative Program (period 2004 – 2007)', 2004.

Fee, Derek. *How to Manage an Aid Exit Strategy: The Future of Development Aid*. London: Zed Books Ltd, 2012.

Ferguson, James. *The Anti-Politics Machine: 'Development', Depoliticization, and Bureaucratic Power in Lesotho*. Minneapolis, MN: University of Minnesota Press, 1990.

Filho, Clayton M. Cunha, André Luiz Coelho, and Fidel I. Pérez Flores. 'A right-to-left policy switch? An analysis of the Honduran case under Manuel Zelaya'. *International Political Science Review*, 4 February 2013, doi:10.1177/0192512112468918.

Fisher, Jonathan, and Heather Marquette. 'Donors doing political economy analysis™: from process to product (and back again?)'. Research Paper. Birmingham: Developmental Leadership Program, 2014.

Fligstein, Neil. 'Social skill and the theory of fields'. *Sociological Theory* 19, no. 2 (2001): 105–25, doi:10.1111/0735-2751.00132.

Fligstein, Neil, and Doug McAdam. *A Theory of Fields*. Oxford: Oxford University Press, 2012.

Fritz, Verena, Kai Kaiser, and Brian Levy. 'Problem-driven governance and political economy analysis: good practice framework'. Washington, DC: World Bank, September 2009.

Fuchs, Andreas, Axel Dreher, and Peter Nunnenkamp. 'Determinants of donor generosity: a survey of the aid budget literature'. *World Development* 56 (April 2014): 172–99, doi:10.1016/j.worlddev.2013.09.004.

Gberie, Lansana. *A Dirty War in West Africa: The RUF and the Destruction of Sierra Leone*. Bloomington: Indiana University Press, 2005.

Geddes, Barbara. *Politician's Dilemma: Building State Capacity in Latin America*. Berkeley, CA: California University Press, 1994.

George, Alexander L., and Andrew Bennett. *Case Studies and Theory Development in the Social Sciences*. London: The MIT Press, 2004.

Glennie, Jonathan. *The Trouble with Aid: Why Less Could Mean More for Africa*. London: Zed Books Ltd, 2010.

Gould, Jeremy, ed. *The New Conditionality: The Politics of Poverty Reduction Strategies*. London; New York: Zed Books Ltd, 2005.

Government of Honduras. 'Declaración conjunta del gobierno de Honduras con el grupo de cooperants G-16'. Tegucigalpa: Government of Honduras, 2012.

———. 'Estrategia para la reduccion de la pobreza: un compromiso con todos'. Tegucigalpa: Government of Honduras, 2001.

———. 'Honduras poverty reduction strategy: progress report'. Tegucigalpa: Government of Honduras, 2003.

———. 'Informe final de la reconstruccion nacional: logros y lecciones del proceso'. Tegucigalpa: Government of Honduras, 2003.

———. 'Plan maestro para la reconstruccion y transformacion nacional'. Tegucigalpa: Government of Honduras, 1999.

———. 'Poverty reduction strategy: progress report 2004'. Tegucigalpa: Government of Honduras, 2005.

Government of Liberia. 'General auditing commission: a blueprint for accountability, transparency, and good governance'. Monrovia: General Auditing Commission, January 2007.

————. 'General auditing commission annual report 2013'. Monrovia: General Auditing Commission, 2014.

————. 'General auditing commission annual report 2014'. Monrovia: General Auditing Commission, 2015.

————. 'Governance and Economic Management Assistance Program'. Monrovia: Government of Liberia, 2005.

————. 'Mid-term evaluation of the Governance and Economic Management Assistance Program (GEMAP)'. Monrovia: Government of Liberia, 15 August 2008.

————. 'National anti-corruption strategy'. Monrovia: Government of Liberia, December 2006.

————. 'Republic of Liberia Truth and Reconciliation Commission, volume II: consolidated final report'. Monrovia: Truth and Reconciliation Commission, 30 June 2009.

Government of Sierra Leone. 'Anti-Corruption Commission annual report 2001'. Freetown: Government of Sierra Leone, 2002.

————. 'Anti-Corruption Commission annual report 2002'. Freetown: Government of Sierra Leone, 2003.

————. 'Anti-Corruption Commission annual report 2007'. Freetown: Government of Sierra Leone, 2008.

————. 'Anti-Corruption Commission annual report 2009'. Freetown: Government of Sierra Leone, 2010.

————. 'Anti-Corruption Commission annual report 2010'. Freetown: Government of Sierra Leone, 2011.

————. 'National Public perception survey on corruption (draft)'. Freetown: Government of Sierra Leone, April 2010.

GPF Secretariat. 'Governance Partnership Facility: interim report November 2008–April 2009'. Washington, DC: World Bank, 2009.

————. 'Governance Partnership Facility: program document (P111816)'. Washington, DC: World Bank, 2008.

Grattan, Michelle. 'DFAT secretary's tough message about AusAID integration'. *The Conversation*, 3 November 2013. http://theconversation.com/dfat-secretarys-tough-message-about-ausaid-integration-19799.

Grindle, Merilee S. 'Good enough governance: poverty reduction and reform in developing countries'. *Governance* 17, no. 4 (2004): 525–48.

Gulrajani, Nilima. 'Transcending the great foreign aid debate: managerialism, radicalism and the search for aid effectiveness'. *Third World Quarterly* 32, no. 2 (1 March 2011): 199–216, doi:10.1080/01436597.2011.560465.

Haas, Peter M. 'Introduction: epistemic communities and international policy coordination'. *International Organization* 46, no. 1 (1992): 1–35.

Hall, Peter A., and Rosemary C. R. Taylor. 'Political science and the three new institutionalisms'. *Political Studies* 44, no. 5 (1 December 1996): 936–57.

Helmke, Gretchen, and Steven Levitsky. 'Informal institutions and comparative politics: a research agenda'. *Perspectives on Politics* 2, no. 4 (2004): 725–40, doi:10.1017/S1537592704040472.

Herbst, Jeffrey. 'The structural adjustment of politics in Africa'. *World Development* 18, no. 7 (1990): 948–58.

Hickey, Sam. 'Beyond the poverty agenda? Insights from the new politics of development in Uganda'. *World Development* 43 (March 2013): 194–206.

Hickey, Sam, Badru Bukenya, Angelo Izama, and William Kizito. 'The political settlement and oil in Uganda'. ESID Working Paper. Manchester: Social Science Research Network, 31 March 2015. http://papers.ssrn.com/abstract=2587845.

Honduran Truth and Reconciliation Commission. 'Para que los hechos no se repitan: informe de la comision de la verdad y la reconciliacion'. Tegucigalpa: Honduran Truth and Reconciliation Commission, 2011.

Hout, Wil. 'The anti-politics of development: donor agencies and the political economy of governance'. *Third World Quarterly* 33, no. 3 (2012): 405–22.

Hout, Wil, and Lydeke Schakel. 'SGACA: the rise and paradoxical demise of a political-economy instrument'. *Development Policy Review* 32, no. 5 (1 September 2014): 611–30, doi:10.1111/dpr.12075.

Hudson, David, and Adriana Leftwich. 'From political economy to political analysis'. Research Paper. Birmingham: Developmental Leadership Program, 2014.

Hudson, David, Heather Marquette, and Sam Waldock. 'Everyday political analysis'. Note. Birmingham: Developmental Leadership Program, 2016.

Hunt, Sarah. 'Breaking the rules, breaking the game: external ideas, politics and inclusive development in Honduras'. ESID Working Paper 52. Manchester: Effective States and Inclusive Development Research Centre, 2015.

———. 'Honduras PRSP update July 2006'. Tegucigalpa: Trocaire, 2006.

Iglesia-Caruncho, Manuel de la. 'The politics and policy of aid in Spain'. IDS Research Report. Brighton: Institute of Development Studies, 2011.

International Crisis Group. 'Sierra Leone: a new era of reform'. *Africa Report*, 31 July 2008.

———. 'Sierra Leone after elections: politics as usual?' *Africa Report*, 12 July 2002.

———. 'Sierra Leone: the election opportunity'. *Africa Report*, 12 July 2007.

Irish Aid. 'Audit report into Irish Aid misappropriated funds in Uganda – Department of Foreign Affairs and Trade'. Accessed 10 April 2017, www.dfa.ie/news-and-media/press-releases/press -release-archive/2012/november/report-into-misappropriated -aid-funds-uganda/.

Irish Aid. 'Uganda Country Strategy Paper 2016–2020'. Dublin: Irish Aid, 2016.

Jackson, Patrick Thaddeus. *The Conduct of Inquiry in International Relations: Philosophy of Science and Its Implications for the Study of World Politics*. London; New York: Routledge, 2011.

Kamm, F. M. *Intricate Ethics: Rights, Responsibilities, and Permissible Harm: Rights, Responsibilities, and Permissible Harm*. Oxford: Oxford University Press, 2006.

Kandeh, Jimmy D. 'Rogue incumbents, donor assistance and Sierra Leone's second post-conflict elections of 2007'. *Journal of Modern African Studies* 46, no. 4 (11 November 2008): 603, doi:10.1017/ S0022278X08003509.

Kharas, Homi, and Noam Unger. 'Set to lead again? New U.S. engagement on global development'. *Brookings*, 28 September 2010, www. brookings.edu/opinions/set-to-lead-again-new-u-s-engagement-on -global-development/.

Killick, Tony. 'Principals, agents and the failings of conditionality'. *Journal of International Development* 2, no. 4 (1997): 483–95.

Kingdon, John W. *Agendas, Alternatives, and Public Policies*, 2nd edn. New York: Harper Collins, 1995.

Kjaer, Anne Mette. '"Old brooms can sweep too!" An overview of rulers and public sector reforms in Uganda, Tanzania and Kenya'. *Journal of Modern African Studies* 42, no. 3 (2004): 389–413.

Klingebiel, Stephan, and Heiner Janus. 'Results-based aid: potential and limits of an innovative modality in development cooperation'. SSRN Scholarly Paper. Rochester, NY: Social Science Research Network, 12 May 2014, https://papers.ssrn.com/abstract=2436625.

Knack, Stephen, and Aminur Rahman. 'Donor fragmentation and bureaucratic quality in aid recipients'. *Journal of Development Economics* 83, no. 1 (2007): 176–97.

Knight, Frank H. (Frank Hyneman). *Risk, Uncertainty and Profit.* Boston, New York: Houghton Mifflin Company, 1921, http://archive.org/details/riskuncertaintyp00knigrich.

Krasner, Stephen D. 'Sharing sovereignty: new institutions for collapsed and failing states'. *International Security* 29, no. 2 (2004): 85–120.

Kuhn, Thomas S. *The Structure of Scientific Revolutions.* Chicago, IL: University of Chicago Press, 1966.

Laffont, Jean-Jacques, and David Martimort. *The Theory of Incentives: The Principal-Agent Model.* Princeton, NJ: Princeton University Press, 2002.

Lancaster, Carol. *Foreign Aid: Diplomacy, Development, Domestic Politics.* Chicago, IL: University of Chicago Press, 2008.

———. *George Bush's Foreign Aid: Transformation or Chaos.* Washington, DC: Center for Global Development, 2008.

Lappia, David. 'Survey report: national perceptions and attitudes towards corruption in Sierra Leone'. Freetown: Department for International Development, 2000.

Lavers, Tom, and Sam Hickey. 'Investigating the political economy of social protection expansion in Africa: at the intersection of transnational ideas and domestic politics', ESID Working Paper 47. Manchester: Social Science Research Network, 2015, https://papers.ssrn.com/sol3/papers.cfm?abstract_id=2598114.

Leftwich, Adrian. 'From drivers of change to the politics of development: refining the analytical framework to understand the politics of the places where we work. Note of guidance for DFID offices'. London: Department for International Development, 6 February 2007.

Li, Tania. *The Will to Improve: Governmentality, Development, and the Practice of Politics*. Durham, NC: Duke University Press, 2007. www.loc.gov/catdir/toc/ecip074/2006035585.html.

Lichtenstein, Joshua. 'After Hurricane Mitch: United States Agency for International Development Reconstruction and the Stockholm Principles'. Boston, MA: Oxfam America, 2001.

Lumsdaine, David Halloran. *Moral Vision in International Politics: The Foreign Aid Regime, 1949–1989*. Princeton, NJ: Princeton University Press, 1993.

Machiavelli, Niccolò. *The Prince* (1513). Quentin Skinner and Russell Price, eds., Cambridge: Cambridge University Press, 1988.

Manning, Nick, and Laura Bureš. 'Institutional and governance reviews'. Washington, DC: World Bank, 2001.

Martens, Bertin. *The Institutional Economics of Foreign Aid*. Cambridge: Cambridge University Press, 2002.

Mavrotas, George. *Foreign Aid for Development: Issues, Challenges, and the New Agenda*. Oxford: Oxford University Press, 2010.

McAdam, Doug, Sidney Tarrow, and Charles Tilly. *Dynamics of Contention*. Cambridge: Cambridge University Press, 2001.

Médard, Jean-François. 'The underdeveloped state in tropical Africa: political clientelism or neo-patrimonialism?' In *Private Patronage and Public Power: Political Clientelism in the Modern State*, ed. Christopher Clapham. New York: St. Martin's Press, 1982.

Moratinos, Miguel Angel. 'Comparecencia del Ministro de Asuntos Exteriores y Cooperacion Miguel Angel Moratinos'. Madrid: Congreso de los Diputados, June 2004.

Moss, Todd, Gunilla Pettersson, and Nicolas van de Walle. 'An Aid-institutions paradox? A review essay on aid dependency and state building in Sub-Saharan Africa'. Working Paper 74. Washington, DC: Center for Global Development, 2006.

Moyo, Dambisa. *Dead Aid: Why Aid Is Not Working and How There Is Another Way for Africa*. London: Allen Lane, 2009.

Munk, Nina. *The Idealist: Jeffrey Sachs and the Quest to End Poverty*. New York: Doubleday, 2013.

National Transitional Government of Liberia. 'Results-Focused Transitional Framework (RFTF)'. Monrovia: National Transitional Government of Liberia, 7 January 2004.

Natsios, Andrew. 'The clash of the counter-bureaucracy and development'. Essay. Washington, DC: Center for Global Development, July 2010.

Nelson, Joan M., ed. *Economic Crisis and Policy Choice: The Politics of Adjustment in the Third World*. Princeton, NJ: Princeton University Press, 1990.

Neumayer, Eric. 'The determinants of aid allocation by regional multilateral development banks and United Nations agencies'. *International Studies Quarterly* 47, no. 1 (2003): 101–22.

The New Dawn. 'New AG indicts John Morlu', 5 September 2011.

North, Douglass C. *Institutions, Institutional Change and Economic Performance*. Cambridge: Cambridge University Press, 1990.

———. *Structure and Change in Economic History*. New York: W. W. Norton, 1981.

North, Douglass C., John Joseph Wallis, and Barry R. Weingast. *Violence and Social Orders: A Conceptual Framework for Interpreting Recorded Human History*, 1st edn. Cambridge: Cambridge University Press, 2009.

North, Douglass C., and Barry R. Weingast. 'Constitutions and commitment: the evolution of institutions governing public choice in 17th century England'. *Journal of Economic History* 49, no. 4 (1989): 803–32.

OECD. 'Paris Declaration on Aid Effectiveness'. Paris: OECD Publishing, 2 March 2005.

Olson, Mancur. *The Logic of Collective Action; Public Goods and the Theory of Groups*. Harvard Economic Studies, Vol. 124. Cambridge, MA: Harvard University Press, 1965.

O'Neill, Onora. 'Global justice: whose obligations?' In *The Ethics of Assistance: Morality and the Distant Needy*, by Deen K. Chatterjee. Cambridge: Cambridge University Press, 2004.

Patel, Priti (Secretary Of State For International Development). 'PRITI PATEL says a well-financed aid budget is just a means to an end'. *Mail Online*, 13 September 2016, www.dailymail.co.uk/~/article-3788169/index.html.

Paxton, Pamela, and Stephen Knack. 'Individual and country-level factors affecting support for foreign aid'. *International Political Science Review* 33, no. 2 (1 March 2012): 171–92, doi:10.1177/0192512111406095.

Posner, Daniel N., and Daniel J. Young. 'The institutionalization of political power in Africa'. *Journal of Democracy* 18, no. 3 (31 July 2007): 126–40, doi:10.1353/jod.2007.0053.

Pritchett, Lant, Michael Woolcock, and Matt Andrews. 'Looking like a state: techniques of persistent failure in state capability for implementation'. *Journal of Development Studies* 49, no. 1 (2013): 1–18.

Reno, William. *Corruption and State Politics in Sierra Leone.* Cambridge: Cambridge University Press, 1995.

Rice, Condoleezza. 'Campaign 2000: Promoting the National Interest'. *Foreign Affairs* 79, no. 1 (January/February 2000): 44–62.

Riddell, Roger. *Does Foreign Aid Really Work?* Oxford; New York: Oxford University Press, 2007.

Riedl, Brian M. 'How to cut $343 billion from the federal budget'. Washington, DC: Heritage Foundation, 28 October 2010.

Rocha Menocal, Alina. 'Getting real about politics: from thinking politically to working differently'. London: Overseas Development Institute, March 2014.

Rodrik, Dani. 'How should structural adjustment programs be designed?' *World Development* 18, no. 7 (July 1990): 933–47, doi:10.1016/0305-750X(90)90077-B.

Rogin, Josh. '165 House Republicans endorse defunding USAID', *Foreign Policy*, 20 January 2011, http://foreignpolicy.com/2011/01/20/165-house-republicans-endorse-defunding-usaid/.

Routley, Laura, and David Hulme. 'Donors, development agencies and the use of political economic analysis: getting to grips with the politics of development?' ESID Working Paper. Manchester: Effective States and Inclusive Development Research Centre, 2013.

Rubin, Michael. '5 questions every presidential candidate should answer: foreign aid edition', 20 April 2015, www.aei.org/publication/5-questions-every-presidential-candidate-should-answer-foreign-aid/print/.

Sachs, Jeffrey. *The End of Poverty: How We Can Make It Happen in Our Lifetime.* New York: Penguin, 2005.

Sanahuja, Jose Antonio. '¿Un nuevo ciclo en la política de Cooperación Española? Prestar atención a los actores y los procesos de toma de decisiones'. Madrid: FRIDE, 2009.

Sandy, Moses D. 'The rise and fall of Robert Kilby'. *Front Page Africa Online*, 18 July 2013.

Scott, W. Richard. *Institutions and Organizations: Ideas and Interests*, 3rd edn. London: SAGE, 2008.

SIDA. 'Honduras: presupuestar la ERP'. The Hague: Institute of Social Studies, 2005.

———. 'Honduras: ¿Qué pasó con la ERP?' The Hague: Institute of Social Studies, 2007.

———. 'Power analysis'. Stockholm: SIDA, 2006.

Sierra Leone Parliament. 'Second public sitting of the Committee on Privileges held at Parliament Building, Tower Hill, on Wednesday 22nd June 2005', 22 June 2005.

New African. 'Sierra Leone's war against corruption', January 1999.

Sil, Rudra, and Peter J. Katzenstein. 'Analytic eclecticism in the study of world politics: reconfiguring problems and mechanisms across research traditions'. *Perspectives on Politics* 8, no. 2 (June 2010): 411–31, doi:10.1017/S1537592710001179.

———. *Beyond Paradigms: Analytic Eclecticism in the Study of World Politics*. New York: Palgrave Macmillan, 2011, https://he.palgrave.com/page/detail/Beyond-Paradigms/?K=9780230207950.

Social Development Department. 'The political economy of policy reform: issues and implications for policy dialogue and development operations'. Washington, DC: World Bank, November 2008.

———. 'Tools for institutional, political, and social analysis of policy reform: a sourcebook for development practitioners'. Washington, DC: World Bank, 2007.

Tarrow, Sidney. *Power in Movement: Social Movements and Contentious Politics*, 3rd edn. Cambridge; New York: Cambridge University Press, 2011.

Tavakoli, Heidi, Rebecca Simson, Helen Tilley, and David Booth. 'Unblocking results: using aid to address governance constraints in public service delivery'. Centre for Aid & Public Expenditure. London: Overseas Development Institute, May 2013, www.odi.org.uk/sites/odi.org.uk/files/odi-assets/publications-opinion-files/8409.pdf.

Therien, J.P., and A. Noel. 'Political parties and foreign aid'. *American Political Science Review* (2000): 151–62.

Tilly, Charles, and Sidney Tarrow. *Contentious Politics*. New York: Oxford University Press, 2006.

Tingley, Dustin. 'Donors and domestic politics: political influences on foreign aid effort'. *The Quarterly Review of Economics and Finance* 50, no. 1 (February 2010): 40–9, doi:10.1016/j.qref.2009.10.003.

Travis, Rick. 'Problems, politics, and policy streams: a reconsideration US foreign aid behavior toward Africa'. *International Studies Quarterly* 54, no. 3 (1 September 2010): 797–821, doi:10.1111/j.1468-2478.2010.00610.x.

Treasury Officer of Accounts. 'Regularity, propriety and value for money'. London: HM Treasury, 2004.

Trolio, Pete. 'Inside the takedowns of AusAID and CIDA'. *Devex*, 19 January 2015, www.devex.com/news/inside-the-takedowns-of-ausaid-and-cida-85278.

UNAMSIL. 'Twenty-fifth report of the Secretary-General on the United Nations mission in Sierra Leone, S/2005/273'. New York: United Nations, 26 April 2005.

UNIOSIL. 'Fifth report of the Secretary-General on the United Nations Integrated Office in Sierra Leone, S/2007/704'. New York: United Nations, 4 December 2007.

———. 'Sixth report of the Secretary-General on the United Nations Integrated Office in Sierra Leone, S/2008/281'. New York: United Nations, 29 April 2008.

UNIPSIL. 'Fourth report of the Secretary-General on the United Nations Integrated Peacebuilding Office in Sierra Leone, S/2010/135'. New York: United Nations, 15 March 2010.

United Nations. 'Transforming our world: the 2030 agenda for sustainable development'. New York: United Nations, 2015.

United Nations and World Bank. 'Joint Needs Assessment – National Transitional Government of Liberia'. New York; Washington, DC: United Nations and World Bank, February 2004.

Unsworth, Sue. 'What's politics got to do with it?: Why donors find it so hard to come to terms with politics, and why this matters'. *Journal of International Development* 21, no. 6 (2009): 883–94.

Unsworth, Sue, and Conflict Research Unit. 'Framework for Strategic Governance and Corruption Analysis (SGACA): designing strategic responses towards good governance'. The Hague: Clingendael Institute, Ministry of Foreign Affairs, 2008.

US Department of State. 'Liberia 2003'. Country Reports on Human Rights Practices, Bureau of Democracy, Human Rights, and Labor. Washington, DC: DOS, 25 February 2004.

———. 'Liberia 2005'. Country Reports on Human Rights Practices, Bureau of Democracy, Human Rights, and Labor. Washington, DC: DOS, 8 March 2006.

———. 'Liberia 2006'. Country Reports on Human Rights Practices, Bureau of Democracy, Human Rights, and Labor. Washington, DC: DOS, 6 March 2007.

USAID. 'Final evaluation of USAID GEMAP activities – Sibley International LLC'. Washington, DC: United States Agency for International Development, June 2010.

———. 'Governance and Economic Management Assistance Program (GEMAP) – IBI annual report to USAID'. Washington, DC: United States Agency for International Development, October 2009.

———. 'USAID activities under GEMAP in Liberia'. Impact Assessment Report. Washington, DC: United States Agency for International Development, July 2008.

National Audit Office. 'Value for money'. Accessed 9 April 2017, www.nao.org.uk/successful-commissioning/general-principles/value-for-money/#notes.

van der Veen, A. Maurits. *Ideas, Interests and Foreign Aid*. Cambridge: Cambridge University Press, 2011.

Walle, Nicolas van de. *African Economies and the Politics of Permanent Crisis, 1979–1999*. Cambridge: Cambridge University Press, 2001.

———. *Overcoming Stagnation in Aid-Dependent Countries*. Washington, DC: Center for Global Development, 2005.

Weber, Max. *Economy and Society: An Outline of Interpretive Sociology*. Berkeley, CA: University of California Press, 1978.

Whitfield, Lindsay. *The Politics of Aid: African Strategies for Dealing with Donors*. Oxford: Oxford University Press, 2008.

Wild, Leni, David Booth, Clare Cummings, Marta Foresti, and Joseph Wales. 'Adapting development: improving services to the poor'. London: Overseas Development Institute, 2015.

Wild, Leni, and Marta Foresti. 'Putting politics into practice: aiming for more politically informed aid programming'. *Developing Alternatives* 14, no. 1 (2011): 18–23.

World Bank. *Assessing Aid: What Works, What Doesn't, and Why*. Washington, DC: Oxford University Press, 1998.

———. 'Reforming public institutions and strengthening governance – a World Bank strategy'. Washington, DC: World Bank, September 2000.

———. 'Strengthening governance: tackling corruption. The World Bank Group's updated strategy and implementation plan'. Washington, DC: World Bank, 6 March 2012.

———. 'World Bank country-level engagement on governance and anticorruption: an evaluation of the 2007 strategy and implementation plan'. Washington, DC: World Bank, 2011.

———. *World Development Report 1997: The State in a Changing World.* New York: Oxford University Press, 1997.

———. *World Development Report 2002: Building Institutions for Markets.* Washington, DC: World Bank, 2002.

———. *World Development Report 2003: Sustainable Development in a Dynamic World.* Washington, DC: World Bank, 2003.

———. *World Development Report 2004: Making Services Work for Poor People.* Washington, DC: World Bank, 2004.

———. *World Development Report 2017: Governance and the Law.* Washington, DC: World Bank Publications, 2017.

Wright, Joseph. 'Aid effectiveness and the politics of personalism'. *Comparative Political Studies* 43, no. 6 (24 February 2010): 735–62, doi:10.1177/0010414009358674.

Wright, Joseph, and Matthew Winters. 'The politics of effective foreign aid'. *Annual Review of Political Science* 13 (2010): 61–80.

Yanguas, Pablo. 'Leader, protester, enabler, spoiler: aid strategies and donor politics in institutional assistance'. *Development Policy Review* 32, no. 3 (1 May 2014): 299–312.

———. 'Making political analysis useful: adjusting and scaling'. Briefing Paper. Manchester: Effective States and Inclusive Development Research Centre, 2015.

———. 'The role and responsibility of foreign aid in recipient political settlements'. *Journal of International Development* 29, no. 2 (1 March 2017): 211–28, doi:10.1002/jid.3269.

Yanguas, Pablo, and Badru Bukenya. '"New" approaches confront "old" challenges in African public sector reform'. *Third World Quarterly* 37, no. 1 (2016): 136–52, doi:10.1080/01436597.2015.1086635.

Yanguas, Pablo, and David Hulme. 'Barriers to political analysis in aid bureaucracies: from principle to practice in DFID and the World Bank'. *World Development* 74 (October 2015): 209–19, doi:10.1016/j.worlddev.2015.05.009.

Index